Inland Navigation
by the Stars

ANNE COLEMAN

Inland Navigation by the Stars

A MEMOIR

www.bpsbooks.com

Copyright © 2018 by Anne Coleman

All rights reserved. No part of this publication may be reproduced
or transmitted in any form or by any means, electronic or mechanical, including
photocopying, recording, or any information storage and retrieval system, without
permission in writing from the publisher.

Published in 2018 by
BPS Books
Toronto
www.bpsbooks.com
A division of Bastian Publishing Services Ltd.

ISBN 978-1-77236-045-5 (paperback)
ISBN 978-1-77236-046-2 (ePDF)
ISBN 978-1-77236-047-9 (ePUB)

Cataloguing-in-Publication Data available from Library and Archives Canada.
Cover, text design, and typesetting: Daniel Crack, Kinetics Design, kdbooks.ca

For those in my generation who can identify with what I describe here, and for all my multitudinous descendants, those of my blood and bone, and those many other younger people I have loved.

Contents

Prologue ix

PART I
Barely Aware of the World 1

Part II
Starting Over 95

Part III
How Beauty Makes Things Possible 173

Epilogue 259

Acknowledgements 261

Prologue

A few years ago I had an experience whereby, for the few weeks that it lasted, my nose was pressed right up against the coalface of my mortality. It was frightening but less so than I would have imagined and it was useful. It showed me that I needed to try to see my life as a finite thing.

My life began, and my life will end. It will end either soon, or, if I am unlucky, very soon. I was given this life (by God? ... by the universe?) and now I need, first, just to take it and hold it in my lap. And then I must lift it up in my hands and study it. It was a gift to me as an unformed thing, a lump of soft clay, mine to fashion into something worthy. So let me look: what is it that I have made?

Across my more than eighty years, I will resurrect past scenes, sift them. I will try to see past and behind them to what else was there. Imagination will be involved but I will harken for the ring of truth. I will hope by the end for an epiphany, to see in a clear light the path I have travelled, with all its curves and tunnels, dead-end side trails and long straight stretches. I will thus "have it," my life. And the people who have joined me along the way for short periods or long, I will have them too. I know I have judged harshly sometimes; I have been mistaken about other people, and about myself, and justified the self I was at the time. I have clarifying to do, and forgiveness to ask.

Our family is full of storytellers and readers and as a literature teacher for my whole adult life I naturally see my life in chapters as a novel, with interwoven plots and repeating motifs. I am its central character of course, but I am also the (supposedly) omniscient narrator: I have a double role. I am both heroine and interpreter. If this story of me is to be a worthwhile one, and ring true, the central character cannot be understood as a static figure but should evolve, rise to challenges, or — sometimes, inevitably — fail to. As the plots unfold, the reliability of this central character may be at times questionable. But we will hope for the insightfulness of the interpreter/ reader to sort things out, ultimately. But will all this be possible? Can this tale have an arc, as any good novel ought to? That should mean that somewhere close to the end there will be the sense of an arrival. But do lives anymore have destinations? Does anyone now feel as certain as Christian does at the end of *The Pilgrim's Progress* when he enters the Celestial City?

I first called this memoir *Really and Truly.* The title hints at doubt. Why both words? I needed the over-emphasis to warn my reader. I will be as truthful as I can. That is all I can promise. The title I have eventually chosen, *Inland Navigation by the Stars*, evokes the sense I want more precisely. I am on a quest: I will find bright sparks of truth but often they will be surrounded by darkness. Clouds may slip over them. I will see them; then I won't. I will do my best.

So what really happened and who was it that it happened to?

PART I

Barely Aware
of the World

I

IN my family I always felt myself to be different. I'm sure most young people think this but I was different at least within my family. I wanted independence in a way my siblings did not. I deliberately stepped aside from the paths my sisters took and would not follow the rules of the day for a girl. This was easier for me than it was for them: our family was more affluent by the time I was of high school age. Somehow our father was able more or less to put behind him his chagrin at the loss of the earlier Coleman family stature, a loss occasioned by his strange and mysteriously irresponsible father. But there was always something a little contradictory in his attitude about social class: he hated snobbery at the same time that he held certain quite fierce prejudices himself.

At any rate my brother went to Upper Canada College in Toronto, and then Bishop's College School in Quebec, and I went briefly to King's Hall in the Eastern Townships of Quebec and then Havergal, a girls' school in Toronto, which meant that from grade eight on I had the blessing of wearing a school uniform. I thereby avoided the morning terrors Ruth and Carol had experienced at public high schools: the distress of having impossibly curly hair; the endless worry about clothes; and the daily contention with the complicated games involving boys, and, equally exacting, other girls — or the pretending not to mind being unable to play them or not being invited to play. And with no boys on the scene I could wait until I was ready to deal with boyfriends. In our summers at North Hatley in Quebec

I had friends who were boys and I had my odd "dream love" for Mr. MacLennan there as well. Dream in the sense that while our unlikely and private friendship was real, I projected onto him a combination of Heathcliff, Mr. Rochester, Prince Andrei and Laurence Olivier as Hamlet. He was a novelist, perhaps the best known in Canada at the time, and we spent time together, talking, going for drives. While I loved him in my day-dreaming way I never was sure what he felt for me. Something, clearly, or our relationship would not have continued as it did for years. But we never touched each other. He was not flesh and blood to me. Men were fantasy figures and I was happy to have them be so.

Of course I couldn't escape the pressures of the day entirely. I was criticized by my sisters for wearing nothing but jeans or shorts, when not in my uniform, and for never being comfortable wearing makeup. I remember — and I was in university by then — Ruth trying to insist I wear a girdle. I was thin and so was she but the point was that the natural shape of one's bottom was unpleasant, actually shameful, and a girdle disguised and smoothed the whole area into a unit, a solid block. The little dip in the middle of a slim girl's bottom was disguised as was the fact that buttocks come in twos. It was the same misogynist thinking as that of the Havergal headmistress who told the whole school, at the end of prayers one day, that the reason our tunics must be worn long was to hide the ugliness of the female thigh, any female thigh. I refused to pay any attention to such notions.

But being an adolescent girl in the late 1940s and early 50s was perplexing, however much I tried to ignore the matter. At the same time it was in many ways simpler than it is for girls now: the sex roles were hard and fast. Stepping aside from them as I did was a clear statement. And the specifics of sex itself I allowed only hazily into my imagination. I knew the fierce and exciting power of it from novels. The haziness of my fantasies did not mean I didn't anticipate it as something amazing and life-altering but I was prepared to wait.

Today a young girl cannot willfully postpone direct knowledge when images of flesh, if not flesh itself (and often that too), are constantly thrust in her face. In the early 50s information was scanty and mostly wrong. I remember a conversation in the Havergal day-girls' lunchroom. While eating we discussed whether a woman, when the time came, obviously after marriage, would enjoy sexual inter-course or would just have to put up with it. I was the only one who said I thought it would be enjoyable, fun even, rather than disgusting. My imagination somehow knew that, however unspecifically. We were all fifteen at the time.

Later, in my first year at McGill, I and several of my new friends were appalled at what someone had heard about oral sex. How could one possibly do something so revolting? Penny, the only one of us who dared ask her mother over the Christmas holidays, reported back that of course no one did that. Her mother had been very sure. The rest of us, as well as enormously relieved, were amazed that Penny had felt able to ask her mother. None of us had discussed sex with our mothers and definitely could not have brought up as rude a detail as that.

Ignorance had its positive side in an age when we could wait until we were ready for sex's overwhelming power to consume us. We could focus on our studies, on music, on art, on our friendships. The down-side, for me at least, was that when direct experience finally came my way I had no way to put it into a saving context. I assumed that the powerful sensations stirred by one man could be stirred only by him. Therefore I must love him. So I did.

My placement in our family affected the trajectory I followed. As the third girl I saw my sisters carve out particular territories: Ruth, the eldest, was studious and an artist. I think her high school years were miserable socially, and then, seemingly overnight, in her first year away from home at university, she suddenly became slim, extremely pretty and very much sought after. She was caught up in clothes and makeup, regularly over-spending her allowance and pleading for more — "Please, Daddy! I've seen a dress at Ogilvy's I would *so* love to have, and really do need." At the same time she studied hard and still saw herself as a budding artist. The kind of true independence I already was saving my babysitting money for held no interest for her. I think she took her future for granted, without even being conscious of any other way her life could unfold, that another choice was possible for a girl. She would marry and be taken care of. And she was right. That was the way it was meant to be for girls like us.

Carol, the second sister, was in the difficult middle position. She was also the prettiest sister, who, from when she was fourteen, caught the attention of boys in a way that terrified our mother. As sex was never openly discussed, mother-daughter upsets were handled so obliquely that Mother's mind could never be at rest. Carol's ignorance and defensiveness fuelled fights they both hated. Carol didn't actually fully understand what Mother was suspicious of and then downright accusatory about. She was innocent but had no words to explain, and wasn't even entirely sure if she really was. Perhaps the evil deed had somehow happened and she couldn't remember properly or hadn't noticed properly? How could that be? But how else was she seen as so very bad? Why else was Mother so furious? The shame about the whole topic trapped and distressed them both.

Mother loved Carol, I'm sure of that, but wounds were inflicted and the scars lasted. Long after Mother died Carol could have moments of overwhelming uncertainty of her love. I could see — not as a child, but as an adult — the significance of something that Carol never could: that our mother was beautiful even at ninety and darling in pictures of her as a young girl. She may have identified with Carol, the one of us who looked most like her. Her background absolutely ruled out frank speech, probably even the clear forming of sexual thoughts. I feel so sorry for both of them! Mother may have had vague memories of early temptation, early unspeakable, even unthinkable, feelings. Perhaps it was as simple as that. There was also the off-stage, lurking figure of our father's younger sister, the family black sheep or black ewe, whom we almost never saw. I met her only twice over my whole girlhood. Might her "bad seed" character crop up in one of us? How could such a thing be headed off?

So then there was the third daughter, me. I had to carve out some position that was unique. I had the same talents: we all were artistic; we all were clever and literary, musical too, though only Ruth and I continued piano lessons for long; we all were, or became, very attractive. I can say that frankly at my age, I hope. But I was by far the most independent. I didn't want to do things just because others were doing them, in the way my sisters both took up smoking and wearing makeup and, in Ruth's case especially, cared tremendously about clothes. I was a tomboy and kept up my outdoor pursuits even as I got into my teens. I was exceptional at math and had an ambition to be an architect — something that I didn't realize until far too late was impossible for me: no one had advised me not to drop science after grade six and architecture required a science background. But I did have a career, if not in that, and one I loved. As our lives turned out I was the only one of the three of the daughters in our family to become self-supporting.

That I was the third girl and not the boy my parents must have wanted by then affected who I became. In fact my parents loved children and I am quite sure, now, that when they saw me they would have loved me at once, despite my being a girl. Even so, when my brother did finally arrive, almost five years later, everyone was wildly overjoyed. It seemed there was no question but that this tiny boy was a superior being. A couple of factors exacerbated both my jealousy and my guilt for feeling it. First, our mother had no understanding of jealousy; if a child showed it, she thought it was evidence of a "bad streak." The child faced crossness rather than reassurance. That response was usual then and not really my mother's fault. The psychology of children was an unexplored area for most people, and any child psychology that did exist was mostly very wide of the mark. The way parents now pore over childcare books and articles was unknown then. And second, luck swept Helen, our nanny whose darling little one I had been from babyhood — I often used to sleep cosily in her bed — into her own marriage within a week of my baby brother's arrival. I don't think anyone considered the blow this must have been for me. It did not even occur to me until recently when I read in someone else's memoir about her pain when her nanny left. But when something is accepted by everyone else as normal, it seems so to oneself. The special category and preciousness of a boy was too obvious for me to seriously object to it for long.

Nevertheless a tangle of roles and jealousies in our family played out in various complicated ways all our lives. Carol and I were mostly very close friends and confidantes but her uncomfortable middle position made it untenable for her that Ruth and I could be friends. Only when there was a falling-out between Carol and Ruth could Ruth and I be close — and that didn't happen until we were adults; the six-year difference in our ages precluded closeness between the two of us while I was a child. Mostly I sensed disapproval from her. But I'm not really sure whom Ruth was jealous of, if she was of any of us. As a child I took for granted her role as important eldest, especially as she was the only one of us exotically born in Africa and thus part of our parents' life there, the stuff of so many stories. It didn't occur to me she might have envied Carol or me. Yet in a picture I have of the three of us taken when Ruth was almost fifteen, Carol eleven, I nine, Ruth looks self-conscious, unhappy and rather plump. Though we are sitting on the dock, she is wearing a dress and I now remember that she never wore shorts that summer. Carol and I both are adorable tomboys, tousle-haired, skinny and entirely unself-conscious. Carol even seems to be wearing a pair of our father's boots. It's difficult to believe Ruth can't have been bothered by her contrast with us.

Relationships among sisters, especially during an intensely sexist era, are at the mercy of the currents that swirl and suck at them. I picture a river with rapids and whirlpools. There are also meanders that can feel temporarily safe for one sister, while another swims strongly out into the swifter water. It is difficult in the tumult to be sure where one is oneself, let alone where the other sisters are. Sometimes it takes a person her whole life to take the necessary breaths. Yet sometimes, as adults, Ruth and I could suddenly be close and that could last even for a few years. They were precious times when our interests and senses of humour clicked perfectly. They made the reversals all the more painful. I am very glad that one of our longer, usually inexplicable (at least to me) feuds ended before Ruth died. She died unexpectedly and it would have been terrible for me had she gone at a time of our being out of touch. Whatever was happening at any given time, if ever she turned to me, I was ready to love her. The sister bond is indestructible, really.

As for Chuck, our "baby brother," despite my early jealousy and even while feeling it, I always loved him and still do. And I think his extreme importance to our father was more difficult and hampering for him than mine as youngest girl was for me. My nose was sometimes out of joint but I was allowed far more freedom and independence. My father's compulsion to indulge and overprotect his son was quite understandable and forgivable but it took me until after he was dead to see it really clearly: he had to make up for, as best he could, his own father's cruelty to and neglect of him.

Parents are simply human beings.

What a totally obvious fact! Yet I had to let the sentence stand alone, for even as a young woman and no longer a child I didn't grasp it. I don't know that I even tried to. I don't think any of us did. Our parents still seemed to have so much power. Yet it was crucial for our adult happiness, and crucial for our love of them, to see and to accept them as fallible and vulnerable human beings. They behaved as they did often for deep and unconscious reasons just as we did, and as I probably still do. They loved us all and they did their best. And they were of an era when most people didn't yet question age-old hierarchical family roles.

But the power they had is interesting to contemplate. I don't see parents today having it, an authority that is automatically assumed and accepted. It was just part and parcel of the patriarchal construct, and a mother, as stand-in authority when the father was away, partook of it as well. Yet our parents were essentially gentle people. I can't remember a serious punishment. As a child I certainly wasn't frightened of them. I was never spanked. There could be crossness — though never shouting; I remember a bad moment on one of the endless two-day drives to North Hatley from Toronto. Our father had to pull over and stop the car — a dark green 1936 Buick with running boards that we had for years; I loved that car: it was a member of the family, the exact same age as I — and attempt to slap the kicking legs of Carol and me who were fighting much too uproariously in the backseat. I don't think the slaps even connected and I strongly suspect he felt guilty for them afterwards, it was so rare for him to lose his temper. Generally our parents enjoyed us. We took that for granted. They loved to tell us stories, and both had lively senses of humour.

2

HAPPINESS was by far the reigning mood of my childhood. There was a balance of order and fun. Ours was a household in which someone was usually singing, someone drawing, someone climbing a tree, someone reading — or several of us doing one of those things together.

I was extraordinarily fortunate. I have friends of my generation who were small children in Europe during the war. One survived the firebombing of Hamburg, another, German but living in Latvia, fled bombardments with her family over and over again, across one border or another, wanted nowhere. They discovered their father, whom they had lost sight of for five years, in the Displaced Persons queue beside theirs, in Denmark. Another close friend, exactly my age, was on one of the trains to newly created Pakistan at the time of the Indian Partition. Almost his entire extended family was massacred by machete before his eleven-year-old eyes. Another friend was on *HMS Athenia*, the first ship to be torpedoed, September 3, 1939, right after World War Two began. She, her parents and her brothers were among the saved. (Their dog perished.) My friend was three years old, fevered with whooping cough and bundled into a pitching and tossing lifeboat. Of course I knew nothing of these other children when I was a child myself.

For my part I had the supreme luck of being born to parents who loved each other and their children dearly and, crucially at that time, we lived safely in Canada, safe, that is, if one's parents were middle class and of Anglo-Saxon background. Other people who much later became my friends spent childhood years in an internment camp for Japanese-Canadians, or, if First Nations, in a residential school. Later Jewish friends had family members who were trapped and perishing in a real-life nightmare. At the time, I have to say, despite the war, there was very nasty anti-Semitism in the Toronto of my childhood. I know this now. Then, it was taken for granted. Carol and I once were chased home from school by a gang of boys shouting "dirty Jews." Our curly hair apparently had created the confusion. We were frightened and felt an unfairness too. We weren't Jewish. I'm not sure we got the point of how much worse it would have been if we were.

As for us, we lived in a new house, built for us not long before I was born, in Forest Hill, an affluent neighbourhood of Toronto. Our house was typical of the area: of stone and brick, it had pretend-Tudor timbering and was large, though certainly not a mansion. We thought it a wonderful house. The back yard was perfect for childhood games, with shrubbery to hide in and enough space to run in, and a particular bush with nicely springy branches from which Chuck and I cut our bows and arrows. The front lawn featured a maple tree in which Carol and I spent countless hours, high up in a green world hidden among the leaves. And Forest Hill was villagey in certain ways: milk and bread were delivered daily by horse-drawn wagons so the streets had daily deposits of manure and a pleasant country smell. Mr. Kroll, a stout vegetable man with very little English and a small truck, rolled slowly through the neighbourhood stopping every block. A knife-sharpener, on foot and ringing a bell, pushed a large flint wheel ahead of him and aproned housewives ran out with carving knives and scissors. The mailman was called Postie and everyone knew him. Cars were few so we played our games of kick-the-can and tap-the-icebox on the road and when snow arrived used the road as a sleigh hill. Forest Hill today is grander and the street life of the 1940s is ancient history.

In the summers we drove in the Buick to North Hatley, a small

Quebec village on the north end of Lake Massawippi where our father had spent a few childhood holidays with his mother's much richer sister, his Aunt Emmy. Those visits gave him some of his few happy memories of childhood, so from when Chuck was a baby that was where he took us every June until school began again in September.

We arrive at the end of a hot day. It has been a very long car trip. We stopped the night before at some cabins with a very smelly picannini kaya — our family always uses those words for outside toilets and we hate them though we like the African words — and today Carol and Ruth have both been carsick and Daddy has to stop the car each time and wait while Mummy and whichever sister it is this time get out and Mummy holds her head as she crouches over. I try not to look. I hate to see the sick. If I do it will make that water come into my mouth which means the sickness will happen to me too. I stare hard out of the other side of the car. Whichever sister it is is always crying as she gets back into the car and I squeeze over away from her because I hate the smell. They suck barley sugar because Grandma says it helps but I don't like the disgusting way it doesn't really taste of anything. But I never get sick so I don't have to have any. Chucky doesn't get sick either even though he's only one. He gets to sit in the front on Mummy's knee except when Mummy sometimes comes in the back and Ruth gets the front seat; I never do and neither does Carol, which is unfair.

    We are at last about to be there. I have almost forgotten to think about where we are going as the driving to it has gone on so long. But then Daddy says, "Who will see the lake first?" and right away we all shout at the same second, "I will! I will!" There are patches of blue water behind some trees. The car stops at a little green hut. It's tucked in under the steep bank so we mostly just see its roof. Daddy says it is our boathouse, but we don't get out. I can see more of the lake, smooth and very blue, with another shore quite far off. Close to the shore that's just below us, an old man is rowing a boat. He leans way back as he dips in the oars and then gives a sudden jerk and sits up straight again, then leans back again. And then he's out of sight behind trees. Daddy has to back up the car after he shows us the boathouse and drives us off the main road and slowly up a steep little lane with trees very close on both sides and meeting over our heads. It's like a tunnel. And then at last we stop.

The house is above us. There is a grassy bank ending in a ditch full of ferns and there are wooden steps going up. The house is white with a shady verandah all along the front. It is a wooden house, which makes it completely different from any Toronto house as they are all brick and stone, and there are vines with big, round, pale green leaves hanging down.

"It's elephant ear vine!" Mummy says. She points to its tiny dark, curly pipes, the size for an old man Dutch doll to smoke. She smiles. "It's a good kind of vine. It doesn't attract any insects." I quickly hope no caterpillars. Do they count as insects? Carol and I both hate them, especially the smooth green kind that hide in big leaves. On the verandah, in the shadow of the vines, I can see a glider swing and four canvas deck chairs. We go in the door and right away I love the smell of the house and the dimness of the room we are in.

I ask, "What does it smell of?" And Mummy says: "Cottage! It's the smell of a cottage."

The living room is square and then we see there is a dining room next to it which has a fireplace, and that's where part of the nice smell is coming from, so I know it's smoke from logs, not coal. On each side of the fireplace is a window seat with pillows. I always like tucked away nooks and I right away plan to curl up in one of them for reading, or pretend reading. I really only look at pictures. I won't learn to read until grade one.

"A wood stove!" Mummy says when we explore the kitchen next. "Look at the flowers painted on the backdrop, so pretty!"

A stack of small logs is stored beside the stove, piled in a big basket, with some very skinny sticks for kindling. We know about wood stoves from when we lived at the Lucky Shot gold mine in Alaska. There is no fridge but behind the kitchen is a shed with what Mummy says is an icebox. There is already a big chunk of sharp-cornered ice in it and she is pleased about that. She lifts me up so I can see the ice and I notice tiny brown bits sticking on it that she says is sawdust. She tells us all how men must cut the ice from the lake in the winter and store it all summer long in a place in the woods where it will keep cool and frozen. I think it must be a deep cave, much bigger than a root cellar, and freezing cold, with ice chunks piled to the ceiling.

We run upstairs to find our bedrooms. Carol and Ruth are faster and they choose the first two bedrooms, but when I get to the last one I am glad because it's the nicest. Carol and I both laugh because we have doors onto the upstairs verandah and Ruth, who has the middle bedroom, doesn't. We will be able to sneak along to each other and no one will know. My room has a big bed, a grownup's bed, with a white bedspread and a pink-flowered comforter folded into a puffy lump. The bed has four gold-coloured posts and the posts have white china knobs at the tops. The dresser has a long white cloth on it and four china things: a little tray, two small pots with lids and a shallow dish. I ask Mummy what they are for and she says, "Why, for you to keep useful articles in," and we laugh because we both think of Eeyore's Birthday. I really, really like my room. This is a perfect house and I will have my sixth birthday here in just ten days.

We all love North Hatley and our cottage, the grownups just as much as the children. Daddy knows it from long ago and tells us a few things about when he was little here but not much. I can't see in my mind what he tells us. It feels too strange. I always can see Mummy's little girl stories but his are different. He doesn't give enough details.

We have a lake to learn to swim in — Ruth already can but Carol and I can't. We rent a rowboat from Mr. Sampson across the lake and try rowing. We often see that old man we saw rowing in that funny jerky way the first day. He is a gardener at a house way up the lake. And we have so many places to explore. First we find a wild place just up the steep bank behind our cottage, with raspberry bushes and some trees, and beyond that we come to the driveway to a big red house. It is one of the houses our Dad used to come to when he was a little boy. There is something sad about that. He shows us a picture of him, then, with his cousins, and he looks too different a person from the Dad I know to believe it can be him. The picture shows a small skinny boy in a funny bathing suit like a girl's. He's looking off at something else, away from the other kids, who are smiling. There is a little girl in the picture and two little boys as well as Daddy. The girl has hair like mine and is about my age.

I ask who she is and he says, "She was my cousin Frances. She died." It doesn't give me a good feeling. Did she die in that house? Did she get polio? Daddy doesn't tell. But we can run across its driveway without really looking at the red house where maybe a little girl with curly hair like ours died and then we are in a very old orchard. The apple trees are almost invisible because they are small and bent low, and there is tall golden rod and milkweed and tall, tall grass, and also some small fir trees. Carol and I make dens in the long grass, each of us stamping down a little circle we can hide in. I lie in mine and watch a ladybug climb a stalk of grass. Ladybugs are lucky to see. It is hot inside my den as the sun darts in through the tall grass and finds me, and I hear birds and sometimes a bee. I hug my knees and sniff my skin. Summer skin smells different from winter skin and nicer, like a biscuit.

Above the orchard — the countryside is all a hill — is the pasture. Carol and I are tremendously excited when we find it. It is so wide, almost a whole land, like a discovered new world in a fairy story, and it slopes up and up until finally there is a forest at the top. It takes us many days to discover it all. There are little groups of trees and some larger ones almost like woods and a big patch of wild rose bushes, and lots of other wildflowers, and there are zigzagging cow paths that we follow one after another, a different one each day until we know the whole pasture. At first there don't seem to be any cows in the pasture but then we discover two, and also the farmer, who tells us the cows' names are Dolly and Daisy. He tells us we can come back when he is milking and we can watch him and maybe he will teach us how to do it.

3

AS we three girls got older there was a kind of withdrawal of our father's natural warmth, or the expression of it. I always sensed the warmth was there, but somehow he no longer knew how to talk to his daughters as we became, one after another, adolescents. Unlike his younger brother, our Uncle Bunny, who kept the conversational channels open with his children as they matured, our father lacked confidence in himself and in us. Or that's how I see it now.

He was a complicated and vulnerable person. He had to become the man of his family at eleven years old. And having to fill that role, impossibly taxing for a child, must still have been an improvement over the frighteningly uncertain life that had come before. His difficult childhood ensured that he locked down a great deal. Even so, such was his strength that he had taken from what small offerings of love came his way — affection, perhaps, from one grandmother, and definitely from a servant in that grandmother's house — enough to forge a loving personality. His mother surely loved him too but my sense is that she was so beaten down — figuratively and maybe literally as well — by her situation, the situation created by her husband, that she could not protect her son. He may have found it hard to trust her love's worth. But I mentioned the servant because I have a sudden memory of a visit our father, Carol and I paid to an old, old lady when just the three of us were driving through Montreal.

Unaccountably we three had gone to Quebec City to a wedding of some cousin of our father's whom we'd never met before nor ever

18

met again. Why Carol and I, and not Mother and Ruth, say, were chosen to accompany him, I have no idea. But it was an adventure and we loved being with him, hearing stories of his African adventures and even explanations of things like road signs and markings. I don't know why I remember that last piece of trivia, but his voice explaining the meaning of the lines on the road has remained with me forever. We stayed at the Château Frontenac. I was eight or nine, and that early hotel experience made me richly enjoy hotel life ever since. This trip was before our father became uncomfortable with us, and having him to ourselves, as Carol and I did that week, made the experience a magic island of time.

Then on the way back from Quebec City we stopped in Montreal at an old stone house. I've no idea now where exactly in the city it was. By that time the house on Beaver Hall Hill our father had told us about may have been destroyed. Or it may have been that house.

It is an old stone house. We know it is old from the smell. It's stuffy and there is a nasty smoke undertone that isn't nice, not like the cottage's wood smoke smell. It's a house unlike any others we've been to. For instance, there are two staircases. We see one at the front of the house. It goes up right across from the front door, with a dark red carpet all the way up it to a landing, and the stairs turn so we can't see if the carpet goes on. But we don't go up that one, and instead go down a long dim hall, through a big chilly kitchen, and there is a second staircase. It is just wood, with no carpet, and steeper. Our father goes up first and fast and Carol and I try to keep up.

Finally we get to the top of the house and are in what we know is an attic because when we look into the small rooms off the hall, the ceiling slopes steeply so that in parts of the room a grownup couldn't possibly stand up, maybe not even a child.

Daddy goes into one of these rooms and we follow him closely and peer around him to see the person we have come to see. He has told us almost nothing about who this person is, just that her name is Hattie and she is very old and weak now and it is important that we stop and visit her. We drive through Montreal every time we go to and from North Hatley but have never stopped at this house before. I wonder if maybe Hattie is dying and that is why Daddy is making this visit.

I find looking at very old people frightening. I dread seeing something terrible, something horrible for the old person having it, and — this seems mean and makes me sad about myself — disgusting for me to have to see. I don't know what might happen to a human body just before a person dies and I don't want to know. I even get a little of that feeling sometimes when Grandma visits. I love Grandma and she is not so old that she's about to die but I sometimes come upon something I wish I hadn't. For example I once saw a strange, sort of flat, pink rubber bag hanging on the back of the bathroom door. It definitely was not a hot water bottle. I asked Mum what it was and she said it was an enema bag and explained what it was for as if it was quite an ordinary thing. It wasn't a bit ordinary to me. Anyway, I don't want Hattie to die right this minute while we are there. I hardly want to look at her but I do. Daddy takes my hand and we go forward to stand close beside the bed so she can see us. If she can look. I'm not sure if she sees us or not.

Her face is very, very small. Her skin is wrinkled and looks like a walnut's shell and is the same colour. Above her face is a small clump of white hair brushed to the side. There's so little of it that I can see bits of her walnut head through it.

"It's Charlie, Hattie," Daddy says. "I've brought my little girls, Carol and Anne, to meet you."

I try to smile. I know Daddy wants us to be friendly and I want to be kind. I can't help looking at the rest of her, or as much as can be guessed at because she's covered right up to her neck with blankets. A white sheet is folded down over the top one so the blanket doesn't rub against her face. Someone must be looking after her, and carefully.

I can see a potty under the bed, but it is empty and clean. Even so there is a smell that makes me feel a bit sick. Is it just oldness? There's an on-top smell of some sort of not very nice soap, but underneath it is something else a bit like poo. I try not to breathe in very often. Which doesn't work. Hattie's whole self is really tiny; the covers barely rise over her body. It could be just a cat stretched out under there, and where what must be her feet poke up is not at all far down the bed. She is much smaller than I am. I suddenly think of the Egyptian mummies in the Royal Ontario Museum. Ruth always makes us have a good long stare at them whenever we go. It is almost impossible to believe they were once humans, in fact not really possible at all. I always think of them as female because of the name. Ruth says they weren't necessarily but I never can bear to connect them with real humans, somehow especially women. They always give me a sort of shivery sinking feeling in the bottom of my stomach but seeing Hattie is worse because she is actually still alive, even if barely, and I can't pretend to myself she isn't a human.

When we leave that house and are driving away, our father tells us as much as he knows about Hattie's early story. It is just like a story in a book, as many of the stories in our family are.

One day my father's maternal step-grandfather went to the railroad station in Montreal to collect something sent to him. He also found there a little girl whom no one had come to meet. He had arrived a little while after the train came in, to give the porters time to unload parcels. Everyone had already left the station. That is, not quite everyone: standing all alone in the middle of the huge, echoing waiting room was a tiny girl-child. She didn't move at all, just stood there like a teeny statue.

She was wearing an old coat that came down almost to her ankles and was missing some of its hem stitching so in those places it hung even lower. A label was pinned with a safety pin on the coat, with her name in a grownup's hand. On her head was a floppy woollen beret. In front of her, its wooden handles clasped in both of her

INLAND NAVIGATION BY THE STARS 21

very small hands, she carried a cloth bag. She looked about six but later the family realized she had to be more than that, perhaps ten. She didn't know her own birthday, nor her exact age. She was probably so small because she'd never been properly nourished. She had been sent over from England, as orphans or just very poor children often were in those days and even much later, to be taken into some household who wanted a child. Her story was rather like Anne's in *Anne of Green Gables*, though Anne was just from another Maritime province. Unwanted children were shipped about the country and the world to help out on farm, or work as domestics in towns, or, if they were extremely fortunate, to live as family members.

But no one had come for Hattie. Perhaps someone had observed the frail little soul and decided, no, there would be no usefulness there.

Anyway, Grandfather Stewart, as he was called, and this is the only story in which he features, took her home for dinner. She stayed for the rest of her life. She had been a fixture in my father's childhood in his visits, though rare, to the house on Beaver Hall Hill. And it was clear that day, by how badly he needed to see her one last time, and by his reaction when he saw the tiny bundle in the bed, that he had loved her. She must have been kind to a little boy who felt adrift in the world, as she had been.

My father, despite the paltry share of love he had known when young, was sensitive, loving and exceptionally kind. He hated the very idea of an adult hurting a young person. I once told him of a girl in my class at Havergal whose father made her eat in the kitchen rather than with the family in the dining room. Her pimples disgusted him and put him off his food. My father's face was stricken at this story; he was appalled by the cruelty of that father.

My father was clever: from both his parents, despite their obvious personality weaknesses, he inherited brains, and clearly from some other antecedent a strong work ethic and strong sense of responsibility. After his father's death my father, still a child, found jobs delivering papers, shovelling snow, any tasks for which a skinny kid could earn a few pennies. However that was inadequate and once into his teens he had to drop out of school in order to provide more. I'm not sure exactly at what age this dropping out happened, but I do know that he remained ambitious for an education. He continued his studies on his own and eventually, as an external student, took McGill entrance exams.

By then a young man he could work underground in the mines of northern Quebec and Ontario and make enough to fund university. The situation was also improved when his mother remarried, which meant he no longer had the full weight of caring for her as well as for his sister and their much younger brother. He chose a profession, mining engineering, that led to adventure and a testing of himself physically and in other ways as well. He was tall but skinny, with light brown curly hair, a narrow face and bright blue eyes. He cannot have found it a simple matter, at least at first, to take charge of teams of men more physically powerful and often older than he, as they navigated the wilderness of Africa, and then the far north of Canada, Alaska, South America. But he did so and he was successful. He had a casual air about his success. He hated pomposity or snobbery. The pick with which he had discovered the seam of gold in northern Ontario that made his fortune just hung in the back shed and was used by us children if we wanted something to dig with.

His children all loved him and we knew he loved us. But we all had difficult moments with him when communication became confounded on both sides. He could be upset by one of us, often out of the blue. It must have been that we triggered something in him that none of us, I'm sure including him, understood. His disapproval of one of us, conveyed only by the look, hung in the air for a while like a strangely stiff grey fog.

Once he came to my boarding school to take me to a film. I was fourteen and for once had felt compelled to put on some lipstick in the face of my roommates' astonishment as I headed out without it. In the darkness of the theatre I was suddenly aware of my father looking sideways at me. Shock and distaste transfixed his face as he hissed, "Are you wearing lipstick?" Unaccountably he somehow hadn't noticed it on our way to the theatre; maybe the light from the screen for a moment made my lips shine. I felt searing shame. But why was it so dreadful? I didn't know. But it was. And I hadn't even wanted to wear it.

Two key women in his early life enacted opposing but equally destructive stereotypes. This was never put into words. That would have been impossible. Underground, fear moved about in our father and inevitably infected us, his daughters. Might one of us go in the direction of the wild promiscuity and general fecklessness of his sister Ruth? Or might someone have inherited the hopeless passivity of his mother? Would that be the better alternative? What sense does a daughter make of such intense paternal emotions when they are expressed only in alarmed eyes, heavy silences, an abrupt leaving of a room? The unspoken messages didn't stop coming even when we became adults.

Our Aunt Ruth was two years younger than our father. I'm sure he loved her when they were children, indeed probably always. When they were young he was her protector from the constantly shifting ground of their family, particularly the raging and erratic temper of their father. Apparently she was a creative, dramatic, volatile girl; in the rare photos I've seen of her she has a quantity of dark curly hair and dark eyes. She was exotic looking, unlike my fair, blue-eyed father, and she played on that. All her life any story she told was a wild exaggeration or a lie. This could be funny and exciting, but also alarming.

For my whole early childhood I knew her only through snippets of stories, vivid as snapshots, the surrounding circumstances never elaborated on enough to figure out rhyme or reason. One image is of my young mother, an Anglican canon's virtuous daughter, being forced by her sister-in-law Ruth to hide behind a pillar in the Biltmore Hotel in New York to spy on Ruth's first adulterous husband. Another scene also comes from the protracted collapse of that first marriage, of Aunt Ruth's widowed, poverty-stricken mother selling her own rings to scramble the money together to pay for the divorce. The legal stipulation was that there be no marital relations between the first court action and the decree nisi. Nevertheless Aunt Ruth went down to the station to see him off to somewhere. These stories are never complete. Was this also in New York? Where was he off to? Of course she simply couldn't resist leaping on the train with him and sharing his berth. It was much too dramatic a situation not to play out. Back to square one with the divorce, her mother's rings sacrificed in vain.

How she then supported herself and her one child, Douglas, is another shadowy area. The details were clearly too unsavoury for us to hear much about them. She worked as some sort of actress, sang and danced in some kind of Montreal clubs; there were many men.

Who saw to the tiny boy, Douglas? It's likely he was left alone much of the time. My very maternal mother, who was our source of any glimpses we got, was appalled at the neglect of Douglas, distressed by the worn and dirty state of his clothes on the rare occasion she saw him. His father was long lost to view when suddenly the little boy had to have an appendix operation. This was Montreal in the mid-1930s and the church, and the Napoleonic Code, ruled the law, as indeed it did for several more decades. A child or a woman could not have an operation in Quebec without a father's (or, for a married woman, a husband's) permission. The nuns at Hôtel Dieu de Montréal knelt in prayer around Douglas's bed — as a child I found nuns sinister figures and I pictured their enveloping black habits, their bald heads under wimples, their severe white faces, their closed eyes — until his appendix burst and he died.

The child must have suffered agony before death took him.

He was eight years old, our cousin we never met. Our mother was sure she would have snatched up any child of hers in such a mortal plight and made a dash for Ontario where saner laws prevailed.

There were also tales of how Aunt Ruth would borrow money from her brothers for some scheme of hers — money of course never paid back. One apparently typical time was when she managed to weasel her younger brother's savings out of him, by pleading and tears. That was my Uncle Bunny, who was then working hard to save enough to start university. The savings she nipped off with he never saw again. Another case of back to square one, that time for poor Uncle Bun.

At some point she essentially disappeared. Until I was ten or eleven, to me she was simply a distressing rumour. Mention of her brought a certain look of distaste to our mother's usually kind face, and if we were lucky, and our father not present, she might reveal a few of the details I've just described, maybe adding another one.

And then I have a brief but clear memory of our stopping, on the way back to Toronto from North Hatley, at a rural farmhouse where the aunt-of-dark-mystery was staying.

Our mother and we children remain in the car, but I can see our father standing some distance away under a yellowing willow tree and talking to a woman. She is standing among fallen yellow leaves and talking agitatedly, her hands gesturing, then clasped. Her look is an imploring one. Is she actually crying? I am too far away to see if there are tears. I have a feeling that she is faking: her movements and expression are too dramatic to be real.

Our father is standing back from her a little. He looks uncomfortable. I know he doesn't like someone to be crying because he's soft-hearted but even more doesn't like a person to exaggerate feelings or even worse, pretend them entirely. We are all consumed with curiosity but our father is silent when he gets back into the car.

We later gleaned — it can only have been from our mother — that our aunt was begging him for the money she needed to board at that farmhouse for a while and write a book. I suspect he gave her the funds, sent them later, that is. I'm pretty sure no money changed hands on the spot.

No book ever appeared.

Another time a couple of years on she came for a brief visit to North Hatley. I remember she started to come for a walk up the hill with us but stopped only a little way up into the pasture to sit in the grass and dream and "commune with nature." I watched her settle herself and was sure she was simply lazy rather than having some sort of poetic moment. My sister Ruth told me afterwards that Aunt Ruth thought both she and Carol had artistic temperaments and talents but that I was a hopeless tomboy with no sort of interesting future.

Probably most family trees have a feckless Aunt Ruth figure lurking in the branches but for our father I am sure she was forever a strong and threatening example of how a girl could turn out. He had loved and protected her when they were children — and look what she had become! Feckless Aunt Ruth had three feckless husbands and, from our remote vantage point, lived a disastrous and irresponsible life. What her life was really like from her point of view is something I can never know. If her childhood family had offered her security more solid than what a brother not much older than she herself could provide, if her mother had been stronger ... and as for her father! But a person in our family could put herself beyond the pale. It was a tough lesson for those who followed, and the scapegoat who provided it essentially was banished forever.

INLAND NAVIGATION BY THE STARS 27

4

THE hopelessly inadequate husband and father, my grandfather Thomas Coleman, is a man of almost total mystery to my generation. His own original family were people of consequence for several generations in Canada, going back to the Thomas Coleman who arrived in the New World from England in the late eighteenth century. He was a United Empire Loyalist who became a Captain and raised a regiment in the District of Montreal, the Canadian Light Dragoons, to fight in the War of 1812. For his services he was given over 800 acres in what became Belleville, Ontario, and built the enormous, very ugly, Italianate Coleman's Castle there (now a funeral home; I've seen it). He was followed by illustrious descendants, the men all doctors, lawyers or other worthies. In my grandfather's generation, one brother, Alfred, became a medical doctor and Thomas a dentist.

My grandmother was eighteen when she met Dr. Thomas Coleman and to that point she must have been a very clever and ambitious girl. He was her professor. He was exactly double her age.

One of seven children she graduated from Montreal High School in 1898 with the top marks in her year. That meant she earned the title "Dux." She was the only family member to go on to university and she chose medical school.

I imagine her as a lovely looking tall girl with curly light brown hair worn drawn back in a bun, the style of the time, and large blue eyes. I have to use my imagination to create the girl Ruth as I've seen only two photos of her and in them she no longer looks young. In one she looks far older than she must actually have been, given that my father as a toddler is also in the picture. She can only have been twenty-one or twenty-two. She is crouching down beside him, not smiling, and is looking up at the camera. Her eyes are serious, perhaps sad. The child is solemn also. The two seem to be in a sort of tenement yard, outdoors but with walls on the three sides one can see and presumably one also behind the photographer. It looks a rather wretched place, outdoors but no blade of grass or shrub in sight. If they are in Montreal, it's not a part of the city I know.

In the other photo she is much older and is sitting on a bench outdoors with my mother, and I think this must be in New York, just before my mother sailed for Africa to join my father. You can see that my grandmother has been a good-looking woman, indeed still is, in a rather haggard way — the large eyes, the high cheekbones — but both women have unsmiling faces. I have no idea what my mother really thought of her mother-in-law. Her loyalty to our father held her tongue, most of the time.

But how did things ever get going between Ruth and her professor? It is a puzzle. She must have worked so hard to get where she was. If she were the one who made the first move, why would she risk everything she had remarkably achieved for this man, so much older than she? It seems more likely to me that he forced himself upon her. But what sort of man does that make him and why was he unmarried at thirty-six anyway? Unanswerable questions. What we do know is that they ran away together a couple of months after she entered his class, in November of her first and only university year.

How I long to know what in the world really happened to the brave and very smart young woman who did something so unusual as get herself into medical school in 1898. Something happened to her. Thomas Coleman happened to her. And the strong, clever, capable and ambitious girl she had been up to then disappeared without a trace for the rest of her life.

We, my siblings and I, always assumed they married immediately, but a distant family connection did some research just this year and found the record of their marriage. It was a surprise. They were not wed until two years after the runaway and after the death of their first child, a son, another Thomas. His death is recorded in the family Bible, without mention of his parents being unmarried at the time. But why the delay in marrying? Did he try to get out of it? Did she? But she would have been so vulnerable, and pregnant; she would have needed marriage. Otherwise, who would have taken her in? Did my father know the truth of any of this and never reveal? I thought that over for a moment and then realized: if he'd known he would not have told us.

What possessed this man to act in a way that meant the end of his professorial position, and then to live a strange, wandering life?

All we know is that he set up dental practices in one town after another, constantly moving his family, as it grew, from one small town to another around Quebec and Ontario. This was surely unwise in a profession that usually requires building confidence in the community.

He was a sadistic man and brutal to my father: one time, at least, he administered a vicious beating with a belt soaked overnight in brine so the wounds would really smart: it was a plotted and elaborated punishment.

It was our mother who told us of that beating, and also that it was actually his sister who had committed whatever the naughtiness had been. Our father protected her and took the blame. And as with Aunt Ruth's neglect of Douglas, here too our mother condemned. She could never forgive our grandmother for not managing to stop it. But our mother had no experience of living with an abusive husband. Fear can be paralyzing. It can leach away power.

My sisters and I have wondered if our grandfather was an alcoholic, or was addicted to drugs, which, for a dentist, we assumed, would have been easy to obtain. Addiction could explain his moving the family so often, unwise for a professional man but necessary for — what? We don't know what drug, available then, would have caused his rages, not to speak of his strange absences for stretches of time. Our fantasist Aunt Ruth, who came to North Hatley again for a visit in her old age, told my sister Ruth and me on a long evening walk that he had been a bigamist and had another family in a nearby town. That was her explanation for his absences, based on scenes "observed" or "overheard" by her as a small child. She was only nine when he died so her spying seems improbable.

She told us another story on that walk. It turned on one of our grandmother's brothers. Remember she was one of seven children, and we know almost nothing about them, bar one brother whom we met once, and Aunt Emmy, also seen only the once. The dramatic tale she unfolded was something we'd never heard a whisper of but she had several details: one dark night our great-uncle rushed into a millenary establishment — a code term for a brothel, she explained — and there he shot and killed his faithless mistress. She lay in a great pool of blood and he fled the scene, racing to hide in the family home on Beaver Hall Hill. Aunt Ruth claimed to have watched from the window there as the police came and dragged her struggling uncle away.

As soon as we got home from this rather electrifying walk Ruth and I could not resist hastening to our father for confirmation, or much more likely, denial, of all this. His face went very pink and his bright blue eyes bulged a little as they did when he was overcome with emotion. He was extremely upset. Aunt Ruth had details wrong; she had been much too small at the time — a toddler — and would not have been staying in that house, and so could not have observed his arrest. But the murder was not a lie, nor was the brothel detail. Our father was upset simply out of shame. He had hoped we would never know of such a deeply unpleasant blot on his maternal side.

As for the bigamy story there is no evidence to support that notion. Certainly no other family came forward after his death. And as for drugs, when he died the family was left destitute. Would a man's financial resources be drained back then by drug addiction as they could be now? In that era, the years leading up to World War One (he died in 1913), laudanum, for example, was readily available and I believe not particularly costly. As well, opium derivatives are calming not enraging.

In the family Bible, in an erased and rewritten entry, his cause of death is recorded as meningitis. However my sister Ruth before she died did research that resulted in a different finding: he died in a mental hospital in Whitby, Ontario, of what was described as "acute mania," whatever that might have meant in 1913. My brother recalls a further detail Ruth turned up: our grandfather died over a five-day period. I don't remember this as part of our sister's findings, and my brother had his death year wrong, but he may well be right about the five days. One thing I'm ever more sure of is how shifting all of our memories, anyone's memories, are. We select, we remove, we add.

Maybe today our grandfather would be diagnosed as bipolar. But I think a person doesn't actually die of that. Maybe he committed suicide while manic. If so and the five-day lingering on death's threshold is true, he must have almost botched the job.

And where was his family during his time in the mental hospital? I have no idea. My grandmother would have been just thirty-three years old, her children, my father eleven, his sister, nine, and Bunny, the little brother, just three.

Whatever he died of the worsening of his frightful affliction over the years must have terrified his family, my father bearing the brunt as far as the children were concerned, though what his mother was going through I can only try to imagine. I, two generations later, would find it horribly difficult to cope with a mentally ill husband — with the fear, the shame, the threat of violence — but I knew that, ultimately, my family would help me. My grandmother's family never did so in any sustained way. There were occasional visits, stays in an attic room. Old clothing might be passed along. My father had to wear a girl cousin's outgrown boots to school, cruelly humiliating for him.

My father himself suffered from several severe clinical depressions in the 1950s and 60s. I know now that the doctors who treated him during those years knew almost nothing about what they were doing. For him his own father's bizarre life and death must have added an extra turn of the screw. As well as suffering the illness, and the horrific shock treatments, cruelly administered daily and for many weeks without anaesthetic, he must have dreaded turning into a replica of the man whose cruelty must have haunted him.

This is not an unusual story. I am sure there is a fantasist aunt in many a family tree (in our case, Aunt Ruth), and many a mad grandfather, or even a great-uncle murderer, spoken of only in whispers, or never, by their descendants. Dead, they are perched safely now among the leaves, as silent as daytime owls. But it's not that long ago, well into my lifetime anyway, that such relatives ranted and flailed about their families' living rooms or brooded grimly in corners. If they couldn't be stuffed into the attic, Bertha Rochester style, or into a locked shed or a boathouse, as two women in my North Hatley childhood were, they embarrassed or terrorized others until death released them. And their dark secrets float down the generations, appearing sometimes in dreams. Subtly they may affect us. We are never told enough to understand, just enough to be uneasy. How can we know if a particular strain of lunacy lurks within us too, and do we encourage or discourage its emergence when we dig out and pass down the tales (as I am doing now)? Or is it best to hide them, as our parents did?

I came across a poem by Thomas Hardy just now. I must have read it long ago, but rediscovering it as I write this, I shivered. It is called "Heredity" and begins, "I am the family face." The "I" of the poem, the face, reappears again and again. It hops down the years and lands in one generation or another. The ancestors are lost in time's mist. Current inhabitants of the face know nothing of them. I have, as did my father, my grandmother's eyes and hair. I was once told I have her hands. What do I carry of my mad grandfather?

Nowadays, with more known about the brain, we have ways, sometimes and if they are willing, of helping such people. And there is help for families even if the sick individual is unwilling to accept any. But a generation or two ago there was silence and deep shame. And I think of our current society's recognition of the need for support for those suffering from mental misery arising out of past events — PTSD. My generation's parents were affected by the Depression, by both World Wars — the first, as children, and the second, in adulthood — with a father or older brother either killed, as was my mother's brother, or returned home often in speechless shock.

I have mentioned several close friends who were children in Europe during World War Two. One woman, now eighty-two, after a full, very busy and happy life as a wife and mother in Canada, at eighty began to experience extreme night-time horrors. Her doctor helped her to recognize that she was experiencing the delayed PTSD she simply had not had time for earlier. In old age she had fewer defences against her memories' surfacing.

All this has always been the human lot, one generation's wars and other horrors hanging, usually not spoken of, in the background of their children and grandchildren.

5

I mentioned my father's Aunt Emmy earlier, the richer sister of his mother and with whom he spent those North Hatley summer visits he remembered so fondly and were the reason for our going there many years later. Aunt Emmy's history was in one way similar to my grandmother's: she married the wrong man. His name was Robert McNeil and he was a wrong choice in one rather key way. He was an alcoholic. Yes, that familiar story. But he was a good choice in another, for her if not for him. There was money in the family and when he left or was sent away, somehow the money stuck to Aunt Emmy.

One of the snapshot images I have in my head from old family stories is of someone coming home: there is a limp bundle of old clothes unaccountably at the doorway. Whoever is returning approaches, puzzled. The bundle turns out to be a man, the erring husband, Aunt Emmy's husband, drunkenly unconscious. That's the whole of the snapshot. So — they had rid themselves of him somehow and now they must do so again. And did. How? Family history does not reveal.

But his backstory is the interesting and lucky part, for Aunt Emmy. His father, also Robert MacNeil, had been a bank manager somewhere in New England. One fine day — those are the words in which the story tells itself (so much happens on either "a fine day" or "a dark night") — he removed all the funds deposited in the bank he managed (I picture him swiftly stuffing bundles of banknotes into a large carpet bag), grabbed his wife's hand, leapt into a horse and buggy and nipped away, to Canada. He crossed the border from Vermont into Quebec and soon fetched up in North Hatley where, with his thieved funds, he bought property up behind the hill to the north of the lake. He built a house to which he added a secret set of rooms in which to hide if the law came after him. He feared a posse galloping up over the border and up the highway to North Hatley. It never came. In the fullness of time the stolen funds, or what was left of them, became Aunt Emmy's.

We visited Aunt Emmy once in Montreal, on our way through. She lived in a large stone mansion on the mountain and had a lover called Mr. Fraser, whose presence made my mother uncomfortable. I suspect she hadn't known he would be there when she agreed to the visit. When he subsequently sent us a shiny tin pail of hard candies for Christmas, she spirited them away. We weren't allowed to eat them — lest we be morally contaminated? Was that when we learned he was her lover? As a child I wouldn't have understood what was involved with the role but later when I did know it was even more of a puzzle. He was stout and old and looked like Beatrix Potter's Jeremy Fisher. I couldn't see the point. But it was clear Aunt Emmy had once been beautiful. Attractive women misbehaving at any stage of life were thick in the family tree. No wonder our father worried about his daughters.

But these flowing streams of life, of biology — brain, limbs, eye colour, the blood moving in my veins, the colour and curl of my hair — all of them connect me to my siblings and parents but also to long dead people. But I wrote "brain" first just now: if the other things come down to me from the dead, what about my brain? Me?

Everyone, depending on our stage of life, is a bud, a leaf or a dry twig of an enormous, endlessly branching system, each of us convinced of our own pulsing and immediate self as a singular thing. I never thought about this when I was younger. It is only now that I see it could be a rational way to accept my mortality. I will be gone but my genetic substance will carry on.

At the same time I have to feel there is an essential individual, Anne, who has created herself out of what was given. Rational or not, I have to feel that.

✦

When I was a small child my father was writing a book, or really not yet writing it but just doing preliminary research. The title I remember well as the project was spoken of for several years. It was to be "Inland Navigation by the Stars." He had spent much of his life in various inland wildernesses — in the Canadian far north and Alaska, in southern Africa, in South America, usually as the only white man, and as such, the leader. The book's purpose was to be a guide for other lone wilderness venturers. All I am aware of about the book, apart from its title, is an image of my father in moonlit darkness of our Forest Hill kitchen, crouching over a shallow pan of a thick, gleaming near-liquid substance, placed on the high kitchen stool. I had an idea it was molasses but my brother claims mercury, which seems more likely, more scientific. The dark surface of the mercury — if mercury it was — caught reflected light. Moonlight? Starlight? Can this be a true memory? It is so odd! What precisely he was doing I had no idea then nor do I now, only that it had to do with his book.

His book was never written (other methods of navigation presumably overtook it) but his attempts suggest to me in some hazy and symbolic way what I am doing in my own book: navigating darkness, a darkness that is sometimes shot with light; I am seeking him, and myself, and all of us who perch, dangle or almost entirely hide, in the branches and leaves of our family tree.

Also I simply want his title to have its life.

6

BUT what of our mother? What dark secrets are hidden among the leaves on her side of our family tree?

Mother's immediate family was irreproachable. There were five children.

The oldest, Edward, was very handsome, clever and athletic. I have pictures of him looking tall and stalwart in the uniforms of various Bishop's University sports teams. He got his BA at Bishop's and then was studying law at McGill but suddenly joined up and became a soldier in the Great War. There was some oddness about that. The story was that he and a few friends joined as a joke, and as Privates. With his education he ought to have been an officer. My grandmother was always bitter about that: his cousins were all officers and they survived. She was likely wrong about his increased risk: officers were killed in the droves, going over the top first as they were expected to do. In any case, Edward was killed on the Somme.

Next came Catherine, her father's favourite daughter — he had her always sit beside him at the table, his hand gently on hers. She died of pneumonia at age thirteen. Then came Hazel, pleasant enough looking but without the beauty of her sisters. (She got to sit down the table, out of sight. I find the insensitivity of that era astonishing! Everyone in the situation took such favouritism as entirely normal and my grandfather was considered a kind man.) My mother was five years younger than Hazel, and the most beautiful of all. There was a late arriver, Ellis, who was born the same year, 1916, that his older brother Edward was killed, and then, before the year was out, Ellis died too. My poor grandmother losing her two sons so close together — their hero, Edward, and the darling ten-month old "surprise" baby: the grief in that household must have nearly sunk them.

Mother's father was an Anglican canon, one of three brothers who were all clergymen. I have a photograph of the three Ireland brothers standing outdoors in a row, their white surplices blowing sideways in the breeze, Uncle Charlie, Uncle Austin and our grandfather James.

No dark secrets so far, but now we come to my grandmother's family.

They were a large group, though that was not unusual in the mid-nineteenth century (Grandma was born in 1869). She had eleven brothers and one sister, if I have the number right, and she was one of the younger ones, with, I think, only one brother younger than she. I am shaky on the details as there was a certain amount of murk in that family, making the facts about some members sketchy.

Several of her brothers also were Anglican clergymen — more rows of white surplices in photos. Another brother had a grocery store in what became Westmount. So far, so upstanding. It was other brothers who provided the murk: they owned considerable property in downtown Montreal, part of which later became the site of the Central Railway Station, and another part, later still, of the Queen Elizabeth Hotel. When the Charters brothers had it, however, there were brothels on the site. I don't know how hands-on the brothers were in running the establishments but they owned them. I do know that early in my own parents' marriage the properties were being hastily sold, and sold for much less than even the land alone ought to have been worth. I have my own, perhaps wild, perhaps correct, notion that the situation became too hot for them. I picture criminal elements bringing pressure to bear and the brothers not being clever enough to play the game to their own advantage. It could easily be true, given Montreal at the time. Or indeed any time.

There was also some other, I think unconnected, skullduggery about money that my grandmother should have inherited and that her brothers tricked her out of. My father tried and failed to sort something out for her but he was too young and inexperienced at the time for them to pay attention to him. But despite the incongruity of ministers and brothel keepers in the same family, and both sets cheating their sister, everyone got along in lively and affectionate fashion, the hypocrisy of the era serving them well. It was all rather like an Ibsen play, except nobody got the comeuppance the playwright would have arranged for them.

There were other stories, set long enough ago that they had lost any sting they might once have had, that my grandmother used to tell us. When she was a small girl living in the family farmhouse, situated more or less at the corner of St Catherine Street and Metcalfe Street in present day Westmount, her own grandmother lived with the family. Her husband had been a sea captain, supposedly. Rank is sometimes enhanced in old tales. He may have been a common seaman. He rarely returned to his homeport of Aberdeen, Scotland. He was a drinker and his wife may also have suspected he had wives in other ports. In any case, after one long absence of his she determined to emigrate with her grown children to Canada, and did so. Years passed.

"One winter's night there came a knock at the door." These are Grandma's exact words. This sort of story is always told in precisely the same ones. The rest of the family being occupied, the old lady went to answer the knock. Outside in the snow stood "an old fella." For some reason for the purposes of this tale it had to be "fella," not a normal word for her. He was clearly an old bum and she made to close the door on him. But he had thrust a foot forward and over the threshold. "Janet, don't you recognize me?" he said.

Looking down, she saw the broken boot he had thrust forward. I picture her cringing with shame at the sad sight of that boot, unsure if the shame was for him or for herself.

"No. I do not recognize you," she said, trying again to close the door.

"But Janet! I'm your own husband!"

"I have no husband. I've been a widow for years." And she struggled with the door again. At this point one of her children heard the commotion and hurried forward to sort out the situation.

There was no escape from the facts for poor Janet: the old man came in, and stayed, for the rest of his life. However, until the day she died, she maintained that he was no husband of hers. My grandmother remembered him well, how he sat in his nook by the fire and pretended not to like the whisky he had to be allowed. He would purse his lips, pretending distaste, and say, "Oh my nasty medicine." And he would take her side and save her when a brother teased by pretending to be a bear under the bearskin rug.

How the stories in my mother's family could have been taken as any sort of lessons is less clear than the ones in my father's. The moral lines are more blurred; rascals are not necessarily cast out. There was more kindness, seemingly, also cheating and probably criminality. There was considerable hypocrisy. But moral lessons, or any lessons, are not overtly passed anyway. It's more subtle than that.

I keep returning to the same theme and images. I always felt, almost no matter how taxing or even dreadful and frightening a situation might be, that my life was richly interesting and I was its heroine. And I would survive. Yet those myriad generations, all those crowds of people, hang in the branches of a towering, hugely towering, family tree — those owls, as well as larks and wrens and woodpeckers, vultures even — and something of them funnels down into me. They were. I am. I am, at the moment. One day I will be past tense too.

One of the most fascinating things of having lived this long and having known several generations is seeing personality traits and talents, as well as physical characteristics, pop up, sometimes skipping a generation or even two.

My elder granddaughter not only has legs like mine but also has my sort of shyness. For both of us our shyness lasted until university when overnight it disappeared. Each in our generation had sat

INLAND NAVIGATION BY THE STARS 41

mostly quietly in our school classes and preferred listening to participating. Teachers' reports always suggested more speaking up. At age seventeen, fifty-odd years apart, suddenly each girl began to talk, sometimes to engage professors and often to hold forth with classmates in debate. Something had clicked on like a light switch and empowered speech. Sarah also has my sort of bookishness and my way with words. We both speak rather loudly and often "know best," and must check ourselves for bossiness.

My oldest grandson's mind also works in ways very familiar to mine. He is a writer too and also has the luck of his Molnar grandfather's athleticism. On the other hand, I see in my oldest great-grandson the same intense, thoughtful consideration before he enters any activity that I saw in my son's face at the same age. I also see the optimism of my mother moving through me and on to some, while others of my descendants have to struggle at times with shadows.

7

MY mother's life, apart from the periods of intense grief at family deaths, was very secure and happy. She was dearly loved, tall and beautiful, musical, a reader, clever with her needle. After high school she took a year of teacher training at Macdonald College. It was there that she met my father who had come with some other boys from McGill out to Macdonald to a dance. He was immediately struck by the sweetness of Jennie Ireland — as her name then was. After their marriage he changed not just her last name as was normal, but also her first. Jennie became Jane, his way of establishing that she was his now. And he took her away to southern Africa where they spent the first five years of their marriage.

The African years had an impact on all of us, not just on Ruth, who was born there. The stories of their life there became family mythology: our father's long stretches out on the bushveldt with his "boys," really men, of course, but everyone used the colonial terminology. Africans were "boys." Children were "picannins." He had encounters with lions, water buffalo and rhinos. Urged on by his "boys" he shot an elephant. He became thin and brown and wore two hats to ward off the sun. He contracted malaria over and over, and suffered worms that burrowed under the skin. At night he gazed at the sky to plot the next day's trek by the stars. He once walked a hundred miles, trying to save a man mauled by a lion. The man, an American would-be Great White Hunter who had somehow at one point insisted on tagging along, wounded a lion and then refused my father's advice to "never, ever follow a wounded lion into the long grass." His torn body — my father had to shoot the lion in order to rescue the dolt — was increasingly consumed by gangrene over the days it took my father and his "boys" to carry him to a hospital. He died just before they got there.

That was a warning all his children took seriously and we keenly awaited our chance to follow it.

Mother went out to him eighteen months after he went himself, when at last he was able to have a sort of home base even if he was still mostly out on the veldt. She kept house for him, with the help of a "boy" called Gibson, in a shack with furniture they made themselves out of dynamite boxes. She had her first baby in a tiny rondavel hut with a midwife in attendance. She always claimed it as her favourite birthing experience, much richer than her later ones, knocked out and oblivious in Montreal and Toronto hospitals and in bed for two weeks afterwards, a nurse sitting by the bedside. I imagine she also must have relished creating her role as a mother far from the influence of her own mother whose Victorian anxieties about a baby's feeding and (especially) bowels, and essential fragility, inevitably would have intruded. She didn't even tell her mother a baby was expected, writing of her pregnancy only when she knew the cable announcing the birth would have arrived. Letters took six weeks. When the baby was a little older, mother had another houseboy, a "picannin" called Saucepan, to help her. His task was to return toys the baby threw out of her cot.

It was that first experience of hers that made me insist, in 1958 when it absolutely was not done, on having as natural a birth as I could arrange in Montreal. I found what I later learned was possibly the only doctor in Canada at the time to allow such a thing. There were no childbirth classes or any sort of instruction so I sent to England for a book I'd heard of, *Childbirth Without Fear*, by Dr. Grantly Dick-Read, and I practiced the breathing exercises, by myself, and in due course pushed out my son Paul while watching in an overhead mirror, both of us fully engaged in the event, though only I remember it.

Nowadays of course this is how most women give birth, and my elder granddaughter even had her third little boy as a "water birth," her husband her only helper as the midwife was delayed in traffic. But in my day it was decidedly not the norm, and I was following in my mother's African footsteps.

My parents' African years inspired, it occurs to me now, the independence I've always sought, my rejection of what others do if I suspect herd-following, my hunger for adventure, also my competitiveness, also my tendency to stoicism.

I did get to Africa, eventually, even if I never had to correctly make the decision about a lion and long grass.

In February 1992 I went to Zimbabwe. In my parents' years in Africa in the late 1920s and early 30s it had been Southern Rhodesia, a colony controlled by a very small group of whites, and it still had that name until not long before I got there. Majority rule was won only in 1980.

The many descriptions of my parents' African life, especially my father's stories, had created the background mythology for my childhood and I had always wanted to go there, to be in the place of his early adventures. I wanted to know my father better by experiencing, at least a little, what had been a such a major creator of who he was: being out on the African veldt.

I travelled alone, and was so for most of the time there, as I wanted to be — I notice my surroundings more when I am alone. I spent time in Harare. I found a small place to stay called the Brontë Garden Hotel (such an apposite name for me who has always loved the Brontës). There was a fascinating variety of other guests: aid workers, Africans in business suits and old "Rhodies." I talked to everybody and found that the Rhodies in no way accepted majority rule and were scandalized and disgusted that Africans were eating in the dining room and not just there as waiters. There were no other tourists but there was a Canadian couple. The husband was taking up a position at the university and they hadn't yet found a house.

From the Brontë I ventured forth by bus (despite warnings from the Canadian High Commission that a white woman couldn't possibly go by bus) to various places, some nearby, some more distant. I took a bus to a Safari Lodge at Hwange, where I went on Land Rover trips into the jungle at dawn and dusk, and I bused down to Bulawayo.

For a while I stayed on a farm with another Havergal Old Girl, Mary, who had married an African. She was now a widow and the matriarchal centre of her late-husband's family. Unlike other white people I visited, there were no fences around her property and the farm was crisscrossed by paths, along which people passed all day, women carrying sometimes huge burdens on their heads, men walking alone or in small groups.

There was a nest of cobras under the windows of my bedroom and there were no screens. I thought of Kipling's Rikki-Tikki-Tavi and at first didn't dare keep the windows open at night despite the heat. I soon gave in. I needed the air. "The cobras never come into the house," Mary claimed. No one explained how one once got into the enclosed courtyard. Luckily no snake awoke me by slithering over my face.

One day while I was still at Mary's, we — Mary, Vu, her son of eleven, and two of Vu's friends — went for a picnic into the Matopo Hills. Some of these hills are enormously high single boulders; others look like haphazard piles of several giant boulders. All are bruise-dark and dramatic, gods in stone. It has been a holy place forever. It is where Cecil Rhodes, in an extreme example of appropriating others' culture, commanded his burial place to be.

We poked into caves to see ancient paintings of hunters. In one, a painting of a rare white rhino gives the cave its name. Mary made a fire by a pretty lake and cooked our lunch. The lake looked tempting. In Canada I definitely would have swum in such a lake. But it was out of the question here owing to the risk of bilharzia. Not to speak of larger creatures. In the diary I kept on the trip I recorded some of the animals we saw that day: baboons, impala, many zebras, hippos, giraffes, wildebeests, monkeys, warthog families, sables.

I am alone halfway up the side of an enormous dark rock the size of a small mountain.

When I realized Mary planned for us to climb it, I stared up at the rearing mass above us and wondered. Vu was scared too but his two young friends, one plump and one skinny, both very black compared with racially mixed Vu, were game and so was Mary.

We all set off and I was fine for some time as we scrambled upwards using both hands and feet like monkeys. My rubber-soled walking shoes gripped the rock securely. In some places I crawled on my knees but I was perfectly safe.

Then suddenly I can go no farther. I am overcome now by the nausea and swimming head that too-high places give me. I take deep breaths but can't control my pounding heart.

So here I am. The rock rears above me under the humming heat of the sun and I can't see Mary or the boys any more. They have gotten above the great bulge of stone by working sideways and then up. I can't even hear their voices.

It is still early in the day — we left the farm at six — but it is already baking hot. I squat on the bare rock. I am no longer dizzy. I am fine now that I know I am not going farther. I am wearing my Tilley hat but can feel the sun through it. I remember the pictures of my father wearing two hats. I can also feel my bare arms and legs toasting. I decide I can inch sideways and wiggle along on my bottom until I get to a small cleft where there is a tiny patch of dappled shade. I settle there, my legs hanging down, and lean back and am more comfortable — until I think of snakes and sit up straight again, pulling up my legs and clasping my knees.

I am looking over Africa. I can see for miles and miles, past the strange surreal stone hills that are near at hand, and past a few low and scrubby moisture-starved trees, to the bushveldt. It goes on forever and forever, until it is lost in haze.

It is entirely strange.

I have seen a million pictures and hundreds of films of it. I have heard about it always. None of that was a preparation for its vastness. The unknownness of it.

What animals are out there? What animals are — watching me, smelling me, about to pounce?

I have an inner tremble all the time in this country when I'm somewhere where a snake may slither over my foot. I can almost see its patterned skin and feel the dry rasp of it against my own. Or a baboon may leap on me, chattering. Or a lion I can't see but which is close by, right now, camouflaged in the shadow, may spring with extended claws. This is unlike watching a nature program on TV. Utterly unlike.

I am glad I am alone at this moment. I want to be aware, keenly aware. I want the full thrill and fear of being here, without the distraction of another human.

I think of how in Canada I am used to being surrounded by wilderness and walking and skiing everywhere on my own. I am used to knowing that bears or moose may well be near me and I am never nervous. Here, I am hyperconscious every second of beauty and of danger. One sharpens the other. I think of the hippos we saw a little earlier, how they rolled in the water, sleek and black and fat. I think of the rhinos for which this area is famous. What animal could get up on this rock where I am? Not likely a hippo. But a lion could.

And suddenly my father feels close, as if I can reach out my hand and he will take it. I close my eyes for a moment and he is here. Almost. I am where he was when he was young, out on the veldt. He is so near I am almost him.

It is so beautiful being in Africa at last.

My life has been about noticing beauty. When I was in that scene, high on that rock in the Matopo Hills, I was excited and frightened, every sense on its toes. I was beauty-struck. At the same time I was aware of my awareness. I knew that I was not just on that rock; I was at a particular point on my own life's path and within my family's history.

I felt my father. But as if I were the parent, I knew more than he did about where we were. He arrived in Rhodesia in 1927 and I was in Zimbabwe in 1992. It was the same place and a different place. I had a much longer historical knowledge of Africa than my father could have had in the late 1920s. And since 1992 it has changed further, and for the worse. I have taken multiple Oxford courses on the rise and fall of empire. I have a vantage point impossible for my father to have had.

What my father was doing in Rhodesia was finding and mapping copper deposits. His work would lead to mines — that was its purpose. He could not have seen the implications. He was a very young Canadian man in a place utterly new to him and was somehow responsible for men of whom he knew nothing beyond their black skin, their teeth filed into points, their tattoos, their tough bare feet. In his diaries of the time, which I have, he recounts every detail of what they encounter. He does not speculate on the future nor does he tell of his emotions. His "boys" constantly urge him to shoot so they can have meat. He is the boss-man, the one in charge, the only one with a gun. In reality they are the ones who know the land. Forever they have successfully brought down game with their assegai spears. They could survive without him; he could not, without them. The land is theirs! But it is slipping away from them and quickly and my father is part of that.

INLAND NAVIGATION BY THE STARS 49

8

MY father's early life seen as a book was almost always firmly closed. Occasionally by some odd chance it fell open and we glimpsed a line of text, never having time to scan a full page. But a phrase — "the belt soaked overnight in brine," for example — would stick, and sting, forever.

My mother's book fell open at many pages, its text brimming with adjectives and adverbs, creating for us images, anecdotes and people we could almost hear and see. I feel about her childhood as if I'd been there too, almost.

I am with her in the buggy behind Leo's swishing black tail as he trots through the village of Buckingham. We are accompanying her father on a parish errand, as she loved to do.

I am sitting on the piano bench beside her as she practices her scales and later when she plays on the radio when she is thirteen. I stand with her as she watches her father shaving the day after the cable arrived from the War about Edward. Papa is crying, his hand trembles and he nicks himself. Blood, tears and soap drip from his chin into the sink.

I am with her when she is nine, on the first day at her new school in Montreal, while she stands with her back tight against the high brick wall of the playground. She is holding her whole body clenched with fear and shyness, until a girl with bouncing braids runs up and says, "Are you our new Minister's little girl?" And it is Mabel who becomes her best friend from that day and forever.

Mother is older but still living at home when I run with her, our hearts beating fast. She is on her way home to the Rectory from her first day of teaching at Miss Dunlop's and she is escaping from a runaway hog outside the Montreal stockyards, while all the men laugh and cheer the pig on.

And then of course there is my mother as "my mother."

A memory from when I must have been about two: I am waking in my crib from an afternoon nap. I am happy because I know my mother had wanted me to sleep so she could nap herself. I climb over the crib rail and run along to her, and we are both pleased with me. How soon did I use words to keep hold of things by naming them? Did the names come right away or jell a little later? I don't know.

And then there was the darkness of a winter morning, yellow light falling into my room from the hall, and my father lifting me up in his arms. My sisters' faces are looking up at us and they are saying, "There are dollies downstairs. One for you!" It is Christmas but I don't know what that is yet. Do I learn the word that day? I understand my sisters; I understand new dollies.

Often these were lovely moments, but not always, or they were mixed. My mother sits holding me on her lap in the operating room while the surgeon and nurses ready their equipment. I am cosy, wrapped in a blanket. I must have felt pain — I had just had an operation at home on the kitchen table to break the eardrum and was about to have a second one to chip away the desperately infected mastoid bone but the pain has been lifted out of the memory. Surely I also sensed my mother's fear. I was three. I vividly remember her softly singing "The Birdies' Ball," all the verses. There was comfort and safety in the midst of hurt. Then under the anaesthetic I dreamed of my teddy Lelly.

Another, more haunting crib memory: I am lying watching the window and the long white curtains that hang either side of it moving a little in the breeze. But somehow floating in the air between the curtains and me are horrible chains of diamond shapes. The diamonds are somehow both black and gold, dazzlingly bright and they are moving convulsively, collapsing and straightening. It is terrifying and I hate it but am powerless to stop it. Even closing my eyes doesn't stop it. I had no words to tell anyone of this at the time but every once in a long while over the years I would remember those diamonds and shudder. I think I was middle-aged before I realized it had been a very early migraine.

Sometimes I told my stories to Carol or to my mother; often I didn't. I had two imaginary friends, Jennie Wren and Dootsy Bootsy, whom I can't remember beyond the fact that they existed, or existed for me. I had even forgotten Dootsy's name but Carol remembered. Mother read to us and sang to us every day and the words from the books and from the songs wove themselves into the stories I told myself. I learned how words and images could express joy and happiness and fun, as well as adventure and danger, and how many different flavours those emotions had and how they were associated with colours and seasons. Mother sang spring songs — "The Birdies' Ball," "A Frog He Would A-Wooing Go" — and winter ones — all the carols and "The North Wind Doth Blow." I learned what grief was from "Now the Day Is Over," a song with suffering and loss in every lugubrious word and note. It was torture to listen to it and yet we begged her to sing it.

We had many books in our house. Every night Mother would sit on my twin bed or Carol's, turnabout for fairness, and read to us: the Beatrix Potters, *The Wind in the Willows*, all of A. A. Milne, fairy tales from a fat red book whose title I forget, Australian children's books sent by Ruth's godmother who had moved to Australia, some American books, *Tom Sawyer* and a book called *The Blue Fly Caravan* that I've never encountered since. There were the strange and wonderful *At the Back of the North Wind* and *The Princess and Curdie*. I can't remember those in any detail, just their mysterious otherworldly atmosphere that we loved. There was darkness at the windows and the lamplight was yellow and we lay so cosily in our twin maple wood beds, with our beautiful mother reading, her dark hair smoothed back in that lovely roll women wore then, her fingers turning the pages.

Later she would go downstairs and we would fall asleep listening to her playing the piano, Beethoven sonatas or Chopin. We were so safe. And across the world other children, children I would later know as adults, crept into cellars to hide from bombs, or were dragged from burning buildings.

9

IN 1940 our family spent five or six months, from May until sometime in October, living in a tiny, tarpaper shack at the Lucky Shot gold mine in Alaska. When we drove down into the valley in our red truck we could see a red band around our shack just under the roof. It looked as if the house was tied in red ribbon, like a parcel, but close to, we never noticed the red ribbon, which was odd.

There was no sort of village, just three or four other shacks and the men's bunkhouse (forbidden territory to three little girls) and the cookhouse. Those buildings were just covered in tarpaper as well, and I remember hurrying past the forbidden bunkhouse as it loomed blackly and ominously in the early October dusk. The men were always so nice to us whenever we met them outside in daylight that it was a mystery how there would be dangers in the tall black house where they slept. Was it dangerous for them too? No. The feeling was that the men themselves were the danger, once inside their bunkhouse. Yet the cook, for instance, was really kind, and made a cake for my birthday with fancy icing, decorated with bluebirds and flowers.

The valley was encircled by high mountains where bears roamed. We were often warned about them but we never saw one. We did often see parky squirrels. Our little house had three rooms. The kitchen was so small that our mother could reach everything from sitting at her place at the table, yet it also had our parents' bed, covered with our father's arctic sleeping bag, tucked into a corner. There was a small living room, and one bedroom with three beds in a row for my sisters and me. The beds had tough grey blankets on them, like horse blankets. There was also a bathroom. Our father went up the mountain every morning in his work clothes, with his miner's hat on (a hardhat with a light), deep into the mine. None of us ever got into the mine except Ruth, a little way, once. Our mother kept house in the shack, cooking on a wood stove, but she often came out with us exploring the lower reaches of the mountains and picking berries.

Those months in that place, as different from Forest Hill and our house there as can be imagined, were a time of peak childhood happiness. For years Carol and I used to say to each other, "Wouldn't it be wonderful if being back in Toronto was only a dream and we woke up still in Alaska?" Books and stories were very much part of that world too. I especially remember the *Just So Stories* from that time, and also a long tale our father would tell us in the evenings. It was called "The Empty House" and he made it up as he went along. I don't remember a single detail, just the slight scariness of it and the fun of our father telling it in that cosy little place which, once the evenings drew in, was lit only by coal oil lamps.

Snow came in October while we were still there and we went for a ride in a sleigh pulled by Mrs. Seski's terrifying husky dogs. It was almost dark when we had the sleigh ride, the days were so short, and that made it even more exciting and for once we weren't frightened of the dogs as they raced ahead over the snow. Those dogs the rest of the time were chained up in front of her shack. We always gave them a wide berth. Seeing us they always pulled up their lips and bared their scary teeth and barked furiously. Their chains rattled as they jumped and strained against their collars. We had to pass them to get to the shack where Billy and his baby sister Helen lived — the only other children at the mine. Billy was six and was always in trouble for doing dangerous forbidden things and I admired him tremendously. Once he fell into a creek poisoned by run-off from the gold processing and we were sure he would die but he didn't.

In Toronto our father read different books to us than our mother did: *Jock of the Bushveld* was a favourite of his because it was set in "his" Africa, and *Twenty Thousand Leagues Under the Sea*. He must have read those several times as I feel as if I spent long stretches of my childhood immersed in one or the other, always in his voice. Books were my favourite Christmas presents; when I recall a particular Christmas, its atmosphere is that of whatever book I first read from the pile under the tree.

There was the year I got *Wee Gillis* and Carol got *Ferdinand the Bull*. It was a Toronto green Christmas, and the same one that Chuck got Tinker Toys. Or there was the wonderful year of the first Christmas in North Hatley when we skied every day and I got two new Arthur Ransomes: *The Picts and the Martyrs* and *Great Northern*. That most of the books I read were English meant that I viewed my own world as if through English eyes. Lake Massawippi and its surrounding hills doubled for the Lake District. Our little sailboat was Swallow in *Swallows and Amazons*. We did read, and over and over, all the L. M. Montgomery books but despite the PEI setting even those had an English flavour. Montgomery's characters' intense love of the natural world and her descriptions of it are Romantic as in the Romantic poets. I rarely encountered Canadian writing otherwise.

10

READING was my joy but as I entered adolescence it also was in a significant way my undoing. Dauntless Nancy of the Amazons was replaced by one girl or woman after another who was fatally undone or at the very least tamed by love. I lived for hours every day within an English, Russian or French classic, not aware of an inner conflict between my desire for independence and a growing yearning for a man who would test me to the limit and beyond it. He must be dramatically, darkly, broodingly handsome, probably foreign — though the passion of a D. H. Lawrence working-class hero also might do, if I ever encountered such. What decidedly would not do would be a young man from either my Toronto or North Hatley neighbourhood.

I shake my head now at how an intelligent girl like me fell into such an obvious and silly trap. Why had I not been able to enjoy those other fictional worlds without losing my common sense? Part of it was the era. I already had the makings of a feminist in me, without even knowing the word, but nothing around me echoed it back let alone encouraged it. All the messages from movies, magazines, radio, early TV when I encountered it had a common theme, whether overt or somewhat disguised. I must live for love. I must find it and then all else would take care of itself and take care of me. That might have been at least a safe goal, were it not for all the novels that ensured that an ordinary man would not do. I required drama and intensity, scariness even.

I knew I was not the meek and compliant girl I was meant to be. I was tall and my walk was too forthright, my stride too long. When I'd boarded at King's Hall for one awful year, I had to go to the gym before breakfast for "walking training" along with girls who had bad posture. I didn't have bad posture but was made to know I must somehow tame my walk, take much smaller steps and put my toes down first. I could do this odd lady-like mincing briefly under the fierce eye of Miss Kaiser, but not otherwise. I was simply unable to hobble myself like that if I wanted to get somewhere. But my walk was the mere iceberg tip of my basic wrongness.

I was learning there had to be a muffling of my true self and a substitution of another or I would bore or alarm any man. And it went deeper than not being willing to wear a girdle, as Ruth did, or walk as a lady ought to. I had no small talk — I didn't even know what it was. When the boys from the boys' boarding school nearby came over for a dance I had nothing to say to them. I knew perfectly well that bringing up my thoughts about *War and Peace* would be out of the question. But on the spot, shuffling around the gym gripped by sweaty boy hands, I was unable to come up with anything else at all.

I had dream loves from my books, Mr. Rochester, Heathcliff, Prince Andrei and many more. Having seen Hamlet, I had Laurence Olivier. Brooding, passionate, often filled with pain and rage over some obscure past tragedy (which I would heal) and darkly handsome of course — such a man might have the kind of power to handle me. I would wait until I could find such a man in real life.

I didn't see the dangerous nonsense of this, or, perhaps more likely, I didn't see the implications. What might a man who considered himself to have power over powerful me do with his power? Or maybe I did sense the danger. It's impossible to feel myself back into that girl's mind. Not completely. Did I think I deserved punishment for my wrongness? Is that why I was allowing myself to be the victim of literature?

All along, beginning when I was fourteen, I did have my love for

Hugh MacLennan, or Mr. MacLennan as I always called him, the writer who spent his summers in North Hatley and with whom I had long talks and a relationship no one else really knew about. But he existed somehow in a separate space. It was a secret that I surely knew all along would never become more than what it was.

II

THUS, Frank.

Frank — born Frančišek Celešči Marcus Molnar — came into my life the summer I turned eighteen. Recently arrived from Yugoslavia, he was teaching science at Bishop's College School (where my brother went) and had taken a summer job as the manager of the North Hatley Club. He also taught tennis, sailing and swimming. He was twenty-six years old, handsome and athletic, also clever. He had thick dark brown hair and high cheekbones and seemed exotic to me. In his tennis whites or his bathing suit, with his summer tan and his strong legs, his beautifully shaped hands, his gleaming very dark eyes, he laid a powerful claim on me.

I met him at the very beginning of that summer of 1954. I had paddled my canoe across the lake to the club for the first time that season. As I approached the club dock I saw a young man sitting on it, his brown arms clasped around his knees. Expertly (my brother and I prided ourselves on being the best canoe handlers on the lake) I drew my canoe tight against the dock and looked up at him.

"This is a private club," he said. He had an accent. Of course. That was how it started.

His past was full of difficult incident. His early childhood was charmed. He was youngest of the four children of the brilliant and ambitious Jula Molnar, she who had redesigned and relaunched a grand hotel in Bled (Slovenia), the Grand Hotel Toplice, of international grandeur and renown. Before the war the court and all the embassies moved north from Belgrade, the winter capital, and spent their summers in Bled. Toplice drew the important and the wealthy from all over Europe.

Molnar is a Hungarian name. Frank's father had been in the Austro-Hungarian Cavalry in World War One. When his regiment rode through Bled he met and fell in love with the young and very pretty Jula Vovk whose family were landowners of consequence in the district. After the war he came back to Bled and married her. He was handsome and charming and athletic: he ran for Hungary in an early Olympics. However, as far as I could understand the story, his wife became the power in the family; he did her bidding and he charmed the guests.

Little Feri (a name Frank later had to abandon swiftly on arrival in North America) was mostly raised by his nanny, Tončka, and the family chauffeur, Tinček. At the same time he was his mother's sweet little favourite. He was a little prince in those early years.

Frank had an old and rather tattered brochure depicting the hotel in its glory days. It was his treasure. He unfolded it and showed me: smiling, beautifully dressed beautiful people sat about on terraces, a lovely lake behind them. The pictures were from a storybook: the smooth green water of the lake, the enchanted small island floating on it complete with its little white church. On the far side of the lake a medieval castle loomed on a high cliff. The people in the pictures, apparently aristocrats or diplomats, wore summer frocks or tennis outfits. They held wine glasses in some pictures, rackets in others. They existed, in the pictures, in a fairy tale bubble. Their confident smiles knew nothing of the abyss awaiting them.

The war swept away everything in that charmed picture. Feri first encountered the horror when cycling home one day and coming upon five bodies lying on the road, lying quite tidily. What had happened? Why were they arranged like that? It hardly seemed real. But blood from their heads was congealing on the hard earth of the roadway.

INLAND NAVIGATION BY THE STARS 61

Soon after, the Gestapo took over the Grand Hotel to use as its headquarters for northern Yugoslavia. Booted feet stomped where the gilded people had played.

Feri, at age thirteen, became political and an organizer. He was expelled from all schools in Greater Germany for his anti-Nazi activities. His brother Miha, age fifteen, had run away to join the Partisans in the mountains. The oldest brother, Sasha, another Olympic athlete, fled on his skis over the Julian Alps to Switzerland. Sister Katka was in boarding school in England. Feri was too young to flee and anyway wanted to do his schoolboy part. He was thrown in jail for three months, then released. His father took him away to ski. I have blank stretches in this story now, though I must have known them once. He can't have simply skied until the end of the war. Somehow he prepared himself for university.

A year after coming to Canada, Frank (the name Feri ditched by then) arrived in North Hatley and entered my life. That summer of 1954 I had had a year away from home at McGill; I had found my feet in a wider world, or felt I had. I was ready for my life to become intense. I was alertly poised to enter one of the European novels I was steeped in, keen for such a chance to present itself. I saw no risk in this. I was hungry for just such a young man as Frank: clever, exotically handsome, and above all, directing at me his fierce gaze.

My relationship with Frank increased in intensity over the next three years. More than once I was frightened by the extremity of his demands for my total commitment to him and tried to break away, but the very thing that scared me was what claimed me. He always managed to pull me back. And I fear I liked the power I seemed to have over him. He vowed he would die if I would not have him. He would stab himself with the Bosnian dagger he kept at the ready. Sitting on his windowsill it passed itself off as an artifact, a piece of decoration, an antique with a carved bone handle. But it was real. I should have taken his threat as a warning of rocks ahead. Instead I was caught by the drama of it. How could I have such power — his life or his death — over a man? I couldn't refuse it. But there was more than that. I did love him.

At the same time, when not in North Hatley with my family I was living the normal life of a young girl at McGill, safe in the women's residence, Royal Victoria College, enjoying my studies and surrounded by close friends. Frank was a flesh and blood figure in my life, but I could still keep him at a little remove. He was more than the dream-hero Mr. MacLennan had been up until then. I knew Frank's warm skin and the feel of his hands. But at the same time I was safe from him, returning each night to sleep in my narrow white bed.

I was aware that he sometimes drank too much, though it was rare that I saw this directly. I would know by his eyes and his mood and if I hadn't seen him for a bit. As time passed I suspected his bouts were becoming more serious but if I tried to talk to him about it he spoke as if they were a necessary result of a situation created by me of which he was victim: I would not sleep with him. His excessive drinking bouts were my fault. The situation would cease to be required once we married.

Thus we must marry.

The reason I didn't sleep with Frank was twofold. Both my sisters had been pregnant before marriage. In that era great shame was associated with out-of-wedlock-sex, and pregnancy clearly proved beyond doubt that a girl had broken the rules. My mother felt this strongly. I felt her eyes upon me, dreading I would follow my sisters' example — and, for that matter, my aunt's and my grandmother's! I did not want my sexual life to be haunted by my mother. At the same time I suspect I was also afraid of the total commitment to Frank that giving in to him would be. I would stall as long as I could. I loved him but I dreaded losing my separate and independent self. Would I have to? He would demand a serious degree of submission yet I couldn't guess just how that would be manifest in my daily life.

I was on a fated path, following a plot I was powerless to escape An inevitability compelled me as if I were the princess in a ballet and a spell had been cast. I graduated from McGill in the spring of 1957, and there was no reason Frank could accept that our wedding would not soon follow. As my wedding, planned for late August, loomed I danced towards it as the princess dances towards death. I felt as if I were approaching a cliff over which I would fall to a doom I couldn't imagine in detail at all. The cliff was one dramatic image I had. Another was of a black curtain ahead cutting off any view at all and behind which I must step — and then, darkness.

The hopeless relationship with Mr. MacLennan moved into greater reality that summer than it had had before, somehow greater than the approaching wedding, the implications of which I could not fully focus on. I spent much more time with him than I did with Frank, who was working in Montreal and came to North Hatley only on weekends. Mr. MacLennan's long-ailing wife had died in the early spring and that summer he was a lost soul. We spent long hours together, listening to the St. Matthew Passion in his cottage or driving around the countryside or going for long walks. I think part of me — maybe much of me? — longed for him to "save me." At the same time I knew how unlikely it was that he'd dare step so far outside what he would have seen as honourable. He was so much older than I; it wouldn't be right.

Surely I must also have sensed that he'd be, quite simply, way too scared to do it. Scared of what would be involved in taking on someone like me, scared of the emotional and sexual demands. I think he did love me. But he had been married forever to a physically frail, otherwise extremely strong and dominant woman, who seemed to me to be many years older than he. I'd always felt she was way more of a mother than a wife to him but that may have doubled the void she left. So how could I have been putting any hope at all on the broken reed that was Mr. MacLennan? He wasn't going to save me!

Now as I try to think myself back into that girl's head I am baffled at how heedless I was. But if I dig down deeper I suspect I was convinced I would survive whatever happened. I was doomed — but it would not be a fatal matter. Not for me, Anne Coleman. I could not really be a doomed princess. It was foolish all the same as plenty of young women marry damaged men and do not survive. Luck came into it too.

So — we married.

12

AT the outset much of our life held promise and pleasure. After our wedding, in August 1957, we lived for two years in a basement apartment in lower Westmount. It was basement, yes, but it was dark-panelled and comfortable, with nice old furniture from home and of course my wedding presents. I worked briefly in the McGill Library, then for about eight months for Mr. Heinemann at the Mansfeld Book Mart, on Mansfeld Street.

I enjoyed that job exceedingly. It was rather menial — ordering and selling books, writing Mr. H.'s letters (typing them slowly with two fingers; I couldn't really type), talking to customers and reading myself in any quiet moment. It was much more interesting than the McGill Library job where I'd been a runner, the person who moils down into the stacks to get books students had ordered. Very few students actually were allowed to take out books, as far as I can recall. The main concern of the librarians was to keep books away from students and lined up tidily on the shelves. But graduate students could send for them, and professors of course. It was a very odd place to work, unfriendly and hierarchical in the extreme. I, a runner, with my meagre bachelor's degree, was the lowest of the low.

The Book Mart was the opposite in every way. Mr. Heinemann was a warmly friendly and fascinating fellow. German-Jewish, he had fetched up in Montreal via Shanghai soon after the war and opened his store where he sold both new and second-hand books in many languages. The place was down a flight of stairs from the street and was rather grubby and very smoky, crowded with toppling piles of books, but somehow cosy, and it was as good as a club for all the displaced European intellectuals of the city. People were always standing about, talking in one tongue or another, laughing, drinking cups of coffee brought in from nearby, leaving things to be looked after, not so often actually buying books. I think everyone was pretty poor. An ancient German baron worked in the store also, Baron von Hahn. He was an aristocrat of the old school, beautifully dressed always in pre-War suits. Heinemann, kind to everyone else, was rather mean to the old baron. He used to send him out into the cold and snow, or late afternoon grey sleet, to post a single parcel. (If I saw him outdoors, he would be creeping along very slowly, lest he fall.) Then, as soon as the poor old chap had returned and taken off his muffler, he would be sent out again. I could read between the lines of Heinemann's behaviour.

I got pregnant almost at once after our marriage. It was what I wanted — to the point that the one menstrual period I had after the wedding distressed me: "Am I infertile?" I watched mothers and babies in the streets and felt anxious. We went out to North Hatley for Thanksgiving weekend and I remember running down the hill towards the lake under the brilliant trees and feeling wildly happy, certain it had happened early that morning. Paul did arrive exactly nine months later.

The pregnancy terrified Frank. He was not cut out for it. Responsibility did not fit with his little prince childhood, a conditioning that had gone very deep, perhaps because so suddenly lost. The drinking binges, which I'd been promised would stop once I had joined him in a bed, began to occur with greater frequency. He could go for a stretch, maybe even a few weeks, and then ... I would know as soon as I saw his face, even just the way he walked if approaching me from a distance, his shoulders held back with special care.

My baby was due in early July and I stopped work at Heinemann's at the end of May. I went out to North Hatley for a visit and then

INLAND NAVIGATION BY THE STARS 67

spent my time preparing for the birth, going for long walks around Westmount daydreaming about my baby, and also typing a manuscript (my slow terrible typing!) for a friend of Mr. Heinemann's.

Paul was born on July 7, a beautiful baby boy. I can still remember exactly the look of him, his wet hair, very dark, a rather squashed nose, the perfect proportions of his arms and legs. I instantly fell in love with him. And Frank did too. "Moy sin," he would murmur in Slovenian to him, putting his face very close to Paul's. Yet the fact of this tiny boy ratcheted up his fears. The binges did not stop.

I told no one. Every day I pushed Paul's carriage up the hill to Murray Park and met two other women, Ilse and Monique, who had new babies too. We loved that park for its wide sloping lawns and huge trees. It was like the garden of a private estate and we preferred it to Westmount Park which was actually closer to all of our apartments. I never told my two friends about Frank's drinking. We talked of our babies, our recent birth experiences, our own childhoods, books (they were readers too).

Ilse's husband was a doctor, Monique's an architect. I imagined they had exemplary lives, that their husbands were solidly reliable men, unlike mine. Frank by then was no longer teaching but had a research job with a drug company. It was a good job with a future but his drinking surely would imperil it. This frightened me, and I assume him as well, though we never spoke of that. He drank the pure alcohol from the lab. I found little bottles of it hidden here and there about the apartment and poured them out.

Between his spells we could be happy. We lived in blocks of time — sane and happy ones alternating with dark and terrible ones. We were on a train that moved through sunlight and then suddenly entered a tunnel. I took joy in my baby and learned a pattern of living in the moment only, good or bad. I was stoic during the tunnel stretches.

Twice Frank tried to commit suicide. Once, he brought home a jar from the lab, and a hypodermic needle. I watched as he injected himself and lay down on our bed to die. He closed his eyes. I sat in the rocking chair nursing Paul and waited. I rocked back and forth. I didn't do anything.

How serious the attempt was I can never know. But eventually he woke up. Another time we were at a party. Our friends' apartment was many floors up and had a balcony with a view over the city. I had Paul with me, a few months old by this time (we were into fall) and was in the living room talking to another woman when I became aware of a commotion out on the balcony. People cast consternated glances at me. I carried Paul over to see what was happening. I knew it had to be something bad as people attempted to stop me. But I saw. Frank had jumped over the balcony railing — but had somehow caught himself. He was so strong! He was hanging down into space, his hands gripping the bar at the bottom of the railing. Two or three men finally managed to haul him up by his wrists and one of them by his braces — which surely could not have held much of his weight.

After that he became worse. Finally he admitted aloud to being frightened and then at last, as winter came on, I convinced him to go to a doctor. I knew the name of my father's psychiatrist. There was an awful weekend before Frank was admitted to the hospital. I was with him when the doctor gave him some sort of medication. He then looked sternly at me and warned that Frank must on no account drink — as if I had the power to police my husband. Somehow we survived the two-day wait and Frank entered the Montreal General. There was a routine. For six weeks the patient had daily shock treatments. That was all that happened. One day it was electric shock, the next the insulin version.

On the days when he'd had electric shock he was peaceful, his mood and his face gentled and smoothed. He was like a friendly animal. But when he had insulin shock he was angry and almost impossible for me to handle.

Whichever treatment he'd had I was expected to take him up on the mountain behind the hospital for a walk. Every insulin day

I faced a nightmare. I would be carrying Paul, pink-cheeked from the cold and bundled in his pale blue bunny bag. The snow was deep and Frank would not follow any path. Burdened by the heavy baby I floundered and again and again almost fell. Frank, furious-faced, leapt ahead. Every little while he turned and yelled, "I won't go back in there. I won't. You can't make me."

I had to talk him down, coax him, plead, until eventually, as darkness was falling, he'd turn and come back to me. No one at the hospital ever asked me how those walks went and it was impossible to refuse to go. Or so I thought. There was no communication between me and any staff member let alone the doctor. It was as if offering me any information, advice or indeed support of any sort never occurred to any of them. As far as I ever could get Frank to reveal, the doctor never talked to him either. This pattern went on for six weeks though Frank did become more tractable towards the end of that time.

On his release from the hospital we went out to North Hatley for Christmas. My parents were good to us and Frank was calm and happy, his best self. We walked in the snow and played with our baby. Maybe there would be no more dark tunnels.

But the "cure" did not last. It helped for a while. For a few months, we were happy, and for my part I connected with Frank's sweetest, funniest self and knew his love for me and for Paul. But then we were back to our switch-about life. Good times, bad times. Sometimes the good lasted a few weeks, even a month or two, making disappointment all the keener when happiness was over, again.

But despite his recurring black demons he was back at work. By great good fortune he had not lost his academic and professional knowledge. That can happen with electric shock treatment. It was one of the reasons, fitting with the times, that women were more likely to get the treatment than men: they didn't need much in the way of brains for housework.

In 1960, on the very January day that Jane, our second child, was born, Frank secured an excellent scholarship from Université de

Montréal and started doing research at the Montreal Cancer Institute, working towards further degrees. We had moved the previous summer to the Montreal suburb of Pointe-Claire. We had bought, with my long-saved babysitting money as down payment, an old, vine-covered brick house with a lovely wild garden. It was the beginning of an extended happy time. Frank adored Jane. He claimed she looked exactly like his mother and would have her qualities of brilliance and creativity. (He was right.)

✛

Jane is born swiftly. She swims out of me, a smooth little seal-baby. The young nurse says, "I have never seen a birth like this. I'm so glad I was here for this one."

I had come to the hospital the night before, and then everything stopped. Nothing. Nary a contraction. "You can have some lunch and then you'll have to go home," they said at the desk. But Jane and I had another plan. I walked up and down the corridor as fast as I could. I wanted to exert my muscles, engage all of them, but especially the crucial ones for this job. And I felt the tightness build; I leaned against a wall; then I walked again; then the tightness, stronger, longer. Finally I couldn't walk any more and I went and lay on the bed.

I ring for the nurse and Dr. Glickman comes into the room with her, bringing on his coat a gust of the cold outside.

It is a frigid January day. He tells me he couldn't come before as his own baby had the croup. We are both pleased at the timing. His baby needed him and I hadn't, but I do now. He sits by my bed. And then within half an hour: my Jane. My perfect baby girl. She is small but a wee bit plump even so, a morsel of a person, and very pink. I hold her and sniff her damp, dark hair that sticks up in quills. Her eyes are dark and gleam a moment. Her first look at the brightness of the world is a swift one, outside the warm and watery dark place where she has been. Then her lids close.

Frank arrives finally and he has wonderful news and this day is flowering with one joy after another. He greets our new daughter first and then he tells me: he has just come from his interview — which I have completely forgotten in my preoccupation — and he will start right away at the Cancer Institute and they will fund his further studies.

I nurse new Jane sitting by my bedroom window. The sun is shining through glittering icicles that hang in a thick dazzling fringe from the roof. It is too cold for them to drip. Day after day they frame my view as I sit there, Jane in a blanket like a papoose, Paul playing at my feet. He knows I can't move and disturb his sister so he does naughty things: he empties all the clothes out of my bottom bureau drawer. He looks over and smiles and dumps the wastepaper basket. He is only eighteen months old, a baby too. I call him to come and look: across the road a small snowplow shoves, and awkwardly turns, and shoves again, trying to heap yet more snow onto the towering piles that line the road.

The pattern of our life seems fixed. I wonder sometimes if the bad periods are getting worse, even if the spaces between are longer. I can't be sure and I never know when the switch will happen.

Every day I push Paul and Jane down Cedar Avenue in the big old English pram I inherited from a neighbour. In the fall brilliant yellow leaves are massed overhead and under our feet, and the children are bundled in the woollen sweaters and leggings I knitted for them.

If it's summer, Paul runs ahead, his brown legs under his lederhosen strong and swift. We are on our way home from the library. Paul has chosen a book entitled *Emmett's Pig* that I know we will read many times before it goes back. He likes all books featuring animals and his favourite book of all, since he was two, when I wasn't sure how much he even understood its very English and rather sophisticated language, is *The Wind in the Willows*. There is one chapter, "The Piper at the Gates of Dawn," that we can't read because it makes me cry even to start it. I can't read the last chapter of *The House at Pooh Corner* either. My poor children, I think, they will never know these books in their entirety. But it can't be helped. Jane already likes story time. She has her own favourite about a ladybug and she listens intently when I read.

In early summers I gather peonies from my garden and put them in every room of the house so their sweet scent follows me wherever I am. In late afternoons I dance in the living room with the children to Harry Belafonte records.

I bake my own bread, remembering how my father taught me. As a prospector in the far north he had to make the bread for himself and his men and never forgot how. I find a recipe and try my own Christmas cakes. The smells richly fill the house; they are a success and I am proud of myself. But I fail with marmalade. It won't obey the recipe and never jells.

Sometimes on summer evenings we race with the children across the grass in a place we call the Running Park, the lovely grounds of an old estate on Lake Saint-Louis just a few blocks from us. When Frank is with us we drive down, but in the day the children and I walk. But it is best when we all go running together, Frank too.

In winters I pull a toboggan and the children hop on and off it. Their cheeks are very pink and Jane, wearing a Fair Isle hat I got her at the church bazaar, has snow on her eyelashes.

Frank brings our morning coffee up to the bedroom on weekend mornings. He gets back into the bed too and both children tumble in with us and we are cosy.

During the late-winter ice-storm of 1961 the power is out for several days. It's like camping, and we love it, all of us warm around the fireplace and a savoury smell rising from the big cast-iron frying pan. Frank is the cook for those days and we light candles and it is an adventure.

INLAND NAVIGATION BY THE STARS 73

In the summer of 1962 we enjoyed a halcyon period, albeit a short one. I remember dressing in a pretty dress, a floral cotton in a brown, peach and green pattern that Ruth had made me — such a dear dress, perhaps the favourite one of my life — and attending, with the children, Frank's Master's Degree of Science Convocation at Université de Montréal. His scholarship would continue as he worked for his PhD. It was a glorious day: his achievement, our sweet children present, his co-workers full of congratulations, and his own pride.

13

OVER the years of our marriage, all the psychiatrists, the sessions of shock treatment, the therapy he'd had, none of it helped Frank in any long-term way and the periods of drunkenness were becoming even more frightening. Frightening for me clearly as I was so vulnerable, but now I can assume they were frightening for him as well, poor man. None of the doctors were of any use at all. I remember a handsome Australian psychiatrist he went to for a while. I accompanied Frank to the last meeting of the supposed treatment and my heart sank to hear the doctor say that Frank should not have to think of himself as someone who could not take a social drink. Oh the hopelessness of that advice!

Frank's good fortune academically was not enough to still his demons for long. There were calm times over that year, but each time his darkness came back he fell more deeply into it. By the summer of 1963, when Paul was five and Jane three, he had descended into a chasm where he lost touch with present reality. I couldn't reach him at all.

He appeared to me — on the outside watching, though hardly detached — to be approaching madness. How could that have felt for him? He tipped at the end of our time together into real craziness and he must have been even more terrified than I was.

He became increasingly obsessed with the injustice of our so different life histories. That his childhood's almost princely status — as he saw it in retrospect — had been so horribly altered by war was egregiously unfair in contrast to my steadily secure and happy Canadian childhood.

And he saw a way to redress the imbalance.

I was appalled at plans for our future that he was insisting on putting into action. I had no one to tell, or so I felt. I must be toughened up — that was the expression he used repeatedly. Of course it was true that until I married him I had led a charmed life. I knew it and appreciated my good fortune. But surely it had not been my fault and punishing me for it now with his planned toughening did not serve any useful purpose that I could see. Jealousy was involved (jealousy of my past good luck) but there was a weird logic to it as well. By toughening me he would equip me for any future disaster, as he, as a child, had not been equipped.

And then that summer there was a crucial shift. Paul also required "toughening." We entered new territory. He feared for both of us, so unprepared for suffering were we. It wasn't sadistic to Frank, or if so, only partly; it was at least partly meant as protection. But it was crazy, nonetheless.

As for his plan, what Frank did that summer was put our pleasant, modest little house in Pointe-Claire on the market. Then, knowing my feeling about a particular east-end Montreal street (the thought of humans having to occupy any of the tenements on it horrified me), he would find rooms for us on it. The move would be salutary. We would discover, and live, in a manner that — I guess this was his thought — would go some way to balance our up-to-then unfair luck with his childhood and youth war experience. The logic of small Jane having the experience too was never explained. He identified Jane with himself for some reason and Paul with me. Perhaps that meant that Jane, at three, was naturally tough already. Both notions of course were crazy.

Having nowhere to turn for help, as I saw it, I simply refused to play. The real estate agent came and put a sign on our lawn; people began to phone him to make appointments to come and view the house; each time, he called to tell me and I packed a picnic, put Jane in her stroller and we three headed out for the day to the park down on the lake. I don't remember how long this went on but the unfortunate agent was getting frantic. I can't remember exactly why. Maybe he'd not even been given a key? I assume they didn't have lockboxes then. Perhaps it was not even legal to have a house on the market and not show it to anyone.

14

MY parents were in Europe that summer of 1963 and ironically they actually stayed for some days in the Grand Hotel Toplice, the hotel Frank's family had lost, first to its use as Gestapo headquarters during the war and then to the Communists, who nationalized it. And so, at the very moment that Frank was completely unraveling, my parents were visiting his parents in their villa outside the village, no doubt both sets of parents talking — or at least smiling and nodding, given my parents-in-law's sketchy English — about the dear family in Pointe-Claire.

In their absence Frank decided we would drive out to North Hatley for the weekend and stay in the family house.

At this stage Frank was essentially drunk round the clock. He came to in the mornings with alcohol still coursing through his veins and pulsing in his head. On this particular day extreme heat and humidity added to the nightmare quality of what was unfolding. I stood on the grass of the front lawn, the huge old trees at the end of the drive standing like sentinels but unable to protect me. The neighbours were behind their high hedges having ordinary mornings while we slipped into another dimension. I held Jane on my hip and Paul held tightly to my other hand and leaned closely into my leg. I was standing still, saying nothing but not getting into the car. I was terrified for the lives of the children and myself. Then, as had been inevitable all along, Frank dragged and then shoved me until I toppled into the back seat, the children on top of me. This was in the days before proper child car seats or even seatbelts for any of us. I put both children on the floor and crouched on top of them thinking if we crashed perhaps my body would offer some protection. In this fashion we careened out along the old highway to North Hatley.

The details of the weekend are vague in my mind as the conclusion was so horrendous they are largely blocked. I do remember sitting with my sisters on our boathouse verandah at one point and telling them something of what was happening and my huge fear of driving back on Sunday evening. Ruth was staying with her children at her father-in-law's house across the lake but had come over to swim with us and Carol was staying with her children at our Aunt Hazel's house, which was on our property just inside the gates to our drive. Both sisters were aghast at my predicament and Ruth especially was adamant that I refuse to go back with Frank and equally clear that I must end my marriage forthwith. "Daddy will look after you," she assured me. I wasn't at all sure of that. Unlike Ruth, I didn't assume anyone else would, or even should, take up responsibility for me. I simply had no idea of where my next life-steps would lead me, or, more precisely, lead Paul and Jane and me. Where I ran, so would they, one under each arm if need be.

The trick was going to be managing not to be forced into the car this time. I determined somehow not to be. And it worked on the Sunday evening, I think simply because of where we were — my parents' house — and the nearby presence of my sisters, not in the same house but not far. Grimly Frank set off alone and the children and I went to bed. It was a hot night and I kept my bedroom window wide open.

Some hours later I wake in the hot darkness to a hissing voice at the screen. It is Frank, of course it is. How did I think he wouldn't come back for us? Of course he would. There was no way he'd ever let me win a power struggle.

INLAND NAVIGATION BY THE STARS 79

"Anne, Anne," he says. His voice is rough and thick. Even from his just saying my name I know he is drunk.

I am sleepy and very scared but I don't dare refuse to open the door; this is my father's house: how can I let Frank break down the door? He is strong enough, and drunk enough, to smash it open like a man in a movie. I know it. He could just destroy the window screen and clamber in that way but it might actually be trickier to do and take longer. I think he will choose to break the back door down. Smashing and crashing will be more satisfying. I know him. These thoughts speed through my brain even as I go to open the back door.

He rages in past me, shoving me so hard that I fall back against the kitchen counter. He yells, "Go get the children up. You're coming with me. Now!" His face is the way I hate it to be, wild and more animal than human. What sort of animal? A mad dog? How can I have so many thoughts when it's all happening so horribly fast?

"Go, now!" he yells and puts his face very close to mine. But he is staggering with exhaustion and drunkenness, even while he is shouting and his spit hits my cheek. "You should have come before. I should have made you come before. How dare you not to have obeyed me then!" It's crazy logic as if we should be able to go back and replay the earlier evening and he is furious that we can't.

I am dazed, half-asleep and terrified. I had lain awake for hours and finally dropped off, and now I can't seem to clear my head. I stumble down the hall and back into the bedroom and start putting our things together. I can't think what I should be taking. The children's clothes are still in the bathroom where I undressed them last night. All I do is throw a few things of my own into the big straw bag I brought for the children's toys, random things. I pull off my nightie and stuff it in. But what can it possibly matter what we have with us when we may be dead? But I am standing in my underpants and I do want clothes on. I grab the crumpled T-shirt I wore yesterday and my blue shorts.

I'm stalling. I can't bear to wake the children. To be again in the car with them, speeding, and in the dark this time: I can't have it happen. I can't let him get us into the car. I can't give in this time. But how — how do I not give in? He is so much stronger than I am.

I hear the toilet flush and then he is in the bedroom. He lurches against the door frame as he comes into the room. Then he falls across our bed, his arms flop down, and he passes out.

In the morning the situation simply resumes. He wakes and I can see from his expression, the way his mouth drags down at the corners and his eyes glitter, that he is raging still and drunk still. I know all his expressions so well. His whole body smells of stale alcohol. It permeates every inch of him. Is that possible? I had thought that people slept off drunkenness, maybe had hangovers if they'd really overdone it. Frank's drinking is way beyond that. Of course what he drinks has to be way, way stronger than the beer or cheap cider boys drank at McGill. He continues to sneak bottles of pure alcohol from the lab where he works.

The weather is still hot and very humid. My limbs and my head feel heavy and slow and time seems to move in jerks. It is exactly like a nightmare, one thing jumping to another over which I have no control. I make Paul his breakfast and myself a cup of instant coffee. But I can't drink it, and Paul only picks at his toast, breaking off bits of the crust and crumbling them between his finger and thumb. He stares down at his plate. I notice for the millionth time his long dark lashes. Then he looks up at me and his eyes are wide and worried. He has caught my mood. And he may well have heard the shouts in the night and was too afraid to come out to me. I hate Frank for scaring Paul. I really, really hate him. Jane is not scared, not yet. She must have slept through the night noises. She is humming quietly to herself and eating her cereal, with her doll, Brown Baby, beside her in the high chair.

By the time Frank gets up Jane has already run down to Carol's, to see her cousins. I'm glad she at least is safe, at least for a short while. But Frank will never leave without Jane.

But this time I try even harder than I had when leaving Pointe-Claire. I am determined not to obey him. Frank shouts at me to come. I am in my father's library collecting Jane's teddy, Grizzly. He is a family member, a Steiff bear sent by Frank's parents. It's crazy: I am collecting a couple of essential things as if we are leaving. But we are not going.

Frank is at the door of the room, waving his arm at me as if he is hailing a taxi, yelling, "Come on, come on!" I don't move. Paul slips past him and runs behind me. He is crying and he clutches my legs. Frank steps forward and grabs me. He grips my shoulders. He shakes me so that my head lurches back and forth. I still don't take a step. Then he releases my left shoulder, swings his arm back and hits me, hard, in the face. For a split second I don't feel it. I just feel the shock of it, and outrage that he had hit me and in front of Paul. And then pain bursts into my affronted mouth and my cheek. I taste blood. My tongue discovers a small, sharp chip of tooth and I spit it out.

I am aware that Paul is screaming. He has been doing so all the time since Frank followed me into the room. "Don't kill my mother! Don't kill my mother!" he wails over and over. His face, contorted with crying and covered in both tears and mucus, peers around my leg to look up at me. He sees the blood. He squeezes even closer against my legs.

Suddenly, a crazy moment: I see my mother's cleaning woman, Mrs. Leonard, in the hall. She arrived before Frank got up and I've forgotten her. She is lugging the vacuum by the door of the room. The vacuum is not on; there is no noise except Paul's crying, and I shout to her, "Call the police! Mrs. Leonard! Please call the police," but she pretends not to hear. She actually pretends not to hear! For a moment I can't believe she has no reaction. And then I know why: husbandly abuse is normal for her. One of her sons is even in jail for some sort of violence. To her this is ordinary. She isn't about to involve herself.

Frank drags me out to the car, wrenching my arms, and forces me in. Paul of course follows, sobbing, my hopelessly tiny protector. Frank rockets the car down the hill and drives up to the little white house in a swoosh of gravel. "Go in and get her," he says. "And be quick."

I hurl myself through the kitchen screen door and try to slam it behind me but he is right at my heels, catching the door as it swings. The two of us, and right behind us, Paul, still crying, erupt into the breakfast scene within.

Carol leaps to her feet, yelling, "Don't hurt my baby!" She is electric with animal terror for her newborn baby girl. Her three little boys scatter before us. Time does that thing again, moving in jumps: I see Jane and her cousin John, and I shout to Jane, "Hide, hide, go and hide!" and she and John disappear into the living room.

Frank stops in his tracks and bows to Carol in his best courtly European manner. She is holding baby Ruthie against her and whimpering with fear. It is another crazy moment like Mrs. Leonard going by the door, the normal and the wild happening almost at the very same time. Frank puts on an ingratiating smile, and says sweetly, "Of course I would never hurt your children, Carol. I see you as the modern Madonna."

He then turns back to me, his expression changing instantly back to fury as he snatches at me and pulls me towards the door the children have fled through.

"Jane!" he calls, again his voice gentle. I know he will not be rough with Jane and hope she has hidden well enough. But it's hopeless: she and John have tucked themselves behind Auntie's sofa; it is only a love seat and I can see their little bare feet and of course Frank can too.

Again I am in the back seat with the children and again I make them sit on the floor. But it's different, the way Frank is driving. Instead of the wild ride we'd had coming out from Montreal on Friday, and the way Frank drove just moments before when he tore down the driveway, we proceed slowly in fits and starts. He keeps stopping the car and getting out. He walks around the car each time, then gets back in and carries on, slowly. He stops at a café for a cup of coffee. Then at Little Lake Magog he decides to have a swim. We never swim here. It's small and shallow and in this hot spell it will be nastily warm. But there are a few campers and a couple of people are in the water.

Frank strips off everything he is wearing except his underpants, tosses his shirt, trousers and sandals into the car, then opens the back door and pulls Jane out. He carries her on his hip and I watch him stepping carefully across the beach. I can't see the sand and pebbles he must be walking on but I'm sure there will be cigarette butts and other litter. It's that sort of place. I really wish Jane didn't have to be taken into that unsavoury water.

At each of the earlier stops he has carefully taken the car keys, and he has this time too: they are clamped in his teeth as he wades into the water. He is taking no chances of my escaping with the car. He can't actually swim while holding Jane and soon he is back and we carry on.

Just before Orford he stops at a little diner right by the road for another coffee, leaving all of us behind as he did at his earlier coffee stop. I peer over from my back seat position and realize with a thump of my heart that he has left the key in the ignition. Instantly I scramble over into the front seat and turn the key.

I have never driven this car. It is a second-hand Wolseley but only a few years old and it is his pride and joy; getting behind its wheel has never been for the likes of me. He is proud of it, with its soft leather seats, mahogany dashboard, and polished brass fittings. It suits the snobbish European sense of his own importance that Canada has not been able to eradicate. I am very scared as I slide into the seat. The gearshift is on the left side of the driver's seat, something I've never experienced, and I've not driven any car at all since he got this one two years ago. Also, without my glasses I have a blurred view of the road.

I don't dare turn the car and possibly stall it. It might give him time to run out. Indeed even as I engage the clutch and pull away with a lurch, I am aware of shouting. The car bounces as I shift to second gear — thank God, thank God, it doesn't stall — and I get into third gear more smoothly. I glance at the rearview mirror and there he is, running hard after us, shaking a fist in the air. Though I can't see his face clearly at this distance, I know it will be wild with rage.

For the first time since I married him I have outfoxed him.

But having not turned the car I am still heading away from North Hatley and towards Montreal. For a flash I think of trying to find my mother's uncle, one of those white-surpliced figures in old family pictures. I know he has a cottage at South Stukely, which is somewhere nearby, but I have never been there, have never even met the man. It's a nonsense thought that I quickly banish. I drive slowly along. I narrow my eyes, trying to see better. There must be a police station in the town of Orford, which can't be far ahead and I must try to find it. And then I become aware of a light blue car coming up behind me and pulling out to pass. As it goes by on my left I glimpse a rage-contorted face at the passenger side window. Frank. Of course.

Once ahead of me the blue car slows down to a crawl and appears to be trying to block my way. I have to swing out as if I want to pass it or I'll bump into it. But I can't pass it. I know we are trapped. That had definitely been Frank's furious face. But then a miracle: a narrow country lane suddenly appears to my left. I make an abrupt decision and turn down it. But then I despair again. This road is narrowing and becoming a mere track. If it's going anywhere at all, it's just to someone's house or farm, and a poor sort of place it must be, with this the way in.

The pale blue car is now looming right behind me again, almost touching my bumper. And the road, as it had to, ends in a farmyard.

I am sunk. A woman comes out of the unpainted farmhouse onto a ramshackle porch, stares for a second at the scene and swiftly disappears inside again. There is no help from that quarter. I get out of the car. All my power leaks out of me and I have to lie across the hood of the car. I drop my head on my arms. My stomach hurts. Inside the car both children wail. I realize they have been wailing right along. I can never outfox Frank. How stupid to have thought I could.

But I have to straighten up and look. Frank and the driver of the blue car are both coming towards me. The driver is a skinny, fair-haired chap with long, hairless white legs descending from very short shorts. His shoes are laced Oxfords, not what a man would normally wear with shorts, a bad sign. He looks odd and he looks worried. He doesn't look at all heroic or powerful, in contrast to Frank, who comes up close to me and then stands, four-square, muscular, tanned and furious. This stranger is no match for him.

But he is not the pushover he looks. He is courageous! He steps forward and inserts himself between Frank and me. I sense what has happened: he has become, over their short time together, doubtful of this man he somehow has been forced into helping. He must have smelled the old alcohol smell to boot. He is bracing himself and he is looking at Frank with extreme suspicion. Amazingly, given my first impression of him, he takes charge of the situation. And even more amazingly, Frank goes along with it. He is still furious but he is also abashed. I can tell by the expression of his mouth, the way he thrusts out his lower lip.

Frank cares very much what people think of him. He is a gentleman and needs people to know he is. At this fraught moment this element of his personality works in my favour. However crazy he is, his need to appear honourable triumphs. It's the same reaction as when he spoke to Carol earlier.

My saviour helps the children into the back seat of his car and I get into the front. We leave Frank to follow in his own car and we drive to the police at Orford. I sense that this poor fellow is relieved to have me as his passenger rather than Frank. Right away he starts to tell me what happened back at the café: he and Frank had both seen me as I started up the Wolseley. Frank had leapt up, seen he'd not be able to stop my getaway and convinced the stranger nearest to him that I was mentally ill and intent on harming myself and the children. I must be followed and caught.

✦

I had thought the police would pay some attention and be on my side but I was wrong. There were two of them and their English was poor but they certainly got the gist of my tale and thought it was puzzling that I would think they could do anything. They shook their heads and smiled with a mixture of ruefulness and amusement. Domestic violence was no business of theirs. How could I have thought it was? A policeman didn't interfere in a husband and wife situation.

However they would let me wait outside the police station until someone came for me, someone I could call on their phone. And perhaps they'd keep some sort of an eye out until that person arrived? I'm not at all sure of that last point. But whom could I call? Both of my sisters' husbands had gone back to the city, as had my brother, and of course my father was in Europe and Uncle Bunny too distant as well. It was going to have to be Ruth's father-in-law, Mr. Harding. I'd call Ruth at his house where she was staying and see if he would drive over and get the children and me. Neither of my sisters could drive.

Mr. Harding was a very formal Englishman. Recently a vice president of American Express he had lived all over the world and had just retired to North Hatley. I had always found him somewhat alarming but as it turned out he was actually kinder and more broad-minded than his son later would prove to be. While we waited for him to arrive we stood waiting right outside the police station window, hoping that if Frank put into action what he kept hissing at me they would have to act. Frank stood very close by my shoulder and said over and over, "Why would it matter if I killed you? I will kill you. For this I have to kill you."

Mr. Harding insisted we drive immediately to the police in Sherbrooke to try to get a restraining order on Frank, which we did

INLAND NAVIGATION BY THE STARS 87

try, but with the same result as we'd had with their opposite numbers in Orford. They were simply not interested. They also added that a restraining order would serve no purpose: as soon as it expired, Frank would be more violent than ever. Mr. Harding, used as he was to being in charge of countless minions, was amazed that he cut no ice at all in this situation. But his support was helpful to me all the same.

The day ended with what could have been a Monty Python farce. The North Hatley policeman, old Mr. Meigs, who had only one arm, stood a shaky guard at the gates at the bottom of our driveway, and my brother, who hurried to the rescue from his job in Montreal, sat up all night in the living room with his .22 rifle across his knees, at the ready to shoot his brother-in-law if need be. I doubt Mr. Meigs was even a real policeman — how could he have been, with his age, frailty and single arm? — but my father was the mayor at the time and I assume he had hired the old chap to deal with the rare traffic offence and such. Standing guard at our gate may have been the high point of his police career.

The next day Uncle Bunny drove over from Thetford Mines and took us into hiding in his home until my parents returned from Europe.

15

IN the months following my terrified escape from my marriage, initially my parents took me and my children in, while I figured out what in the world I was going to do. What felt unfair to me but was unquestionable — literally I felt I could not question it — was that the whole ghastly period I had been through, Frank's drinking to the point of craziness, his violence, the end of my marriage, was worse for my father than for me. For days his face was steadily fraught. He heaved deep sighs. I, the cause, just had to keep my head down.

A young woman had made a disastrously mistaken marriage. Her husband had become crazed. The woman and her elder child, a boy, had been his special victims. There was a huge difference: I had escaped. But what echoes there must have been for my father. No wonder he identified always with my son Paul. He cared desperately that we be safe but he was hard on me. He wanted to make sure I realized my fault in what I had brought upon us.

Sometime that fall he took me to Pointe-Claire to arrange about the house, its sale and the moving out of the furniture. We had had to get a court order to sell it; even though ownership was in my name, a wife in Quebec could not sell property without her husband's permission. It was the same as for an operation: women and children were essentially men's property. When the sale went through, only $5000 was realized, given the market just then and the mortgage. As I had borrowed that amount from my father, to top up my babysitting savings and make the down payment, he took the whole sum back on the spot. I did not question that, though now I am amazed. It would have been wonderfully reassuring to have that nest egg.

When we got to the house it was in a mess. Frank had been living there for several weeks on his own, probably steadily drunk. An old house can quickly descend into apparent squalor if no one sweeps anywhere or washes the kitchen floor or cares about anything. My father sternly upbraided me for my bad housekeeping. The specific he chose to focus on was the dust on top of the door frames.

On the way back to North Hatley I had to ask him to stop so I could eat something. He was shocked at me again: he himself was much too upset to eat. "I've had to make myself eat when upset while I was pregnant, while I was nursing a baby," I wanted to tell him. "I had to for my health, for my children." But I said nothing.

Within a month of my runaway a decision was made, essentially by my father. An article had appeared that summer in the weekend magazine telling of a need for teachers in Canadian universities and colleges. My father drove me over to Lennoxville to meet with the chairman of English at Bishop's University and suddenly I found myself enrolled in a master's program. That the university was in Lennoxville, just ten miles from North Hatley, and that I and my children could share an apartment with my brother who was completing his bachelor of science, were strong points in favour of Bishop's rather than McGill.

I made several trips into Montreal during that first year of my studies, to meet with a divorce lawyer. That grandfatherly man was shocked at my father's treatment of me, which he saw as punitive. Were I his daughter, he claimed, he'd be sending me around the world on a cruise after what I'd been through, not making me knuckle down to my studies. I felt badly done-by but not for long. I was too much like my father not to know that getting down to work was the answer for regaining my pride and self-respect, and most importantly for acquiring the means to support myself and my children. To even up what he spent on my divorce, my father gave my two securely married sisters new kitchens.

Henceforward I was going to be an independent woman and the sole parent to my children. I was twenty-six, still a young woman, and my future was my own. I didn't know how I was going to take the reins into my hands, but I would.

As for Frank it was the end for him of his chance at a normal happy life. His excessively indulged early childhood had been interrupted by events that were no fault of his: war, and at age thirteen a German prison, later a Communist one; his favourite brother essentially destroyed by spending the war in Bergen-Belsen camp — Miha had come home in 1946 speechless, literally. He had joined Tito's Partisans at fifteen and been captured right away (a bourgeois boy, he was used as fodder). He had no words and no will to tell what had happened to him. Frank was a victim of a violent and dislocated world. He was not a bad person but a damaged one.

My father's strong initial disapproval of both Carol's and my choice of husband was based on prejudice (neither had an Anglo-Saxon background, Frank's being Slavic, Vince's Italian) though only in the case of my husband was there any actual reason for fatherly alarm. His voiced objection to Frank was entirely to do with Frank's being Yugoslavian. He never saw fit until after I'd left Frank to bring up to me the signs of alcoholism he apparently was aware of before the marriage. Why he kept silent about his observation (based, as he told me years later, on the rather too urgent way Frank kept having his glass topped up at a North Hatley cocktail party) I can't know. But I wonder now if on some obscure level he was feeling that if I insisted on Frank, against his advice — the voiced advice which was wide-of-the-mark and bound to get my back up — I would have to face the music and learn my lesson the hard way. Which in time I did. Father-daughter relationships can be vexed in complicated ways a daughter does not figure out for years.

Even after our weddings Carol and I dreaded seeing that shadow cross our father's face, say if one of our husbands spent what in our father's frugal view was too much, for a young man, on a car. Yet once when Frank, yet again, was released from hospital where he had been treated for depression and alcoholism, my father came to stay with us to be in charge of the daily tipple Frank had to have to forestall delirium tremens. He did this in a matter of fact way and even with a certain amount of humour. In a crunch he would take charge and his kindness would overcome his censure of the situation. In serious trouble his was the hand I wanted to hold.

My father's treatment of his daughters when they made mistakes was well intended but not always fair (and definitely was not fair when contrasted with his much more lenient treatment of his son). It was the right thing for me to go back to university, but an earlier "lesson" Carol had to have was wrong. When she at age sixteen had entered Bishop's she surely had to have been the prettiest girl in the freshman class. So much was made of her that she managed to fail a course, German. Her excellent reading skills and high intelligence worked for her in the other courses but German required actual hours spent memorizing vocabulary.

As a consequence she was made to drop out of university and do a rather menial job until she was old enough, eighteen, to go into the nursing program at Toronto General Hospital. She did well in nursing and married a wonderful doctor. Our father's tough decision did not ruin her life. But she should have had a choice. She could have done that necessary memory work in the summer, taken a supplementary exam in the fall and carried on. Amazingly, none of us suggested that she should do that, such was parental power then. It was not questioned even among ourselves.

That my marriage ended in craziness and violence helped throw up a barrier to full memory and it can still get in the way if I am not careful to hold on to this new way of seeing. I created a narrative for my years with Frank that I could bear, and that became settled in my mind. The process took a while to do. I knew I could never go back to Frank, for my children's sake (especially Paul's) — that I had to hold firm and never weaken in my resolve. The few times I saw him later, I recognized how broken he was at the loss of us. He was destroyed and I knew he would never recover. But I could not for a moment show concern for him. I told myself I had to be cruel to be kind.

After some weeks had passed he was allowed by the court to visit the children, to take them out for a few hours though not beyond the town of Lennoxville. One time I agreed to go out with them, Frank, Paul and Jane, for a pizza supper. It was a mistake: I could see a fearful hope in Frank's eyes that this could signal I was relenting. It was cruel to have gone with them and I knew I must not do it again.

Part II

Starting Over

16

OVER most of my first year at Bishop's I slipped in and out of a kind of recovery mode, though at the time I would have had no words to describe the process to myself let alone to another person. In those days no one suggested that I should seek a counsellor or indeed any sort of outside support. I think there were no such people then. I knew not another soul who was in my position, or had been in it and got through it. I didn't know what was normal to feel, under these circumstances. For months I had a huge scream inside me that needed expulsion yet could not possibly be allowed to escape. In our tiny apartment I could not possibly upset the others — my children! — even by weeping, let alone emitting screams, and when, on the weekends, I climbed the forested hill behind my parents' house, the children always came with me. Even inside my head I willed stillness and held a clamp on my emotions.

Professor Gray was the head of the English department and my advisor. I was taking his course, Spenser, Milton and Donne. He was a rather dry Englishman who read his lectures from notes that his students all joked were dog-eared and yellowed survivors from his own university years. I suspected they were. Outside of class I quite liked him; I did not expect to feel emotion in his classes. However, one day he wrote an early sixteenth-century poem on the blackboard. It was one I'd never seen before:

Western wind when wilt thou blow
The small rain down can rain.

Christ if my love were in my arms
And I in my bed again.

It pierced me. For a moment my defence melted. I tilted my head
back to hold my tears in place.

During the early weeks I left the university after my last class and
walked through the quad, passed through the cloisters and headed for
the road and the bridge to the town of Lennoxville. I passed our place
and went up the hill to my friend Cynthia's to collect the children.
That fall was wildly beautiful with red and yellow maple leaves, first
brilliant against an impossibly blue sky, then scattered, still blazing,
on the grass of the quad. Then there was the wide, dark and sleekly
moving river with its water birds, ducks and a few geese, once a heron,
readying to fly south. Sometimes it was too much. My defences were
stripped and I felt the world too piercingly. I was relieved when the
leaves were all down and brown and sodden under my feet as I walked.

It was even better when the frost began to seal everything including
me. The winter was bitterly cold with frequent snowfalls. I remember
the bone-reaching pain of the wind on my forehead as I hurried along
Main Street to Church Street, taking care not to fall where fresh snow
covered the ice. I wore my scarf pulled up over my mouth and cheeks
and breathed moist wool. But I welcomed the cold and the endurance
it demanded. It didn't seem a punishment, more a necessary passage
to test me and at the same time hold me safe. It was the correctly
extreme season in which to learn a new way to exist. But even at the
time, somewhere in my body, perhaps even in my mind, I was aware
that this was a chrysalis stage: I was on ice; in the fullness of time —
and the coming of spring — I would emerge into something else. I
was not a girl for indulging despair, I told myself firmly. That's what
it would have been, for me, an indulgence. Weakness. I repudiated
weakness. As for the scream, it never had the satisfaction of emission
but it leaked away somehow anyway.

And surprisingly enough I had my moments of joy, even during that difficult early time. My default mode has always been happiness and it began to break through more and more. One major pleasure in that year was that Chuck lived with us. Looking back I know it was an amazingly patriarchal arrangement: he was the one to whom our father had given a car to drive back and forth to the university and somehow our timetables never allowed for me to have a ride with him. As well I did all the shopping and cooking and such cleaning as happened (I suspect ours wasn't the tidiest of dwellings), as well as washing four people's clothes in an old washing machine that was "semi-automatic," an optimistic description that meant I really washed everything by hand. In 1963 this was taken entirely for granted by both of us, as well as by anyone around us, certainly our parents. Girls did household tasks. Girls walked while men rode.

I wasted no energy on resentment. It didn't even occur to me it was unfair, I was so glad of my brother's presence. Even now, looking back with chagrin and amazement at my pre-aware feminist self's acceptance of my servant's role, I have to say the bargain was worth it. Chuck and I had — still have — the same sense of humour. Our shared laughter made up for a lot, however black the jokes sometimes were. He would play his guitar and sing in the evenings while I made our supper, and he was endlessly patient, funny and kind with Paul and Jane.

Jane still had her crib, placed now end to end with my bed, but every evening, as soon as I closed my book and turned out my lamp, she climbed up, balanced for a second on the crib's end, then jumped down onto my feet, crawled up the bed and snuggled in with me. Every morning, the first one awake, she slipped downstairs to do jigsaw puzzles on the rug right beside the couch where Chuck slept. He claimed she had a way of making little grunts of satisfaction with each piece correctly placed. Every morning he tried unsuccessfully to doze through the grunts, but he never complained. His long-ago disrupted sleep is still a joke between them.

For the children I think his presence made our situation feel almost normal: two grownups, two little children, a proper balance. A family. Almost. Chuck's best friend Clem often came over as well, and the two of them played their instruments, guitars or banjos, and sang. There was always music in that apartment: my singing (to the children their nightly song-sets), Chuck's singing, often Clem's joining in, and Joan Baez, Bob Dylan and Ian and Sylvia on the record player plus my Bach Inventions on the piano. My emotions found expression both in the wailing folk songs and in the comforting, mathematical, thought-ordering patterns of Bach.

Cynthia was also a crucial element of our Bishop's life. My former McGill roommate now married to a Bishop's professor, she was at home with two little boys. Ian was Jane's age, Peter, two years younger. She took for granted that she would include Jane in her care for full days and Paul (who was in morning kindergarten) for afternoons. She was an extraordinarily generous sister-person. My children had known and loved Cynthia since birth and her warmth and steadiness eased them, and me, mightily.

After that first year Chuck left and went on to do graduate work at McGill, but a new friend, dear Karen, moved in across the road. We walked together to the university every day, our gowns floating out behind us, and with our height, and with each of us having long thick hair in a fat, single braid (not a common style then) and with our long swift strides, we must have looked a duo to reckon with. I wish I could be vouchsafed at this moment a glimpse of us as we were back then when we were young! I can call us up now only in my imagination, looking back over decades. We were beautiful and we didn't properly know it, either of us. More importantly Karen became another almost-family member, eventually marrying Clem. We are close to this day.

I must emphasize a truth: I have been incredibly lucky with friends. And friends — among whom I include members of my blood family — have been my beloveds really, far more than any husband or lover I ever had, though I didn't see that obvious fact for ages.

I believed I was supposed to value a man, be he husband or lover, over mere friends — though never over my children. I always knew they came absolutely first. But for certain quite long periods of my life I assumed a woman's need for a man held primacy. Even though, really, it was never true for me.

Over that whole Bishop's time, especially when I was singing, reading, walking or snuggling with Paul and Jane, or spending time with Chuck or Cynthia, and later Karen, my awareness of my chancy, truly alarming situation seldom impinged. It seems amazing to me now. I wonder at myself, the strength of my impulse to be healed, and how happiness overtook me often and often even during that first year, without any of the professional support and counsel and talk-therapy assumed to be essential today. I was so unworried! Yet what did I really think was going to happen to us? A portion of Frank's salary was garnisheed for us now, but I knew he'd likely soon flee back to Europe. How did I think I would manage? It astonishes me now. I put my trust in my own good luck, I guess, but not exactly consciously. I would get my master's degree. I would find a job. It would all work out. It had to, so it would. Such naiveté!

Yet it did work out. I was lucky.

For my particular personality (and I certainly do not generalize) I think now that the fact that I knew no one else in my position was a plus, as was the fact that there were no articles in magazines or newspapers about women like me. I did not know how despairing I ought to feel, how perilous I should realize my future was likely to be. I didn't even realize that we had become "poor folks."

That Lennoxville apartment was our refuge for two important years of my life and I still feel affection for it. It was the narrow back slice of an old, white clapboard, turreted Victorian house on Church Street, a block up from Main Street. We entered our separate tiny domain through the back porch of the main structure, our door to the left of Mme. Chahier's kitchen entrance. She was old — almost certainly not as old as I am now but she seemed ancient to me then. A widow, she lived alone, though her nun-daughter often visited. Neither woman had more than a word or two of English but they smiled and nodded and patted a child's shoulder or smoothed hair off a small forehead when we converged. Frequently Madame left a pie or other baked treat for us on the ironing board she kept out there on the porch. I remember the nun-daughter, one day in spring, trying out Paul's new little bicycle and her long black habit getting caught somehow — she was decidedly large to be folded on a child's bike, let alone with all the trailing heavy fabric. She laughed and laughed as we disentangled her.

Our slice of the house had two rooms downstairs, a kitchen, with my round pine table and the chairs, and the dough box under the window, and, through an arch, a small living room where Chuck slept on the couch by night. My desk and its chair were in that room, also my piano. The desk had once been my mother's and the chair her father's. The chair was oak, broad-seated, heavy and solid, with sturdy arms; he had sat in it to write his sermons. Almost every object in my life has a history. At that Lennoxville point I think I probably still possessed the Bosnian dagger, though it has since disappeared. On the other hand, my grandfather's chair, with its happier provenance, is now in daily use at my son's ranch.

My still having my piano may seem anomalous with my description of the tininess of the apartment and the necessity of paring down my life, but I had kept it for a reason. Our father had suggested to Ruth that she keep it for a while, just until I was in some better state and could house it again myself. Her boys could try piano lessons and Ruth could decide if they should buy piano of their own. But Ruth agreed to take the piano only if she could keep it. She and Michael were not about to pay for tuning and whatever else it might need after being moved if I were ever going to demand it back. Was this mean? It felt so to me at the time, though chiefly it perplexed me.

I felt that were I in her shoes as rich sister, I'd have been happy to fall in with the plan, and happier still if my calamity-struck sibling's situation improved so she could reclaim her instrument. Now I suspect her resistance was unclear even to her.

Ruth was extremely clever and also artistically talented. Crucially, her mothering instinct was a paler thing than Carol's and mine and I've come to see that a woman does not choose her version. A purely maternal and domestic role could not have been entirely fulfilling for Ruth. Yet in that era a middle-class woman was seldom able to see any way out, especially if they had a Victorian-style husband as she did. *The Feminine Mystique* might have been written for her. I remember an advertisement in all the women's magazines sometime back then: in the photograph a lovely thirtyish woman is sitting awkwardly in a child's desk. She is at a PTA meeting. Her expression is one of bafflement and distress, and somehow exhaustion as well. The caption states that she has a MFA (Master of Fine Arts) and the solution to her problem is Valium. Ruth did not turn to Valium but I knew women who did or who drank secretly to achieve the necessary lulling and dulling. There were to be more examples of Ruth's lack of sympathy with me, but at that point, with regard to the piano, our father simply shook his head over what seemed her selfishness and he and Chuck moved it into the Church Street apartment.

There were other features of the slice. The downstairs floors sloped rather drastically. They were partly covered by my braided rugs but there was enough bare linoleum for Paul to run toy cars and trucks downhill. The stairs that wound tightly up from a corner of the kitchen had such a shallow depth that only small children could ascend without being on tiptoe. Immediately upstairs was a small room with Paul's little bed tucked under the eaves and his toybox under a large window that looked out onto the long narrow backyard. The other room upstairs had my double bed — also tucked under eaves — and Jane's crib. At three and a half she was still a tiny person and I decided she didn't need a real bed yet. Nor would there have been space for one. There was a bathroom — the only one in the apartment — off this bedroom, with toilet and tub but no sink. We used the bath tap for tooth brushing and washing hands. The bathroom ceiling sloped so steeply over the tub that adults had to crawl into the water from almost a hands and knees crouch on the bath mat. My bed was covered with the patchwork quilt I'd made for my wedding.

That quilt! I'd pieced it together with my own hands and had the final quilting done by a North Hatley woman. (She charged $25 for that enormous amount of handwork and it actually seemed a lot to me at the time.) It was in a pie pattern. Each pie had sixteen pieces and was stitched onto a white square. The white squares in turn were bordered by bands of turquoise. The bright colours and small intricate patterns of the pie pieces held memories of various former summer dresses — mine, my mother's, my sisters' — that I had cut up to make it. And it had covered my marriage bed for almost six years. The past was present in it in a way that was alternately comforting and confusing. I still have that quilt somewhere, folded and stored away. It became tattered over the years of children's jumping on it but it holds too much history to be thrown away. Not yet, anyway.

In winter it was very cold upstairs in that house as the only heating was an oil stove my father installed in the kitchen below, but we took for granted the cold floors and the thick frost on the small, deeply inset bedroom window. One was either in bed under the covers or darting swiftly in and out of the bathroom or sitting in hot bath water, the ceiling almost meeting the top of one's head. It was not a bath in which to languish.

I became very fond of that apartment. It felt real. It was a bare-bones place, primitive, its life and atmosphere created by us. At the end of our two years there, when we were about to leave it, Cynthia and her family, expecting another baby, were considering moving from their attractive quite large modern house to something even larger. Ian (age four) suggested he'd like it best if they took over our place.

The rent of the Church Street "slice" was $45 a month.

An image: Paul crosses Church Street, carefully looking both ways, and sets out to walk the two blocks to the school. He is in kindergarten now. He has a new life, a new dwelling, a new family arrangement and he has started school. I watch him stepping out and I can see the seriousness with which he is being "a big boy." He is taking on many new things now, including that he has no father anymore living with us. He has told me he plans to rise to the challenges. Since he was about three he has made behavioural plans and has told me of them. The first time he did so he came to me and earnestly announced, "Mummy, I have made a new plan. I won't cry any more when a babysitter comes." Until then, on the rare occasions in Pointe-Claire when I had a neighbour girl from down Cedar Avenue to babysit, he would cry and cry, upsetting all of us, the young girl, me, Jane, as well as himself. Quite on his own he had seen that the crying only made matters worse.

Now I watch him enacting part of his latest "new plan," walking to school by himself. His thick brown hair has been tidily cut for school by the North Hatley barber. My father insisted on it and took him there himself. My father does not hold with little boys having haircuts done casually by their mother, a mother who usually allows the hair to get much too long first. He wears a red viyella shirt and grey flannel shorts, both bought in England for him by my mother. He is beautiful, with his large, slightly slanted, long-lashed and dark grey/hazel eyes. No one has ever pinned down their precise colour. Once, when he was four, he overheard his unusual eyes being discussed by his aunts. He told me afterwards, "I have private eyes." But I am watching his back at the moment and cannot see his face. I am so proud of him for the courage and care with which he taking on his new life when he is still so small really. As he reaches the curb he turns to give me a wave. I blow him a kiss.

✦

Another image: It is Jane who is in kindergarten now and this is her first day. She is only four and she is not ready for this. After all Paul was five before he had to start school. The children are sitting on little chairs around a table and all the parents who brought them have gone except for two: I stand behind Jane's chair; Professor Arthur Motyer stands behind his daughter Gillian's. Both little girls are sobbing. Gillian has long light brown hair, carefully brushed and braided, I'm sure by her mother, to be tidy and pretty for this first day of school. She is blue-eyed, tall for five, and English looking. Jane's hair is darker brown and short. She does not look English. Her dark brown eyes, swimming with tears, are Slavic and she is tiny for her age, younger than the usual age for kindergarten. She seems at this moment an adorable baby still.

Neither little girl can bear her parent to abandon her; each keeps turning to clutch a parental hand. But we have to go! Arthur must teach a class and I must be a student in the class. The lecture hall soon will be full of impatience and perplexity if Arthur does not arrive and for my part I don't want to miss his class either. He is everyone's favourite professor, the most brilliant and the most demanding of his students. We share anguished glances and finally we each peel off our little girl's fingers and escape. Loud weeping follows us down the hall. We are almost crying ourselves. Later that day I hear how Paul, now in the grade one classroom, heard the crying and fled his own class to come to the rescue. Somehow everyone calmed down.

At the end of my first year back at university, as spring was in the offing, I was more conscious than I could remember ever being before of the newly snow-free lawns and fields. After a winter that had lasted an eon, the brown, flattened grass seemed to be charged with latent energy as it waited for the warm rains and the sun. I felt the urgency of it in my body. There was a tension in the trees too, in their buds, which were still clamped tight yet already swelling with promise, nearly ready to break open. All of that invaded me and built inside me. Air with the cool, water-earth smell of spring blew into our open windows.

I too was ready for something, waiting for it. I admitted it to myself. I wasn't sure what it was. I felt younger than I'd been for years, an adolescent again.

17

THE children and I throughout that year almost always went home to North Hatley on the weekends. Late on Saturday mornings we took the bus, boarding it outside the post office on Main Street. The trip took half an hour and we arrived in the village just as the noon whistle went. Then there was a walk up the hill, circling past the ballpark and passing, farther along and higher up, Mr. MacLennan's house. It would be boarded up for the winter as all the summer houses were from September to June.

Then, just after we passed the Parkins' cottage, perched well above the road and also boarded up, we entered the gates to our property. Through them, we climbed again, took another left turn, and beyond the pine tree in the middle of the circle drive, our house was in view, waiting for us. I use the word "our" again and again, as if I were still a child of the family, the property and house mine as much as anyone's. Yet that wasn't quite so. My mistaken marriage had put me at least partially beyond the pale. I had to earn my right to be fully within the family fold. But we were allowed to come for weekends. My father strongly identified with my children, now essentially fatherless. He saw himself especially in Paul.

Now, however, with the long summer holiday looming not far ahead, I knew by some sort of osmosis that our staying with them for the whole of it was not in the cards. I was not looking forward at all to spending summer in the Church Street apartment. For the school year it was fine, but in summer, the summer that would shortly be upon us? I envisioned how hot and stuffy it would be trying to sleep in those small rooms under the eaves. It would be quite unlike our Pointe-Claire old house with its large wild garden bordered by tall hedges and brilliant with peonies and poppies, and with Lake Saint-Louis at the end of the street. I was spoiled by the kinds of summers I'd always had.

As it turned out I found a way to be in North Hatley after all.

North Hatley had long been literary place but until recently that had been the case only in summer. Mr. MacLennan (for years my secret friend), novelist and professor, for years had come for several months, as had Frank Scott, the poet and law professor. He had a cottage that he shared month about with Blair Fraser, then the editor of *Maclean's Magazine*. The Frasers I knew well as I babysat their younger son Graham in my teens but as an adult I became friends with Frank. He was a stork of a man, ancient, very tall, with long skinny white legs, usually exposed to view as he favoured shorts for summer wear. He had a large boney nose and one blind eye which gave him a piratical look. He came to all parties and thought he was young. He did have a lovely artist wife of his own generation (reportedly long ago the mistress of Norman Bethune) but he generally had a girlfriend, decades younger than he, in tow. He was brilliant and very funny. There were Harvard professor-writers too. All of these were late-June arrivals. They would settle into the cottages opened and readied for them by local townswomen. These intellectual men — they all were men, though of course their wives came too — were all members of the Club, which opened in late June. But now there were year-round writers and professors as well as the summer ones.

The poet, professor and literary critic D. G. Jones had bought our old house from my father in 1963. Our family had lived there, sometimes just in the summers, sometimes year-round, from when I was five-almost-six until I turned twenty-one. In 1948 we had it winterized and enlarged from the charming cottage it initially was. I'm not sure it was as charming thereafter but it was still loved by us all. We moved out of it in the summer of 1957 — the fateful summer at the end of which I married Frank — to our new house high up on the hillside above the village. For several years my father rented out our old one to various families and then in 1963 the Joneses bought it.

By 1964 a whole row of professors and writers resided on the little lane, formerly our lane, one level up from the lake: as well as Doug Jones, there were Professor Joly of the University of Sherbrooke, writer Ron Sutherland, chair of the English department there, and Ralph Gustafson, poet and English professor at Bishop's.

It is an early spring Saturday and the children and I are walking along the road by the lake. We had come over to North Hatley on the bus from Lennoxville as usual on that morning and now it is the middle of the afternoon and we've come outdoors again. I am restless. I've no idea what to do with all the spring energy inside me. Studying and caring for my children aren't enough. I have been hibernating like a bear all through the winter and now I'm out of my cave, up and about and sniffing the air.

We have walked fast down the hill and now head westward along the lake. Lively smells have been released by the sun, earth, green things I can't name as well as manure — a horse has passed recently. Widening patches of wet grass are exposed. I hear water running under the soft ice and slushy snow at the edges of the road, which itself is bare, wet and black. The ice in the lake has a rotten look, uneven, grey and coarsely granular. Here and there dark channels of water have opened where the ice has drifted away from the bank. The lake ice always takes longer to entirely melt than the snow and ice on the land but the process is starting.

We come along beside our boathouse, locked now of course. The dock's sections are piled in a tidy heap on the verandah. But there is activity down at the lake edge and child voices. That in itself is a surprise but then I stop and stare in shock: a child is out on the ice. Two smaller children, a girl and an even littler boy, are on the shore and are the ones calling. The boy on the ice is only a little bigger than Paul, seven or maybe eight. The ice he is standing on must have shifted and he is balanced on what has become a shallow and now tipping iceberg. An expanse of dark open water distances him from the shore and that dark space is widening as we watch. The voices of the two children on the beach are shrill and anxious. There are wooden steps going down to the beach and I start quickly down them, Paul and Jane behind me. I am the adult here and I must save the situation.

But the boy acts before I can figure out what to do. He leaps. I see his legs scissoring. He is wearing too-short trousers and I glimpse astonishingly thin and white ankles — and then he is in the water. It is not very deep, as I knew it wouldn't be, but it is near freezing and well above his knees. He staggers, almost falls sideways, rights himself and then wades lurchingly towards shore. The girl is crying now. "Oh Sky," she is wailing. "I told you not to go out on the ice."

Sky is shuddering with cold but he is laughing, or trying to. On shore he stomps up and down once or twice in his sodden running shoes, which squelch in the slush and wet pebbles. He is wearing no socks. Who can these raggle-taggle children be? I grab the boy's cold wet hand and start pulling him up the stairs. "We must run!" I say. "You have to get out of these clothes. You need to get warmed up!" I can see that the stagger he did to keep upright in the water soaked him right to his waist all up one side.

The other four children follow, scrambling up the steps behind us. Paul and Jane are both staring with extreme interest at the drama unfolding, transfixed by such naughtiness, a boy going out on the melting ice! To them such small children being down at the lake without a grownup is amazing.

"Where do you live?" I ask. I am thinking fast: what would be the nearest occupied house? The ones along the lake are all summer cottages still boarded up for winter. The little girl is the one who answers me. "It's not far," she says and she takes quick steps past me out into the road, leading the way now. She at least is wearing boots.

"What are your names?" I ask. They are not poor children; I can tell this from their voices. So who are they? I know most children in North Hatley.

"I'm Tory," the little girl says, "and he's Sky, and he's North." She points at each brother. "And our last name is Jones." She looks at me, and then away again, and smiles shyly. She has a narrow, very pale face with pointed features and large hazel eyes. She is a fairy girl, thin and pretty, with an almost dancing, nervous way of moving.

I now know who they are and where we are going. And indeed it will not be far, just up a short rather steep hill and along to the second house at that level, a large white shingle one. I know there will be a low stone wall at the road and steps going up, and a big old maple tree, one I looked at every day from my childhood bedroom, a friend. We turn the corner — and the tree is gone! I am stunned for a second, as if it had crashed down (silently!) and been removed just as we climbed the hill.

I clench with nervousness at the prospect of going inside, as I decide I will have to do, to accompany sodden Sky. Ever since we left this house, seven years ago back in the early summer of 1957, I have had it intact in my mind: my childhood home. It has still been mine in my imagination and now will no longer be. The Joneses cut down my maple tree. What else will they have done? Certainly another family's identity will have been imposed. I brace myself to meet it. I am also plain curious.

I actually have met these children's parents once. A couple of months ago Cynthia had them for dinner in Lennoxville and had me as well, as she always did when she gave a dinner. Doug and Betty. I had been struck by Doug, by the intensity of the way he looked at me. When Cynthia introduced us he gave me a steady deep stare that went on longer and with a more piercing intensity than usually happens when one first meets someone. He kept doing it over the evening. He talked to me more than he did to anyone else too, in a low, slightly nasal voice. His eyes stayed in my mind for several days after that night, though because of the distraction of them, I can't now remember many details of what he actually said to me.

Tory opens the front door and we troop into the vestibule, where I expect sodden running shoes and boots will be removed, but the Jones children stump on into the hall where they leave damp and muddy prints on a white rug. The rug is the first surprise. It covers the hardwood floor from wall to wall and is made of some thin, rough fabric, perhaps glued or stapled onto the wood below. A rather dirty springer spaniel that had been waiting on the verandah comes in with us as well. Sky heads for the stairs and squelches up them, kicking off his runners and pulling off some of his clothes as he reaches the landing and stuffing the sodden bundle under one arm. The runners he leaves behind him on the landing. The other Jones children take off their jackets and boots and throw them back into the vestibule. My children and I take off our boots and stand them tidily near the door. We are behaving as if this is still my mother's house or as if it's anyone's house where there are normal rules.

The kitchen is another shock: the room is so dark! All the appliances are very dark brown — a style I've not seen before; the long table in the bay window is dark wood and in the middle of it is a large and long aquarium, the water green-black. In our day the room, with its west-facing bay, was bright. Now all the light is swallowed up.

The people in the room strike me next. There are three of them. Doug is sitting at the end of the table smoking. He lounges in a slump on his chair, one arm loosely on the table, the other bent, the wrist limp, the hand carelessly dangling the cigarette, which he then brings slowly to his lips. He narrows his blue eyes and smiles at me. A peculiar thought occurs to me: with most people, you never think of the skeleton inside them. With Doug, you do. There's so little in

INLAND NAVIGATION BY THE STARS   113

the way of flesh on his bones. At the same time he's quite beautiful, if a man can be that.

I am invited to sit down, and I do, and I explain why I am here, how Sky got so cold and wet, falling into the lake. His mother surprises me — this house is full of surprises — by barely listening. She doesn't leave to go to Sky as most mothers surely would. Instead she offers me tea, or a beer. Doug is drinking a beer. I accept tea and she fills the kettle. She appears delighted by my visit. Why?

There is a young boy sitting at the opposite end of the table to Doug. He is familiar to me from a history class I am in, though we've never spoken, and he smiles at me in recognition. He is an attractive boy and unusually foreign-looking, for Bishop's, which has an otherwise uniformly Anglo-Saxon student body. I've often watched him as he enters the lecture room, walking with a springy confidence and then stopping to look about for an empty seat in a slightly dramatic posture that makes his black gown swirl behind him. He has very thick black hair and exotic features, yet very blue eyes. Apart from a few teen-age spots on his forehead, he is attractive. But certainly too young for me.

"This is Michael," Betty says. "He's boarding with us this year."

18

AS spring goes on I drop in on the Joneses often. I continue
to be fascinated by the oddness of this household. I am taking my
own part in it because I am increasingly drawn to Doug and his blue
gaze and the things he tells me. They are literary things, not ever
intimacies, but his intensity makes them feel intimate. I know this
is probably not a wise or good thing to be doing, allowing myself
to be fascinated by this man. And I don't even know if I'm imagining something that isn't real at all. But it's not just Doug that keeps
bringing me back to the house. It's the household's off-centredness,
or non-centredness, the way energy pulls in one direction and then
in another, and I don't know what I even mean when I think that.
It's the way Betty keeps pressing me to come back. And the children,
they are probably the main pull. They are so appealing — and no one
but I seems to find them so. At one moment I decide that the family
draws me in by its very unwholesomeness, these people operating like
a drug I can't resist. But then I have to wonder how much of the "evil"
magnetism is something I am imagining and projecting onto them.
After all I am lost and off-centre myself.

I am not mistaken though that the focus in that family is very
much on the adults, on the literary talk that goes on all the time
between the parents — or really just between Doug and a few friends.
Other writers, poets, a literature professor or two are often in attendance. Betty flits about, always seeming to be on the move, and light
on her feet despite an advancing state of pregnancy. She never settles

in one place and seldom joins in the literary talk. Their circle makes me think of a smaller Bloomsbury Group, and the children are like Bloomsbury children, free, shabby, slipping in and out, or like those in the novel *The Constant Nymph*. They are not really the point for anyone.

Young Michael is an anomaly in the house: he seems the most centred somehow, the most sure of himself. He moves about among the separate entities that make up what seem to be different camps, sometimes playing a game with the children as if he is another child, sometimes laughing — almost flirting — with Betty, and sometimes being a part of the literary group around the kitchen table. I gather he writes poetry himself. His youthful energy is in sharp contrast to Doug's lethargy, the collapsed or crumpled way he sits. Michael leaps up and down the stairs or jumps up out of chair with that springiness I have noticed in his classroom entrances.

There is an ongoing irritation on Doug's part about Michael though: the boy takes a daily shower in the bathroom right above Doug's chair and water drips down onto Doug's head. He grumbles about this. That shower leaked in our day too; our father gave up on trying to fix it and forbade us to use it. It's a puzzle that Michael goes on irritating his host. Some sort of male territorial thing going on perhaps. Michael seems sunny and uncombative otherwise.

Of course I have to take into account that it is fascinating to be in a house where I had lived myself for so much of my life and to see it under a new, so different, dispensation. I am surprised to find it is easier to bear when it is so different. But I am not often really painfully reminded of our old life here. The emotional atmosphere is the main thing that is different but the décor is as well. My mother created in her houses what I would now call English Country House Style — it is the style I favour myself to this day. It involves Persian or Turkish rugs on hardwood flours, comfortable chintz-covered sofas and chairs, white curtains on bedroom windows and a sense of order. We had dogs and cats that came in and out too, as the Joneses do.

We were never nagged about the state of our bedrooms, our clothes or our shoes, but somehow, in our day, order almost magically prevailed. I can see that Betty has given thought to her redecorating, at least at the outset, and has tried a modern look: long, striped burlap curtains frame the tall window over the stairs; the thin white carpet I first noticed covers the floors. This was a mistaken choice with dogs, cats and careless children in and out in all weathers. Jugs of dried grasses gather dust here and there. My mother had fresh flowers, some potted plants, never dead things. Ours was a happy house where a young person, or indeed anyone, could feel safe. There was the calm and solid centre that was our mother. And our father could not be more different from Doug Jones.

Silly and extreme images come to my mind when I'm not at the Joneses but am thinking about them, which I do when walking back and forth to the university: the house, without our family in it and instead under occupation by this new one, is full of energy-cross-currents, like water just below a water-fall; or it is a fast spinning top, somehow lurching off balance. But tops lurch like that only when they are slowing down. How can a house be slowing down? And perhaps the intensity in the air, the source of which I can't pin down, is just me! I don't think so but how can I know? And I keep going back.

My identity shifts about. It's a fluid thing these days: I am no longer a wife, and I am a student again. In those two ways I am back to an earlier self. But I am also a mother now. That is the most important factor in my life. Because I am a mother, and on my own, I take my studies more seriously: I am preparing myself to earn our living henceforward. It's hard to get my mind around this, hard to believe it can be real. When I was at McGill my studies had no particular aim. None of us thought of careers: we all knew we'd simply be wives. Our degrees, the Fine Arts professor said, would make us better mothers. That made one sort of sense, but now I'm not sure of his logic. Higher education might equally have made us dissatisfied with domesticity. I suppose he thought of us as creating more cultured homes than our less educated sisters, which would be rewarding for us, presumably our only reward. But some homes shake apart — and then what? Of what practical use were the art classes?

I'd been nervous when I approached the first set of exams before Christmas. What if I'd lost my edge after six years out? In November I'd gotten a rather low mark on an early history essay. I'd done first class work in history at McGill. Had my brains dulled in the six years of my marriage? Now the May exams are coming up but I feel surer. My academic wits are awake.

19

I may have felt my wits were awake that spring but they were still dozing in one regard. The same thing I took for granted in the other parts of my life, assuming it to be normal, operated academically as well: both the courses and the professors who taught them were products of an embedded male system. And as I took for granted I would do all the housework, I took the academic situation for granted too.

This may seem puzzlingly obtuse of me. One might think that academic matters are at enough distance from family life and matters of the heart, intimate life, to be looked at rationally, especially by a good student such as I. But of course there really is no distance between the academic world and intimate life. They mirror each other. Virginia Woolf knew that: she published *A Room of One's Own* in 1929, long before my student days at McGill or later at Bishop's. And I had read it! I had read several books by her and knew about her life; I had read Charlotte Brontë; I had read George Eliot. But I had no way to imagine integrating into my life what those women writers had seen, and the truth of which I recognized when I read their work. Nothing and no one around me ever reflected back to me or spoke of such a way of looking at the world. Waves of feminist thinking, and even some valiant action, had arisen in earlier times, but in the 50s and early 60s as I was growing up those waves had receded out of sight and mind, leaving the sand as smooth as ever.

All that is not to say my time at my two universities was wasted. Far from it. I learned a great deal from my professors. It's just that neither they nor I recognized a huge hole in the English and history curricula. Where were the women?

Over my four years at McGill I had only two women professors. Both were in the French department. One was a stern old ogre whose beady stare froze my tongue whenever I tried to speak her language; I came close to failing her class, she unnerved me so. But the other was the young Madame Eva Kushner. She inspired and encouraged her students, and her courses were the only ones that were conducted in the way I, much later, would emulate.

The model back then was the lecture. A student took notes while a professor held forth. I respected my male McGill professors and learned from them but almost never dared speak in class. That was true even in Mr. MacLennan's classes, he who was my friend. No one did. He was so scornful of how ill-educated we were. He did do one thing that echoed his own Oxford time: he had us, though just once over the whole year, come to his office and read aloud an essay we'd written. This felt very important but he didn't actually say much about the essay beyond a few positive comments, in my case at least, and really it was nothing akin to the weekly meetings he had had with his Oxford tutor.

Mme. Kushner was unique in my experience, inviting participation and helping her students understand even very complex ideas; she also encouraged us to work out our thought processes aloud and come to our own recognitions. It was exciting — I still remember the discussion and debate we had about existentialism. She required us to think and created a respectful classroom climate that meant we could dare to. Other amazing things about her: she was young and pretty; she was married with one small child; the second year I had her, she was pregnant again. A woman academic who was also having a woman's life.

As for the other professors, even in small classes where discussion should have been possible, and even when I think they would have liked an exchange of ideas with students, they had no idea how to stimulate such a thing. Professor Gray used to try to get us going, especially in his Literary Criticism class, but it never worked. Arthur Motyer was better at it, yet even he, much as I liked him, had such a princely presence that few students spoke up. The only woman professor I had, Dr. Harper, who taught me both Anglo Saxon and Middle English, was a good teacher in the old mold. She was like a schoolteacher with her drills and quizzes. I thought she was very old yet she couldn't have been: forty years after those Bishop's classes she had Cynthia and me to dinner at her seniors' residence in Victoria and she looked exactly the same.

Professor Harper was old-school in more than one way. I remember her distressed eyes and furrowed brows in class one day after she had asked how many of us believed in the fires of hell. I can't remember just what we were reading but the question must have been relevant. Nary a hand was raised. We were embarrassed and sorry we failed her in this and she was worried for us, kind soul that she was. Another aspect of university teaching in those days: essays had almost no internal marking or comments, and nothing at the end but a letter grade and perhaps one word or one phrase. Some "very good" essays were handed in year after year with new cover sheets and final pages. Students kept track of how the grade differed, rising or falling a little, from year to year.

I didn't exactly formulate at the time my thoughts about all of these professorial practices. I took them for granted. But later, when I began my own teaching, I knew I wanted to be a Madame Kushner-style teacher: I would be the expert in the room as best I could be, and what I had learned from my professors was enormously helpful there, but I would also see students as individuals worth respecting and hearing from. Both roles were always important to me. I never wanted to allow myself to tip too far into the second role, as many teachers did in the 70s, allowing their classrooms to descend into cacophony, a noisy sharing of ignorant views.

But those realizations were ahead of me: at Bishop's I was mostly happy to listen and to read. I discovered many works I'd not delved into before. At McGill in first year English we had had to read Book I of *Paradise Lost*, but now we had to read the whole thing and I loved it — never mind Milton's misogyny, which I didn't bother paying attention to in my enjoyment of the poetry. I was fascinated by a course I took given by Dr. Masters, Eighteenth Century Thought. In Ralph Gustafson's Modern Poetry course I found I loved Hopkins and Auden and other poets I'd not read much of before. Ralph was another one who tried, unsuccessfully, to get discussion going: either he lacked the knack or the class was too unused to anything but a straight lecture, probably a bit of both. Not a single course included a woman writer. In Medieval History we once had to create our own essay topic and I had the idea of trying to do something about women of the time. I thought there could be an aspect of social history I could explore. Social history — and I wouldn't have known that term — had never been touched on by my professors but I suspected there must be something in it. Dr. Thaler could give me no direction at all in how to even start to look, and I became discouraged. There has to have been material, however scrappy, buried in the library, but what with my busy life, I chose something simpler and male.

Within that period of spring awakening I was asked — I forget how the message came to me — to go to Montreal to meet with Frank's psychiatrist. I assume it was thought I might have some illuminating things to say. This was new, as his previous doctors had never thought it important to speak to me. I had no intention of returning to Frank, whatever transpired, but I agreed to go. I probably fitted it in with one of the trips I made to see the divorce lawyer.

The psychiatrist's name was Dr. Stuart Smith, and I remembered him as a distant figure from McGill, years ahead of me. I think he had been involved in student politics. While I was with him, after we discussed Frank, I thought it only fair to sneak in a question of my own. I told him that I was puzzled about sex, now that I was no longer married. The physical had been a strong element in my marriage to Frank. But was it natural and normal to feel its loss, to miss it, and with urgency? Was it normal to feel those needs awakening in me? Whom was I thinking of? Obviously I was thinking of Doug but not only of him. The urges were more widely focused. And maybe I had it the wrong away round: maybe my urges were creating my attraction to Doug. It was just my own self, creating the trouble. And trouble it certainly was, I learned. Dr. Smith was unequivocal: my feelings were definitely not normal. A woman's sexuality existed only in response to a man's, her husband's. It was impossible, or at any rate very wrong and abnormal, for it to exist, as it were, on its own.

I found that only briefly daunting. I was pretty sure he was wrong and that there was nothing abnormal about me. But I do find it dismaying that the psychiatric thinking then was so wide of the human mark.

20

O<small>N</small> the long Easter weekend of my first year at Bishop's I go down to the Joneses. It is warm, almost hot, yet still not fully spring. There is still that feeling of urgency in the waiting hills, and in me.

We are sitting on the edge of the verandah, our feet on the brown grass. It is still too early for the summer furniture to have been brought out, if indeed this careless household will follow such a seasonal custom. It is just Betty, Michael and I; the children are playing on the side lawn. I am wondering where Doug is. He may still be sleeping in — but then I see him coming along the road. Improbably, he has been for a walk. Even more improbably, he is walking with a young woman. And he is holding her hand. They are walking along slowly, talking, oblivious of the three of us sitting on the verandah. But then he sees us. He gives his rueful smile (his smiles always have that quality) and he doesn't drop the young woman's hand. Nor does Betty look at all concerned or even puzzled; she smiles back at them and stands up to walk towards them as they come up the steps. Her pregnancy is now like a basketball but does not show at all from the back.

I stare at the young woman. And the word "woman" is the correct one for her. I decide at once that she is a very different expression of a female from those of us who still consider ourselves girls. She has the air of someone who discounts mere prettiness. I find her appearance disquieting in its severity: she should not be attractive to Doug but clearly is. This spring, on days when we can, all the young girls I know, and I as well, are wearing flowery shifts with short skirts and our hair is long and flowing. If it is curly, like mine, it is allowed to be itself. Even I have given in to the new fashion of pale lipstick. It's as if everyone is allowing herself to blossom in an ultranatural, but of course quite conscious, way. This woman is clearly not having any truck with that. She is wearing a pale grey blouse, like a school uniform blouse, and a long dark skirt. Her dark hair is dragged back, its curl — I can tell it is curly from the way it is fuzzing up a bit in the damp air — as tamed as possible. And Doug is looking at her with the very gaze I find so compelling.

She is a serious intellectual. Oh dear. I am not a serious intellectual.

"This is our friend Peggy," Betty says to me, and Peggy slides me a swift, uninterested glance. Doug has dropped her hand but the two of them walk past us and through the open door of the house. I hear her voice though not what she is saying and the two of them laugh. Her voice and her laugh have a low nasal quality.

I feel very confused. There is something unnatural and sick afoot in this household. Why do the two who have disappeared into the house seem to be a couple? Of course I am very jealous.

Later we all sit around the kitchen table. Several other people have arrived and the room is full. Peggy sits in Doug's usual spot and he is at the far end, facing her. She reads aloud a poem, not one of hers, I think — though she is a poet too. The poem expresses the poet's (I assume a man's) disgust at female fecundity, the disgustingness of birth. I deliberately block specific details but I am upset. The men appear to enjoy the poem, but does Peggy? I can't tell. Peggy's voice is a perfect vehicle for the poem. The men around the table all enjoy it. She, like them, is a poet, a writer — and that means she is more than a mere woman. No one objects to the hostility of the poet's images in a house full of small children and where a pregnant woman is flitting in and out of the room. For her part Betty appears to be paying no attention whatsoever.

INLAND NAVIGATION BY THE STARS 125

On the last evening of the holiday weekend we all drive over to the university to see the latest in the Ingmar Bergman film series. We arrive late and have to sit in the front row, in the seats where one must lean back and stare upwards and the movie people are huge and distorted. The light from the screen falls over us brightly. At one point I glance along the row and observe the others: Doug is again holding hands with Peggy; Betty, farthest along and right on the aisle, is — yes, she is — holding hands with Michael. She lifts his hand to her mouth and kisses his fingers.

Peggy leaves after the holiday weekend and returns to her own work. I think that she, like me, is a graduate student, but at a much more prestigious university (Radcliffe or even Harvard itself?). She is far more important than I am. I don't think she even ever noticed I was about. Certainly she never spoke to me.

Soon after that weekend the situation is finally explained to me. Despite my discomfort with the adults I remained magnetized by the family, and of course I loved the children. Peggy no longer in the immediate picture, Doug was back to gazing at me.

Betty calls to me: "Anne! Will you come out here? I need to discuss something with you. Please!" She is out in the kitchen and the others are all heading outdoors, the adults to sit on the verandah on the newly dragged out chairs, the children to play.

While Betty always was keenly welcoming, she rarely conversed with me. Usually, for example, having pressed the children and me to stay for supper, she would be seemingly in a brown study at the table, leaving the talk up to Doug and me and sometimes Michael, the children having their own ploys and jokes at the end of the table away from the grownups. But on this day she wants me, and on my own. She takes me into the little hallway between the kitchen and the back porch, where we have to stand very close together.

"I'm leaving very soon," she says, looking me in the eye very directly.

I notice that she has very pretty eyes, large and a warmly rich brown. Bambi eyes. I'd not thought before really about her looks. She was almost ten years older than I and very pregnant and I'd simply not considered her attractiveness. Maybe I had not wanted to.

"I have a proposition for you," she goes on. "I wonder if you'd consider coming here, with Paul and Jane of course, and just for the summer. It would be a great help to us, and the children are very fond of you. You must know that."

I did know that. Especially the two younger ones, Tory and North. They used to draw close to me, whenever I was there. Sky too, though less obviously. Tory had taken to climbing on me, curling an arm around my neck and snuggling against me, closing her eyes, tucking her face into my shoulder as if this might be a secret behaviour no one else would notice. She was a tall little girl and her thin legs would dangle down. She was a big girl for lap-sitting, especially on someone not a relation, but I was happy to hug her. I was starting to love her.

But where was Betty going? How was she going anywhere, when she was having another baby in about six weeks? How was she going anywhere but to the hospital in Sherbrooke when her new baby was ready to be born? And then she'd be only four or five days in the hospital, not the entire summer. Then — and she was excited: I could see in her sparking Bambi eyes how she had been leading up to this — she tells me she is leaving the family. She is leaving for good. The new baby was not Doug's. She would be flying to Mexico for a quick divorce and then would join her lover in Ontario.

Her lover? Her lover. Truth swirled and settled. Several puzzle pieces, wildly unlikely ones not so long ago but recently hovering, landed on the table and clicked into place. Michael. A boy. Several years younger than I, even. Presumably he would leave first, or as soon as the exams were over.

This was why she had seemed to court me, why she had been so welcoming and issuing of invitations, even while not especially liking me as far as I could ever tell or even trying at all to get to know me. This was the reason for my sense of the household's dislocation, my sense of a top's once-whirling energy slowing, the top lurching off balance. Things — children! — falling here, falling there, unattended. A marriage had come asunder and it must have done so almost a whole year before.

The word "asunder" comes to me because I had rent my own marriage asunder and sometimes thought of what I had done in those biblical terms. Actually, even as I heard the words spoken during my wedding I had been caught by them. I think I already sensed that a rending asunder was ahead for Frank and me and that it would be at my hands. Those words in the marriage service sound so brutal and physical: "What God has joined together, let no man rend asunder." Rending asunder is what happens though. The words are right and true. A brutal tearing of the spirit and of the flesh. Yet this couple, Betty and Doug, had remained in the same house all the year after the rending, with her lover there as well. While she burgeoned with the basketball that was Michael's baby they, all three, lived as characters in a play, enacting a pretence of normalcy.

"Strange" would be too small a word.

It comes to me now that I substituted the word "rend" for "put." The marriage service actually says "let no man put asunder." Of course it does! But I am leaving the incorrect "rend," as it expresses what I felt to be the truth. Marriages that end are torn apart. Even if no physical attack occurs, a marriage ending is violent. "Put" is too mild for what is done.

But these "renders," Betty and Doug, had not fled from the scene, or not yet. Maybe it was not a tearing apart for them. But how not?

"I need to start fresh," Betty tells me. "I am an artist, and here, in this family, I am not able to pursue that. I've not been allowed the space or the time to realize my talents. Doug never gets up before noon." That is clearly a bitter grievance. "I am a talented woman!

I deserve more freedom than I have had here!" She believes this. She is adamant. Then she pauses and looks away from me. A small and tender smile comes and goes. She sighs. Smiles again. "Michael is very young," she says. "He is beautiful. And he will allow me freedom. He is only a boy, after all."

21

AND that was how it came about that I and my children spent the summer in North Hatley after all.

Because of course I agreed. How could I not have? I needed, or at least really wanted, a way to be in North Hatley, not to have to spend a hot and stuffy summer in the slice. Paul and Jane could swim and play with their cousins, as was only fair. Above all, I was seriously drawn to the mystery of Doug and I already knew the neediness of those children. I had begun to love them. At this distance I can't be sure what was the strongest draw. All of them worked together.

That I should move in just as Betty moved out has to have presented an interesting situation for the village gossips. At my parents' insistence my younger cousin Charlotte came to stay in the house for a while, to circumvent open scandal, though, as I learned only much later, her presence did not exactly stop all tongues. But North Hatley was then, and likely still is, very forgiving of errant behaviour. Of course people enjoy watching dramas being played out, but new arrangements are soon accepted. Over the generations almost every family has had its moments. I'm sure my mother smarted over what people thought but "rose above."

Once I was living in the house the need for my presence was almost overwhelming in its starkness. But I wasn't overwhelmed. Not I. Who else but I would have had the energy and love to deal with those bereft children? Who else would endlessly sing songs to them every night as they tried to settle to sleep? Who else would strip the soaking sheets from the beds every morning? Who else figure out what to do with those mattresses that had been soaked nightly for months? (I tracked down soft plastic sheeting to encase them, first scrubbing them and drying them in the sun.)

Doug was a man of the times and a poet to boot. Poets were allowed to float above the mundane even more than ordinary men. Think of Wordsworth and how sister Dorothy and wife Mary slaved for him, and quietly too, so the great man had the silence and peace he needed to think and write. There was no question of Doug's noticing any of the rest of us as he lay sleeping in for the entire morning, and, once up, sat like Wordsworth, thinking and writing at his desk. There was no question of his doing a clothes washing or cleaning anything. He certainly would not go food shopping or cook a meal. He stayed up very late every night and talked. I stayed up every night to listen, and very fascinating he was. Betty had been quite right about his rising. I was the one — as she had been — who got up soon after the sun rose to make breakfast for the children and start the household tasks.

The children were very quiet, very good. They hardly ever spoke of their mother. After a while — I forget just how long — only Sky was wetting the bed every night. He and Tory and little North stuck close to me. Steven, the eldest, was more remote. Was he more distressed than the others, as eldest and most aware, or less distressed, as already more independent? I had no way to know, he said so little. My only clue was that when they chose the songs I would sing to them every night, sitting on each child's bed in turn, he always wanted "Bye, Baby Bunting."

As far as I understood it they had had no warning their mother was leaving, let alone for good, until she was going out the door. Yes, there had been months of her distraction and a strange atmosphere but how do children figure out what an atmosphere is about? I didn't figure it out myself until Betty told me. A mother disappearing is the nightmare dread of any child. Surely it could not happen outside a dark fairy tale. But it had.

INLAND NAVIGATION BY THE STARS 131

How did I do all that work for that family without ever thinking that their father could do some of it? I'd thought Betty, complaining about her burdens, implying they were a reason to run away, had been tiresome. What else would a married woman have expected?

I lived there with Doug and the children only for a couple of months. It was far from a long time but even so I have to shake my head at how I just didn't see it. Yet again — as with Frank and then with my brother — I accepted the fact that I would do all the life-care of a household and even feel proud that I had the energy and the love for it. Again I had a situation that felt like a family: a man, a woman, children — six children this time. That it was in my own old home, however different the furnishings — and the bedrooms were much the same — gave it almost an inevitability.

It was probably also inevitable that I ended up in Doug's bed. A man and a woman in a house with children, a configuration marriage-like, almost, and this time the man was not my brother. Perhaps it was more my doing than his, the start of that? I can't remember. I've lost the moment it began, and whether by repressing or ordinary forgetting I can't say. I'm sure he never was in love with me. Those intense gazes of his that had so struck me when I first met him turned out to be simply a quite unconscious trick of his eyes. His daughter has the same way of gazing at me even today, and while she and I do love each other, it's not a sign of that; it's just an inherited trait.

Whether I loved him I can't say. I don't think I could have when we never had intimate conversations at any point, even though our "affair" lasted for months after I left the household, almost for a whole year. There was not enough there to constitute love. I wasn't even the only woman in the picture. There was Peggy, from even before I knew about the state of the Jones marriage. Peggy visited sometimes for a few days at a time during the following year, when Doug was still coming to me. I'd know when I didn't hear from him that she was there or about to come. Later I gathered from gossip that this had long been a pattern with him: at least hand-holding, and maybe more, with someone else. Another element in Betty's final turning to her beautiful young boy.

My brother was incredulous that I was attracted to Doug and all these years later he still is. To him and to our friend Clem, Doug was not the kind of man worthy of the sexual attention of a woman like me. He was the opposite of the athletic, obviously handsome Campus King men they both were — that was not a term they used themselves but one I teased them with as they had so many girlfriends — and certainly he was the antithesis of Frank who was so very masculine in his darkness and strength. But I found him beautiful, in his slim tall-ness, his tanned skin (he was almost always indoors yet he was tanned, in my memory anyway) and especially in his face. Those intensely gazing eyes, the fine bone structure, the serious set of his mouth: that face made a claim on me. There seemed to be a thrilling promise in it. My undoing has always been intensity in a man.

Such a degree of intensity usually turns out to have its roots in something other than love, some kink of personality. It could have its roots in sex but not necessarily love and I wanted love as well. I wanted both, to my ultimate chagrin.

Doug also had the air of a wounded creature, a further draw. I soon got the point that he was troubled by more than the recent weird year he had lived through. Had I but realized it, his essential unhappiness went beyond anything I could ever provide some sort of caring-poultice for. His family history had been fraught from the very beginning.

His mother came that summer for a visit so brief I barely remember her all these decades later. She left a steel-grey impression, but if that was her dress, her hair or just her aura, or all of those things, I can't now say. She was beautiful, I do remember thinking that, but she also had a cold and forbidding quality. She had experi-enced tragedy: an alcoholic, weak and useless husband; one son dead as a little boy, drowned; another son murdered recently, indeed the very winter that had just passed. He had been shot by his male lover and buried in a shallow grave in the lover's basement. The walls of the lover's house were full of bullets from previous gunplay — so was it really murder or an accident? I never heard the conclusion, if there was one. Doug had had to identify his body in Montreal. He showed me a poem he wrote about it. I don't know if the poem was ever published but I remember an image from it: a drawer in a morgue is pulled open by the attendant, there is a rush of freezing air, mist in the warmer room. Through it, the brother's face is waxy white. And dead. Doubtless I am creating my own image of it now, not having seen that poem since 1964.

No wonder that their mother, with that grief still a living thing, when visiting briefly her one remaining son, emanated a steely chill. But I gathered warmth had never been a quality of hers. Her grief must have been complicated as well, in that intolerant time. How would she have felt about that son being gay, being shot by his gay lover?

The shooting of the brother made all the odder the quantity of guns I found under the stairs. In the cupboard where, in our day, out-of-season tennis rackets and such things had been stored, I discovered a toppling stack of guns. The next-door neighbour Ron Sutherland, who became my friend that summer along with his wife, Jean, told me how he'd been woken one morning by his daughter Janet, age four, waveringly pointing a rifle at him. It was so heavy for her she could barely hold it. He leapt out of bed and to his horror discovered it was loaded. Small Janet had not intended a tiny-tot patricide but there could have been a shattering outcome if she had managed to pull the trigger. I could not have the guns in the house where I was caring for a herd of small children and I took them up to my parents' house and put them in Chuck's cupboard. Doug was perplexed by my concern but didn't object to their temporary new location.

I was very severe, very unbending in my judgment of Betty for leaving. A mother who left small children "to find herself as an artist" and to join a much younger "beautiful lover" was incomprehensible to me. Her children's unhappiness wrenched my heart. Her flight was against nature. Terrible. She had to be a bad woman. The guns in the house added an extra helping of blame on my part. She had to have known about them.

I have long realized that it is impossible for an outsider to understand another marriage, especially a young inexperienced outsider arriving late in a tangled drama. I had no right to make a judgment. But of course I did. Yet I never had had the chance to know Betty really. I had observed only her surface and at a time in her life when she was deliberately engaged in a charade. We never had an extended conversation, the longest being when she announced her departure.

Betty was born a generation, perhaps two, too early. She must have seen no way out except the drastic one she took. It was all or nothing in those days. The house itself, the state of it, was symbolic: when she moved into it, which was only a year or so before I first visited them, she had made an effort. The white rugs, the modern curtains, even the arrangements of dried grasses, other details I now forget — was she giving her marriage one more attempt, a fresh start in a new place? Or, on the other hand, was she doing her best to make the house nice for them before she fled? But the place and the people within were in disarray by the time I saw it in early spring.

Betty had artistic ambitions as a girl and got a BFA degree, as my sister Ruth did. Betty thus had the same art professor as Ruth and I did at McGill, Mr. Lyman, who liked to state that the value of a woman being educated in art was so she could pass on an appreciation of it to her children. I did not find him at all inspiring and had him only in my first year but both Ruth and Betty persevered in his classes for the whole four years. Mr. Lyman didn't allow that a woman might become an actual artist herself; by allowing them in his classes he was providing a sort of social service: families would benefit, culturally. I think again of that lovely and miserable woman in the Valium advertisement, with her supposedly useless MFA.

Women with strong maternal instincts, and who found children's development, including their conversation, fascinating rather than boring, were far luckier. I actually was that sort of woman. Had Frank's behaviour not become so extreme I would not have left as I did. I would not so soon have gone back to university, and then to work, not while Paul and Jane were so small. Once the children were in full day school I might well have been drawn to the classroom again. But back then, if a woman was not satisfied with full-time domesticity, and finally could take it no longer and fled what had become for her a trap, her children really suffered. Of the families I knew well, where the mother escaped in that manner, the children never wholly recovered. The fathers then, having had no role at all in child-care, were at a loss how to fill the void the escaping mother had left. And they had to go to work. I believe Doug, for example, loved his children but what was he to do, how was he to discover how to double-parent, without any skills for the greater part of the job? After my time with the family I know he did the one thing he knew to do: he read to them every night.

It is very different for my granddaughters today. The elder, Sarah, the one most like me (as I've earlier mentioned), has a degree in English but shares with her mother, my daughter-in-law, the ownership and operation of an exceedingly successful bakery café. Sarah and her husband, Greg, share the care of their three little boys, Henry, seven, Daniel, six, and Rufus, two. Her younger sister Rebeccah is a practicing veterinarian, mother of Annabelle, age two, and with another baby due in September. She and her husband Chad share the care of Annabelle. The fairness of such arrangements would have astonished me long ago. The husbands, Greg and Chad, would have been the stuff of impossible daydreams.

Smoke! I am at the end of my Jones-connected history and the oddest thing occurs to me: I have neglected to mention something that pervaded everything in life at that time — smoke. It was entirely taken for granted by everyone then, and for a long while afterward too, at least for ten more years, that in vast majority of houses, including in the bedrooms, kitchens and dining rooms, plus in cars, planes, trains and buses, restaurants and college and university classrooms — everywhere one can think of — there was a thick grey haze of smoke. I never smoked a single cigarette myself, but my hair, my clothes, every breath I took in an indoor environment has to have been saturated with smoke.

We simply didn't notice because it was everywhere, a fact of life. It was actually akin to the sexism of the time. With its presence assumed to be normal, no one noticed it. Doug chain-smoked so that house must have been thick with it, and the house of my marriage must have been, as well. Frank smoked. The haze would have been less in my own old family home as my father smoked far less, though when he did, it was a pungent pipe or cigar. At least he only did it downstairs, and mostly in the dining room on occasions when he and visiting Uncle Bunny would talk for hours, moving from the table to sit in front of the fireplace. This all came to my mind as I thought of those evenings of Doug talking — I was the audience — until a very late hour in a room that must have been chokingly polluted, a fact ignored by both of us. But I can see him, in my mind, lighting one cigarette after another, drinking one beer after another, always from the bottle, and holding forth endlessly. Smoke and sexism — only Doug talked — funny how they went together.

I have always been an early-to-bed person but I couldn't bear to leave him even though I had to be up and feeding breakfast to the group. I felt it was worth it then and I still think it was. He taught me how to look at literature, how to think about it and how to teach it. I asked questions from time to time but I'm pretty sure I didn't say much else. I was very busy listening. I wanted to remember what he said.

When I sift through the memories of that time and try to weigh my gains and losses, I have to come down on the side of gains.

I learned a great deal, literarily, as I've described, but as well it was more emotionally rewarding than it was painful. Especially I had come to love those Jones children. For several years, until I moved out West, whenever I was at my parents' house visiting, somehow Tory and Sky would sense my proximity and appear, Tory to sit on my lap, Sky to be near me and play with Paul.

I have a vivid image — it feels like a poem — towards the end of my relationship with Doug. It is a morning in the spring of 1965, almost a whole year since I began my involvement with that family. Doug has climbed the hillside to me the night before, up to where I am spending the weekend at my parents' house. (They are away.) There had been a light fall of snow in the early evening as he walked up, and I am watching as the warm spring sun lifts his tell-tale foot-prints from the grass. Soon they will be quite gone.

There may not have been love between us but there was a caring. We were both hurt and needed comfort, and we found a simple, human-animal comfort with each other for a while.

22

THE point of my getting a master's degree in English was to prepare me to teach. It had been my father's decision for me, in those shocked first days after my runaway when I could barely open my eyes to look about me let alone decide anything crucial but very soon it made sense to me too.

All the same as the goal came closer I couldn't envisage the transition in specifics. I had been a mother and wife for six years. That chapter over, I'd reverted to being a student again for two years, experiencing a kind of second adolescence, even though I was a mother as well. My brother and my new friends were all several years younger than I and somehow I had slipped backwards and joined them. But now I would be a breadwinner and one with more responsibility than they had, these twenty-one-year-olds who were considering graduate school or travel or all sorts of things out of the question for me. I had to buckle down to life in earnest.

For some months the lawyer my father found for me had had a portion of Frank's salary garnisheed (a new word for me) but that arrangement would end as soon as Frank left Canada, which he did, returning to Yugoslavia in 1965.

I knew from that point, in practical and financial terms, I must fill a role my upbringing had never hinted would be mine. I didn't know another single mother, not a one. Within a few years more of us would be about, including my close friends Cynthia and Sonya, but when I did my flight in 1963 nary a model was in sight. I would be stepping on untrodden ground.

At least I would be the one in charge of everything, not Frank, who had unraveled so drastically. That was a plus. As well, and this I couldn't know the value of until much later, there was another positive side to my having to create the role. The terms "single mother" and "broken family" weren't yet in common usage. I didn't have a label and I didn't see myself as a victim. There were no advisors of any sort, no daycare arrangements. I had to do this on my own. Given my personality, this was, oddly enough, good. I had a challenge to rise to. My great good fortune was that I had the brains, health and inner wherewithal to rise to it. I suppose there has to have been some slightly modernized version of the old workhouse but I knew nothing of it and no one mentioned it. I just had myself, myself who now had to get down to work. Of course I strongly suspect now that my family would not have let the three of us sink beneath the waves, but then I didn't consider that. My father had made it clear I had much to do to redeem myself. There would be no handouts.

So — teaching!

Nothing in my courses related to how to teach, apart from the examples the professors provided: they stood or sat, and spoke, reading from notes. This was taken for granted as the way it was done. Few of them had much engagement with individual students or any interest in our reactions to them or their ideas. I now found myself wondering how they, long ago (they were mostly quite old), had summoned the nerve to take on the role of deliverer of wisdom. I suspected that Professor Gray, for example, who seemed a very shy man, may well have started out nervously, but when I had him as a professor he'd been teaching for over twenty years. I'm guessing (now when I've had my own thirty-five years of teaching and have known many Professor Grays) that he early on figured out an unvarying routine as a way of coping. Having such a routine is a bit like wearing a uniform. It can make a person feel almost anonymous and thus protected from the reality of other humans' responses. Professor Gray read from yellowed notes, he never left his chair to move about the room and he didn't even look around at us much even though we were close to him, sitting around a conference table. I liked this professor. He was a kind and nice man but he was an example I hoped not to follow.

Some professors read dynamically and one or two even strode about the room and made eye contact. These few appeared infectiously engaged by their material and eager for us to understand it. Professor Motyer at Bishop's was like that, as were, earlier, wonderful Madame Kushner, Professor Mladenovič, and to some extent Mr. MacLennan at McGill. Actually Mladenovič never strode about: he was too plump and old, plus had to be close to his ashtray, but he could be exciting while sitting. Before McGill I had had a number of excellent teachers at Havergal, but that was high school. I was thinking of teaching at a college or university; the models of Miss Muckle or Miss Bevan presumably would not serve.

Very soon now the power in a classroom would be mine. I would step forward several paces; I would turn 180 degrees and face my erstwhile peers. I would open my mouth and speak wisely, impose authority. I wanted to see eyes spark. I wanted to be a Motyer or Mladenovič, or best of all, a Madame Kushner.

What magic would descend to make this possible?

Some crossings of life-thresholds are a birthing of a new self.

Having written that, I think of my actual childbirths and the confusing moment of stasis that happened each time, just before my body entered the next and final stage of labour. It was the moment, especially the first time, when I came closest to fear. Then, after a pause that went on almost too long, came the pushing impulse. I became nothing but my body, engaging in all-consuming convulsive action, until Paul, small and squirming, his face squashed and red, was in the world. In a blink I was reinvented as Mother. But that long pause as one awaits translation into a new creature is, while it lasts,

INLAND NAVIGATION BY THE STARS 141

like a single note of music sustained and sustained, or like a holding of the breath almost beyond the point of bearing.

Other rebirthings of mine were trickier, fear-clouded. Particularly the unease I'd felt all through the summer of 1957 leading up to my late-August wedding. I was not able to picture a future self. I have described earlier my disturbing images, one of falling off a cliff, one so high that as I fell I could see no bottom, another of being pulled behind a curtain into darkness. It would be too late to undo my own fatal impulse that had brought me to the brink.

There was not much of an echo of that anteroom here. Teaching did not bring dreams of death or eclipse — I knew classrooms too well for that — but even so my future was teasingly difficult to envisage. Would it work, my slipping into new "teacher shoes," then stepping in them to the front of the room? The images that haunted me before my marriage were of self-diminishment, a kind of near-death ahead. (Though, an aside here: I can't let those many times revisited memories pass unchecked. I don't know for sure that I took those dark suspicions entirely seriously. Surely I knew even then my tendency to self-dramatize. I doubt that deep down I feared for my identity's survival, but I sensed there would be a serious testing of it.)

In any case passing beyond this new threshold would be a test of an opposite sort. Becoming a teacher would not be a loss of identity and power but an increase of both. Student Anne, until now safely in her desk among her peers and exemplary in her role, would metamorphose into a new person, Mrs. Molnar, Teacher. A miracle would have to happen on the spot.

I thought of further models to reject: I remembered the hopelessness of certain graduate students who had taught first-year sections at McGill that I'd had the bad luck to be assigned to. There was a young man who taught first-year math — supposedly. In fact he stood facing the blackboard, chalking swiftly and indecipherably on it, muttering to, even chuckling with, two or three boys who had already done trigonometry and who huddled at the board with him.

Their heads were close together; no one else heard a word. Also at McGill there had been a young woman graduate student in English who attempted to hold seminars so we would have a chance to discuss what we heard in Professor Duthie's mass (but wonderful) English lectures. She was possibly shy and had no idea how to lead a discussion. Very soon I didn't even bother to go.

It would be easy to do better than those pathetic souls.

I thought of the model Doug gave me. When I was with him, much of the time he treated me as if I was his student. Preparing myself, I relived those evenings.

He talks and talks. I am curled up on the couch, listening to him. I watch his face, his intense blue gaze which is mostly not directed at me but at the fire he has made or at the smoke from his cigarette which spirals up clouding my view of his face. He smokes one cigarette after another. He takes sips of beer from a bottle which otherwise dangles dangerously as he holds it loosely by its top between two fingers. I think he may drop it but he doesn't. He pauses for thought and frowns. I am fascinated by the look of him and by his voice which makes everything he says intense, almost as if he is revealing a secret. When he reads a poem, especially when it is one of his own, the words carry a heavier weight of meaning than they could in any other voice. Sometimes he gives a barking laugh, usually not of humour, more of mockery, and as often at one of his own just-voiced thoughts than at anyone else's he may have been quoting.

At first I am flattered by these apparent lectures he gives me every evening. After a while I am pretty sure he is not thinking of me at all, or not as a specific person. I am simply a pair of ears. I am not expected to comment. Maybe I don't matter any more than his old springer spaniel who is also with us and is sleeping through the flow of his master's voice. Even if that is so, I listen keenly.

What he is holding forth on is how patterns of ideas, of literary themes, of symbols, and of moods, arise from national and regional preoccupations. He tells me that writers write out of a need to discover who they are within a specific landscape, mental and physical, and to discover also the voice in which they can best do so. He gives examples from England's literary history, century after century. Writers have a role beyond that too. As individuals embedded within a particular people's history and spiritual journey, they are the interpreters, perhaps almost Shelley's "unacknowledged legislators." He sees a weakening of the human sense of power, with the dawn of the modern age, especially our own contemporary age. He compares Robinson Crusoe's self-confident survival on his desert island with the complete mental deterioration of William Golding's Pincher Martin on his.

He often speaks of Canadian literature, working it into his thesis. He sees a dominating fear in how Canadian writers develop their characters, how they occupy our landscape, a fear that arises in them out of their lostness within a vast and dangerous nature, a fear arising also out of a dual inheritance of Scotch Calvinism and Roman Catholicism, religions based on guilt. He cites my old friend, Mr. MacLennan, whose characters exemplify this, fearful of allowing themselves to experience joy.

I listen and I plan to remember as much as I can of this. When the time comes I will use these ideas, make them my own and build on them.

I finally get sleepy on these evenings though. As I get into my nightdress and settle into my bed I think of Mr. MacLennan. Doug rather dismisses him, yet I learned many of the same or at least related things from him as well. Both men look at evolving patterns moving beneath the surface as human social consciousness evolves. Both men see the writer as expressing what is emerging out of a history and a place, and naming these things. They both also see a day when Canadian writing will be worthy of consideration as literature, a day they personally are ensuring will come.

If Doug, now dead, had read what I am saying here, he might well have disagreed with how I have summed up and inevitably simplified what he said all those years ago. What I can say truly is that he was an influence. He set my mind stirring in new directions. Over my life of reading, listening and teaching I honour first my own initial reactions to a text. Then I reread, consult other wiser people's opinions, accept some of them, or don't, and come to more considered ponderings. It is a process that never stops even now when I am no longer a teacher. I am always evaluating and testing new writing I encounter against what I think I know, and I'm sure I caught from Doug a way of looking for evolving patterns, for ideas moving beneath the obvious, perhaps only barely emerging into the intellectual air. I also certainly got from him an idea quite new to me: taking seriously the writers of our own country. Canadian writers had never been considered worthy of attention in the schools or universities I'd attended. Doug was convinced they were worth looking at, that Canadian writers were contributing to "Literature."

I was so lucky in my timing! Both these men's approaches were the opposite of what emerged a couple of decades later and seemingly overnight: Literary Theory. It swept academia. My personal luck was that the new jargon-wracked (and pleasure-wrecking) language of structuralism and deconstruction and all the other newly invented "isms" surged in an engulfing wave over the universities very near the end of my teaching career.

23

BUT teaching itself had been waiting in the wings for me for some time, hovering offstage yet unconsciously sensed.

On a day in early fall during my early life as a wife the children and I are going for one of our daily walks. Jane is sitting up alertly in the old English pram our neighbour across the road, Audrey, gave us. Audrey's children are in high school, travelling into the city every day to go to private schools. Her house is behind a high and thick lilac hedge, as is our house, but hers is a much larger property. They even have a swimming pool, which she invited us many summer afternoons to use. Jane's round dark eyes are keenly taking in every detail of every hedge, tree or passing person. Paul is running alongside or nipping ahead and then waiting for us before the next cross street.

We are just coming up to the elementary school. It is a couple of long blocks down our street towards Lake Saint-Louis. The day is one of those lovely early September ones, the sky brilliantly blue and the huge old trees that arch over our heads making the street a tunnel are just starting to turn. Here and there among the green mass is a single branch of red or yellow leaves. Paul picks up a perfect yellow maple leaf from the sidewalk and runs back with it and gives it to Jane. She holds it by its stem and twirls it.

The school is set on a sort of island, the road diverging on each side, and as we circle around to the right of the playground I look over at the building and think of what is happening inside. It is about two-thirty and I have a sudden vision of how exciting it is, the start of a new school year. For me it always was the real New Year, much more than January 1st could ever be. As I walk more slowly I can almost touch, in my imagination, a smooth, cool, light green notebook. I can see it centred on a desk in front of me, a desk of some pale wood, with an inset inkwell. The notebook is just waiting to be opened but is still pristine, its pages nicely tight together, not sprung a little as they will soon be. I had loved that anticipatory moment, and I had loved the active moments that would follow.

I stop pushing the pram and just stand there. I yearn suddenly to be able to sniff the smell of a clean, pink eraser and the wood of a just-sharpened orange pencil. I wish for a powerful second or two that I am not outside but inside, sitting at a desk.

Later that winter I am perched on a stool in my friend Shirley's kitchen. She lives a block below us and has an older English husband and two small children, Tony and Cindy. All four children are playing in the living room, Cindy, a year older than Paul, is showing Jane how to dress the dolls, and Paul is being bossy with Tony who is only three. I am listening to be sure things remain happy in there.

Shirley and I often meet up as we are both readers and we enjoy discussing books. We talk of other matters too, our children, our families, her brother-in-law who was a Spitfire pilot in the war and has just been visiting (and whom I think she may have a crush on) her husband. Today, because of a book Shirley has been reading, we have been discussing religion and speculating about its existence behind the Iron Curtain now. Suddenly, forgetting the listening I should be doing for Paul in the next room, I am telling her of my speculation that it is still a powerful thing in Yugoslavia, perhaps even more so for being forced underground. I am explaining to her the complexity of the country, with its three religions, historically. I am telling her why the population of the whole of Yugoslavia is only 9% Muslim, but of Bosnia-Herzogovina 33% Muslim, and what the significance of this fact might be, both now and in the future. The topic fascinates me and I go on and on.

Poor Shirley! I suddenly see myself: I am holding forth; I am lecturing as if I were addressing not one woman but a whole roomful of people. She is standing at her sink filling her kettle — we are going to have a cup of tea — and looking over her shoulder at me with some amusement. I have to stop and laugh.

But afterwards, walking home up the snowy street, both children tumbling in and out of the snow banks, the sky a very dark grey-blue behind black bare tree branches as the daylight goes, I feel an odd sense of dislocation, as if another self took over for a little while back at Shirley's. What could it possibly mean, that feeling that had come over me, that sudden powerful need for a lecture hall! It was just silliness, I tell myself, and rather embarrassing. Who do I think I am?

24

IN my teaching career I had only two jobs. For both of them, my most effective reference letter was from Mr. MacLennan, who had never seen me teach but knew me very well and presumably trusted me to pull it off. My first job lasted five years, my second, thirty, ending only when I was ready to retire. Thus I had thirty-five years of teaching, winging it all the way and loving it so much that I feel to this day that I may have, perhaps just before I die, some sort of comeuppance. Some boss-figure (God?) could come forward and demand back thirty-five years' worth of my pay. "You never actually worked. You just were enjoying yourself." It would be true.

I am in Montreal for an interview with the headmistress of Miss Edgar's and Miss Cramp's School, a school for girls. I walk up, and up, as the school is much farther up the hill than I'd realized and I get hot in my suit. At the top of Wood Avenue is a steep flight of stairs that take me to the next level of Westmount and to the street I've been looking for, Mount Pleasant Avenue. I worry about arriving in a lather from hurrying up those stairs and try not to walk so fast but don't want to be late. To arrive both sweaty and late would not be good.

My suit is my best outfit and I've read that suits are appropriate for an interview, actually essential. It was tailored for me a couple of years earlier by a European dressmaker as a gift from Frank in one of his happier phases. That was another life and I was a different person then, a girl who could not have imagined this day. I recall standing in my slip in that dressmaker's little stuffy room. I think she may have been German; her English was very poor — she can't have been in Canada long. There was a whole sad story there, no doubt. She was tiny and stooped and I towered over her, feeling huge, as she held her tape measure against bits of me, and turned and wrote the numbers down. The suit is made of pure wool cloth in shades of pale green and grey-blue. I dare hope that I look my best. It is important that the headmistress, Mrs. Graham, approve of my appearance. I must seem ladylike and a fitting role model for the girls.

I finally arrive and stand for a moment taking some deep breaths. I am quite nervous now that the interview is upon me. This main part of the building is only a year old, as the school has made a move from downtown to Westmount. Beside it is a big old mansion to which it is attached by what must be a long corridor. I go up the steps, in the front door and into a wide and sunny entrance hallway. It is appealing and I think maybe this will become a completely familiar place to me, but I don't want to count my chickens so I quickly dismiss the idea. I take a few steps and see, to my right, an office.

The school is very quiet as it is the Easter holidays and the girls are all at home. In one way I wish they were here so I could get a sense of the school as a living place; in another way I am glad they are not here. The sight of a crowd of real-life girls I might be having to impress and take charge of would be scary. I am scared enough at this moment. I don't want too much reality.

There is the sound of a typewriter in the office and I walk towards it and see a middle-aged woman working there. She is thin and has a chin that recedes into her neck.

Within a minute or two she ushers me into the inner office and there is Mrs. Graham, the woman I have come to meet who will decide my future. She comes forward from around her desk and smiles at me and shakes my hand. After all my fears of being intimidated I find her friendly and not at all alarming, a pretty and slender woman with short grey hair, somewhat older than my mother but not old, and not a bit like an academic, more someone I might meet at tea party of my mother's friends.

Our conversation doesn't touch on literature. She doesn't quiz me on my knowledge of Milton or Shakespeare; she asks about my own schooling — which she must already know from the curriculum vitae I sent her. She is obviously pleased I went to Havergal and she tells me that Miss Edgar and Miss Cramp had both originally taught there before coming to Montreal and starting their own school. We talk of this and that: I guess she is trying to get a sense of me. I like the sense I get of her, that she is gentle, that she has a sense of humour.

She takes me out into the hall again and shows me the portraits of the Founders, oil paintings, gold-framed and hanging on the wall in places of honour.

"The Board of Governors are meeting today," she says. "I'd like you to come and meet them."

To my slight surprise I already know two members. It's just the kind of organization they would be members of but I'd not been aware of the fact. They are Mrs. Mary Webster and Mrs. Barbara MacTaggart, whom I'd known from the North Hatley Club since I was a little girl. I'd sometimes sailed with Mrs. MacTaggart's son Donald when we were younger, and I'd also sometimes crewed for her in the races and liked her. Mrs. Webster is a very nice woman too but she had got my back up just before I married Frank. It was reported to me that she'd said to someone my relationship with him was sure to have been "just a summer romance," and she was apparently sorry it had turned out rather differently and we were actually to marry. Of course she was right in her misgiving but I still feel slightly hostile towards her for knowing best. However, she smiles at me very pleasantly and I can't help responding in kind.

I leave the school to walk down the hill again feeling I had presented myself well and had been liked but chagrined that Mrs.

Graham left things up in the air. I'm not good at living in suspense and I had hoped she might tell me the verdict right away, even though my father has told me that normally a person waits for a letter of acceptance — or rejection. But a letter comes within the week: they want me and I am to start in September. I must arrange a day to return to the school in the summer to collect the curricula and books that I shall need to prepare for my classes. Further, the letter says that Jane will be able to attend the school and enter Primary, their name for grade one. I will pay no fees for her but will pay for her lunches. A hot lunch is served to girls and staff every day.

That Jane can attend, and free, is a major bonus and I picture her wearing a tiny version of the school uniform, which is almost exactly the same as my uniform at Havergal, a dark green tunic, green bloomers, green knee socks. The only differences are the shirt colours — pale beige at Havergal, white at miss Edgar's — and of course the school ties.

I didn't realize for years that both pull and snobbery very likely played their roles in my getting that position. Even Jane's free attendance was probably down to both things: another new teacher that year had a daughter entering grade one and there was no offer of a free place for that child. The mother hadn't gone to Havergal or a school like it, nor did she belong to the North Hatley Club. It was unfair but it was the way things worked then, and so smoothly and naturally that I didn't even notice.

Within a very few days of teaching I love working at Miss Edgar's. I am clear in my mind that teaching is the right career for me despite its having more or less been thrust upon me by chance and circumstance. I really like the school. It doesn't have the castle-like grandeur of Havergal and the grounds are not nearly as large but I like its modern simplicity of style, its brightness. The senior classrooms are sunny and cheerful with large windows. The Junior School has a different but also pleasant atmosphere as it is in the old Westmount mansion I'd noticed at my interview.

Both sections, Senior and Junior, still add up to a small school with only one section of each grade, and about twenty girls as the largest number in a class. In Jane's class there are only nine little girls with an extremely pretty young teacher — Miss Partridge, I am first told, but then she turns out to be Mrs. Archibald, having married during the summer. She has smooth, thick blond hair curving under in a pageboy style and her class at once loves her. Their classroom is in what must have been a sitting room or library of the old mansion. It is very cosy, with curtains and cushioned window seats. I can't imagine a more pleasant classroom for Jane.

The school has thought of everything: there is even a comfortably plump and white-haired grandmother-person, Mrs. Rennie, who has a small room with a cot where a girl feeling unwell or just missing her mother can go for a small lie down or cuddle. Jane is the youngest and the smallest person in the school but I've been told that others in her class are also only five, even though with birthdays very soon, and she should fit in.

Jane and I walk to school on the important first morning for both of us. I am wearing a bright green skirt and matching sweater and have tied my hair back with a green and white silk scarf. I had thought long and hard about what to wear on this first time of meeting my classes and decided my suit would not do. It was too hot for a September day, so I decided on my next nicest outfit. I didn't consciously plan to wear the school colours and I just realize I have done so as we walk up the hill, both of us in green, and I hope it doesn't strike my students that I am trying hard to be one of them. Oh dear!

Paul will walk with his cousin Eric to start at Westmount Park School. I wish I could have gone with him for his first day too. That Paul can't set off with us every morning gives me a bad pang. He doesn't have to leave the apartment until twenty minutes or so after we do, so he will phone his Uncle Chuck and talk to him. And I

INLAND NAVIGATION BY THE STARS 153

wish so much my sister Ruth had been willing to give him lunch. I had thought she might, as she will be making lunch for her own boys every day, but she refused. I'm not sure if her husband, Michael, was at the bottom of it or if it was her own decision. I suspect it was both really and I am not entirely surprised as it fits with the earlier business about my piano. She also refused to have Jane for afternoons. Jane needs a place to be every day from after lunch until I get home at four, as Primary lasts only for the morning. Our parents think Ruth could help with this but needless to say given the other lesser things she has refused, she won't. Luckily, as it has turned out, my close friend Judy will do this instead. She simply took it for granted as if she were the sister rather than my real one. Judy, like Cynthia in Lennoxville, is a true, deep friend. And the janitor's wife in our apartment building will give Paul lunch every day. She doesn't speak any English and I know if he could have lunch with his cousins it would feel friendlier for him.

I hate it that Paul is the one to suffer most for our changed circumstance.

My parents are quite fed up with Ruth about this but she won't relent. She came over to my apartment in Lower Westmount the day after Dad and Chuck had moved me in. I was in the tiny kitchen ironing the long green curtains I'd made for the living room. She was quite pink in the face and defensive and didn't stay long. The point of the visit was to tell me not to expect that we'd be invited over to their house for Sunday dinners or anything of that sort. Michael didn't want to have to see me, given that I'd not taken his advice that I must return to Frank. He judged me an immoral woman who had left her husband, never mind the circumstances. I already knew by then about her refusal to help with Jane's afternoons and Paul's lunches, so it wasn't a total surprise, but it still stung. I simply can't imagine being so cold to a sister, and as for being unkind to her children — well, I've put it out of my mind as best I can. I have Judy and will soon have other friends. And Chuck will always talk to Paul on the phone to help ease lonely moments. But he lives all the way downtown and Ruth lives only two blocks away.

✦

Some things in families, my family definitely, can never be discussed openly. I came to recognize — though not at once — how Ruth was herself caught. I forgave her long ago, though we never brought it into the open. Yes, she went along with her husband in banishing me from family gatherings at their house, and she refused to help with Jane or give Paul his lunch, but when I properly awoke to feminism I gained a better understanding of women in her position. In 1965 I was too hurt and surprised and at a practical loss as to what I would do. But Ruth had her own frustrations, as I explained earlier.

I have a memory of her reading Simone de Beauvoir at the time when I was a new mother of one and she already a mother of two. De Beauvoir's negativity upset me and I wanted no part of her disgust with the female body, as I interpreted her feelings for it. My body had made my baby. My mother-tiger love for and protectiveness of Paul were stronger forces than any I'd known before. And my baby had more than doubled my vulnerability: he too was at the mercy of Frank's instability and more important than myself. But *The Second Sex* made sense to Ruth. At the same time she would have felt powerless to do anything with the emotions the book awakened. She had a husband who loved her dearly — and who was totally Victorian in his views about women. She had never had the urge for independence I'd had since childhood and I'm sure could never have imagined supporting herself. It would not have seemed in the realm of the possible.

Being lumbered with yet another little boy needing his lunch was a last straw, especially when her younger sister was stepping out into the world.

25

I am form mistress of the Upper Eleven, the highest grade in the school. I enter my classroom and the girls all stop talking at once and stare at me. I stare back and try to smile in a natural way but my nervousness makes my lips stick to my teeth. The girls look worryingly sophisticated, despite the green tunics, green knee socks and white blouses and that they can wear no makeup. Butterflies flutter in a crowd in my stomach. Is this going to work?

"Good morning, everybody," I say. "I am your new form mistress and my name is Mrs. Molnar." I turn and write my name on the blackboard so they'll see how it is spelled and I have a flash of my first day at Havergal and Miss Muckle doing this very thing and announcing that "Muckle" was a Scottish name. The memory gives me courage and I say, "Molnar is a Hungarian name, and was my husband's." I pause and then add, "But I am no longer married." I know right away I shouldn't have said that. It will give them fuel for conjecture and gossip. But then I recognize that if they don't know my story's outline already, they soon will. So many North Hatley summer people live in Westmount. I will have no secrets here.

The girls are instantly friendly and also seem respectful. They smile back at me and I suspect they are probably pleased to have a young woman as their form mistress. I saw a couple of old-style ogres in the staffroom: they could have landed one of them I suppose. I read the list of their names aloud, looking about to see each girl as she raises her hand. I want to get everyone straight right away and it will be easy as it is such a small group. Then we all file out and walk along the hall to prayers, which are held every morning in the gym, one of my prefects tells me. This is totally familiar as we always did the same at Havergal.

The teaching day is beyond bewildering. And endless. I meet one group of girls after another. I walk up and down the halls, up and down the stairs, moving from classroom to classroom, each time facing a new group of girls. How can I interpret the ways they stare at me? Are those stares admiring or does that girl there, the one with the tiny smile, know me for someone who has no business pretending she is a teacher? And how about that girl with that grave expression, is she about to frown? Is she anticipating being bored by me? What about the raised brows exchanged between those two? Are they mocking or intrigued? By four o'clock I am exhausted. I wonder if every day will be like this, require this enormous energy. I must keep all these girls engaged and learning, and well behaved, and above all, liking me. And I must do so every day. I must do it tomorrow.

I teach all the Senior School English classes, which are broken into three subjects, literature, composition and grammar. The English curriculum was laid down years before by a very ambitious woman. Mrs. Graham probably told me who but I forget and in case she did I don't want to ask again right away. The idea is that the girls study the great English works in chronological order, starting with Beowulf and working up through the centuries, ending with the Victorians. It seems to me to be a good idea in theory, and fits with my own view of including the historical, but I think that surely some texts must be awfully challenging for the younger girls. I know from the curricula I was given back in the summer that form four (grade eight in a public school) has to read Beowulf, in translation of course. I think we can probably have fun with the monster Grendel and his even more monstrous mother. But that class also has to read Spenser's *The Faery Queen*, which I had to read at Bishop's and both disliked and found hard going. At least I love and understand Bacon's *Essays* myself, which will help considerably when we come to them, but his language isn't easy.

I know what I want to do as a teacher, if I can. I want to inspire in the girls a love of reading even more than I care about meeting the academic goal of introducing them to the Great Works. But I'm hoping to achieve both. I want the girls to discover that those old texts are not dead words on a page but are living things, human things. They can reach us across the centuries if we know how to listen to the voices speaking within them.

I discover when I study the timetable that I am teaching Elocution once a week to form five. There is no specific curriculum for the course. I imagine that at some earlier stage in the school's history the purpose of the class was to foster lady-like speaking voices in the girls, perhaps even English accents. Miss Gillard, the headmistress at King's Hall, fruitlessly attempted to impose English voices on the girls when I myself was in grade eight. After prayers in the gym on Saturday mornings she would walk up and down the rows as the whole school chanted, "I hawd to lawf to see the cawf walk down the pawth a mile and a hawf." Our ridiculous "English" accents lasted only until we left the gym. There is no way I'll be following in Miss Gillard's footsteps but there is no guideline as to what precisely I am to do.

I murmur a question to another teacher at our morning tea break on the second day, "What exactly is Elocution supposed to be?" She raises her brows and replies, "I think you can make it whatever you want it to be. Reading aloud with expression? Memorizing poems and speaking them? What else can it be?" We both laugh at the vagueness. I decide that under my regime we will read plays and poetry aloud and it will be a chance for me to introduce more modern works, or at least as modern as Shaw and maybe Barrie. Ibsen may be too advanced for that grade. We shall see.

As time passes, in my real Literature classes as well I gradually slip in a few more contemporary things. I discover that the younger girls love me to read aloud. On Friday afternoons when they have worked

158 ANNE COLEMAN

hard all week I read chapters from Llewellyn's *How Green Was My Valley* and Rumer Godden's *The River*. The girls' eyes are both intent and dreamy as they watch me, or gaze at the trees outside our window, and listen.

26

THE rather amazing thing about Miss Edgar's was the freedom I was allowed. I was expected to cover certain works, and I did so, but how I did so, and whether we studied only those works or moved into other more modern realms — well, no one ever asked. And the girls responded. The composition and grammar classes I enjoyed as well. I'd always loved writing myself and I valued precision in language. Many of the girls did too. I had learned how to write essays with Miss Muckle at Havergal and how to organize academic writing with Professor Mladenovič at McGill. I taught the girls simply what I knew, and many of them were very bright girls. We daily had lively discussions; we laughed a lot. I don't think I ever had a single discipline problem in my five years at Miss Edgar's, and no parent ever complained about me. I did have the occasional dicey moment. At the end of my first term I discovered I had to put on each girl's report separate marks for composition and grammar. I had combined the two all term. "Needs must," I said to myself, as I made up grammar marks for five classes.

Teaching there for five years as I did meant that I taught students year after year as they moved up through the Senior School. Thus I knew some of them from little girls of twelve to young women of sixteen or seventeen. I got very fond of them and close to many as if I were an older sister or young aunt. Fifty years later I can call up their faces and their personalities and live again certain classroom moments.

Doreen has chosen to do a project assignment on *The Pilgrim's Progress* and produces something quite amazing to me. It is colourful, with an overall effect of green and pale orange, the colours balanced beautifully and making a swirling shape, showing his voyage's path; when I look carefully I can see all the harrowing details Christian encountered, executed in tiny perfect drawings. A work of art.

I assign as a first sentence "It was a dark and stormy night," pointing out the cliché it is but challenging them to create a story based on their own experience that will transcend cliché. Anne M. writes of her anticipation of her older brothers' return from boarding school for the Christmas holidays and how her excitement turns to acute worry as a blizzard threatens to make their return impossible. A train held up, stuck in a drift, a taxi skidding off the street and into a snowbank, brothers — pink-faced and covered in snow — finally arriving on foot. She tells it well, recreating her tension and her ultimate delight. The whole excitement of Christmas anticipation bound up in family love is in the tale.

Diane M.'s story is on another, far darker, emotional level. The writing of it has to have caused a sensitive girl pain. I can only hope that her putting it down on the page helped. She has, and more tidily than usual, penned word after difficult word. Perhaps it is a message to me, her teacher, knowing I care about her or perhaps it is a way to push the facts off a little, to create a distance from them.

Her storm is a summer one: it is late afternoon and black clouds are hanging low over the water; there are rumbles, then huge crashes, of thunder, blinding dazzles of lightning. The power fails. Night falls, and total darkness.

Why is there no candle? She is in her bed, frightened. Then she sees flickering candlelight under the door, hears hushed voices out there in the hall. She knows something terrible has happened. How? She doesn't know how she knows it is terrible but she does. She creeps

INLAND NAVIGATION BY THE STARS 161

to the door to listen. Whisper, whisper, whisper. Women's voices. Her mother, her aunt. She strains to hear. And does. Why has she tried so hard to know what she cannot bear to know? Her father has committed suicide. Suicide. The sound of the word hisses like a snake. He has shot himself in their boathouse down at the lake's edge. The adults' hushed voices fade as they pass down the hall.

The girls tell me many private things.

Diane C. lies crying on the floor one afternoon when everyone has gone home but the two of us. She is telling me, between sobs, of her difficulties with her mother and how her father tries to be on her side and how that makes things worse.

I become close to two sisters who are orphans and are being cared for in an uncle's home. There is money and there is everything they need but especially the younger girl seems lost. She talks to me, she teases me. We are friends.

There are two shy, quiet girls who are the nieces of the man who shot Doug's brother and buried him in his basement. I think of that shallow grave and wonder if they know. I suspect it would have been kept from them, another of those whispered secrets that haunt a family.

Susan is a brilliant girl who understands everything she reads in subtle ways that impress me. I strongly suspect that she is smarter than I am and I find that exciting. I want her to realize it too. She gives a book report in class one day. The assignment is to speak about a book they've read that they want to convince the rest of us to read too. She has chosen *Brideshead Revisited*, which as a Catholic girl she particularly identifies with. She offers us many insights I'd never have thought of myself, let alone her fellow students.

But Susan is a difficult challenge to me and one I am ultimately unable to meet in one important particular. She is so bright and yet is unable to spell any word longer than "the" correctly and sometimes not even "the" comes out right. There is really no way that I am aware of to correct this strange weakness but I try to convince her she can still succeed. There are dictionaries, I tell her. But I know they are only of use if she can spell enough of the word to look it up! Still, I encourage her to apply to the colleges she wants to. The Miss Edgar's students often aim for the American women's colleges and thus write the SAT exams. These are multiple choice, and we are hopeful. Susan, to our delight, is accepted at Smith.

I receive many, many confidences. I feel honoured that my students trust me. Really I love these girls, which is a funny thing when they aren't my family and once they are out in the world I may never see them again, but I truly care for them.

Sometimes I have to chastise them, even if I find what they've done funny: Mrs. Graham discovers in horror that someone has written a tiny "fuck" on a poster in the senior girls' common room. It is up to me to deal with the unseemliness of that, and I do, though we have some smiles together, the senior girls and I. On another occasion loud cheers are heard from the locker room where the girls are just arriving and taking off their coats: word has just been passed along that Mlle. H. was mugged the previous evening. Mlle. H. is an older teacher from France, one of the ogre-style survivors of the era when some teachers' main teaching tool was fear, still a present-tense weapon for Mlle. I know at least one girl who has to throw up daily before French class as she has confided in me, and I feel badly that I have no way to control Mlle. beyond telling Mrs. Graham, who also fears her, I suspect. I understand the cheers, but again it is my role to have them cease and explain why they must.

Reflecting now on how almost miraculous my teaching success has to sound in the telling, I have to acknowledge certain significant qualities in the girls I taught. They came from upper-middle-class homes where almost certainly there were books and periodicals and parents with a habit of reading. Plus it was at a time in social history when, as in my own fairly recent childhood, the balance of power had not shifted to the young. That was about to happen but had not done so yet, or not in Westmount at least. A measure of respect for an elder was natural — so long as that elder was not sized up as unworthy of it; bullying of teachers of course has always gone on if a teacher somehow seems to invite it. Also, I was (and still am, I'm afraid) naturally somewhat of a showoff and I was also tall and slim. I could speak in a carrying voice. (My dear friend Cynthia found she could not be a teacher as her voice was too soft.) But above all I really liked the girls — that was most important — and I was eager to share my love of literature with them. They sensed both things right away.

An aside, jumping forward: there are things I wish so much now that I'd known then. For example, Susan's now-obvious dyslexia. That was a word that had never reached my ears nor the ears of any teacher I knew then, though the condition must have always existed. Even today, actually curing dyslexia is assumed impossible. Many school districts have programs to assist children with dyslexia. They teach various ploys to work around it, though not everywhere is even that that much attempted. In Berkeley, California — so very surprisingly for such a famously academic city — there is currently no help for dyslexia within the public school system. But my daughter, who lives there, pulled her youngest son William out of school determined to help him. In grade four he could neither read nor write with any ease and his teacher was doing nothing but humiliate him. Mathematically brilliant but clearly dyslexic, William was made to feel totally stupid. He had to be, literally, dragged along the road to school as every moment there was so wretched. He couldn't sleep at night for dread of school.

Jane, a math not a reading specialist, put her full attention to the problem. She used her knowledge of the brain's plasticity and connection to the workings of the whole body. It took several months and much effort and patience, on William's part as well as hers, but together they effected a total cure of his dyslexia. People tell me this is impossible but William, now thirteen, reads and writes at university level. Unfortunately we can't send Jane backwards in time to reassure and help Susan.

+

When I began teaching at Miss Edgar's I had just emerged from a time of testing in my life, and now I found myself in a place where I discovered strengths and talents I'd barely known that I possessed and there was nothing to trammel their flourishing. I was in a place where I felt free. What happened next, how I moved forward in my life and cared for my children, was entirely up to me and to no one else.

At the same time I was surrounded by what was very familiar. Miss Edgar's was a smaller version of Havergal, the school where I'd been happiest — young and powerful and yet safe. If I exaggerate my satisfactions at Miss Edgar's a little in my memories, I forgive myself because those memories still give me happiness and do no harm. I acknowledge the large role that sheer luck played, the luck of my family background. Even more important was the era. We were all learning together, the girls as students, I as a becoming-teacher, without the enormous distractions of today's electronic devices and social media, and also just before the drug culture and the sexual revolution. It was a far simpler time for all of us in which to be young and find ourselves.

27

MY last year at Miss Edgar's was different. Our very pleasant Mrs. Graham having retired, we had a new headmistress. Mrs. Graham had been in the mold of one sort of girls' private school heads in that she was a gentlewoman with no particular academic credentials. She had taught as a young woman for a year or two and then spent many years as a wife before assuming her role as headmistress. It was largely because of her that I had been able to find my own feet as a teacher in the way I did. She never interfered. I suppose had I been less able her complete trust might have been a mistake, but not one that would have worked for long. The parents surely would have complained; they were paying fees after all. As it was, the one criticism she had of me in her four years was that I wore my skirts too short. And I'm afraid I carried on doing so.

The new headmistress was in the same mold insofar as she was a very attractive, beautifully turned out woman with little background save a year or two of teaching many years earlier. However, her manner was very different from Mrs. Graham's, more formal, more concerned with establishing firm rules. Both women were childless widows but the new head lacked Mrs. Graham's warmth. I suspect she was less comfortable with young people. Perhaps she was shy. Her husband had been a military man; she may have felt more comfortable using his rather rigid model. She tried to create and maintain a tightly run outfit.

I carried on in my own way in my classes but I sensed her suspicion that too much enjoyment happened there. She would sometimes suddenly appear at the door and stalk in to investigate what I was up to. At that point the girls and I would automatically swing into something other than the free-wheeling discussion we might have been having and plunge into a lesson on essay outlining. We never talked about our tactic; we just did it and we all knew why.

Luckily she never arrived at a moment we'd have found hard to explain: Mary G., for example, a tall thin beautiful girl with wildly curling dark hair, writhing on the floor as Satan and staring with an aghast expression around the classroom while another girl declaimed the text: "Round he cast his baleful eyes that witnessed huge affliction and dismay ..." She likely would not have got the educational point of really getting into *Paradise Lost*.

At the end of that year over half the staff left Miss Edgar's and the new head herself lasted only one further year.

28

AND my social life for those five years we spent in Montreal? It was the liveliest I have ever known and the most fun. The city was the centre of a pulsing world, the culture changing rapidly, freeing the French from their churches and opening up their education system, not to speak of their expectations, and freeing the rest of us from all sorts of strictures. Revolution was afoot on every front. Discotheques burst on the scene and we all rushed to them to dance in the new free ways to the new music. Expo came and whirled us all into the preparations and then the events. My two best friends, Judy and Lisa, were at the social centre of the city and gave the liveliest parties and I was at them all.

A lot of this ended in tears of course, with the FLQ Crisis on the one hand and the arrival of drugs, initially just marijuana but soon stronger things as well. Several friends sank into quicksand. By the end of the decade the mood had changed to something much more serious. But at first, before it all went too far, the excitement of change was in the air, the Canadian version of the 60s, paler no doubt than the Californian, but lively enough for us ...

Various men came and went in my life. Two I especially remember: Tony, an English public school chap, much older, who had been in the war and even taken part in the Great Escape, though not as one of the leaders who got out first, and he was recaptured. He was a dear man but he was very proper, very much in the English, buttoned-up, gentlemanly mold. He had been sent to boarding school at age five

— no family member even accompanying him — on a ship from Dar al Salam, where his father was stationed. He had to learn very early — at five! — to pull all his emotional needs deep, deep inside himself. He revealed to me once that his father had committed suicide, but not why, when or where, or how he, Tony, felt about it then or now. I think I revealed feelings way too readily for him to cope with and seemed almost a hippy to him, though I was far from being one of those really.

The first time we went on a picnic together I was in charge of the food. I made egg sandwiches, wrapped them in wax paper, grabbed a few apples, put the lot into a paper bag and that was that. Next time he took charge. Out of the trunk of his car came a large wicker picnic basket. We ate cold chicken off actual plates, sipped wine from real, stemmed glasses and had raspberries and cream for dessert, blotting our mouths with real cloth napkins. It was a lovely treat, the first of many, but ultimately I wasn't nearly proper enough for Tony.

Another love, a little later, was the art master at Miss Edgar's. I actually think I had more pleasure with him than with any man before or since, more play, more laughing. It was as if we were both children together. But after a while, that I was "a grownup" (a term he used for me but definitely didn't apply to himself) became hard for both of us to ignore. I was responsible for two children, rather than one myself. I cried a lot at the time but what has remained with me is the fun we had. I also have a thought of him sometimes when I make an omelet: he taught me how to lift the cooked edge of the egg and tilt the pan so the uncooked part slips underneath.

I also remember a rather alarming French philosophy professor with whom I had a brief fling and a black chap who was teaching English at McGill. And others. Montreal in the mid-1960s! There was a spirit in the air, an awakening to possibilities, a tossing aside of certain old rules. In my group of friends, who mostly weren't yet thirty, we still felt young and innocent, whatever we did. Most of us were responsible with at least one part of ourselves — jobs, children

— but a few of us were moving too far towards the wild. Not I. I could play, but as a single mother (and still the only one in my set) I was my children's only security. I never forgot that.

It is an early spring evening and I arrive at Lisa and Bart's house, having walked the ten blocks from our apartment. I enjoy walking at this hour through the city, looking at lighted windows and speculating about the lives glimpsed within. The sky is not yet dark, but the still-bare trees are black against it and people's lamps are on. And I love this arrival moment: a party, a house I know well, a big party with close friends and also those I've not yet met. I feel adventurous. I may encounter someone new and thrilling. There will be dancing, and everyone in this instance will be dressed in white. It is a White Party. "Theme parties" are happening again, as I've read they did in 1930s London.

I go in the door into shadows. Candles cast the only light. It is like entering a cave and we are all anonymous, simply young. And beautiful.

I can see the white dresses everywhere, short and fringed, or long, loose and swirling. Men are in hospital whites or a white caftan a wife has run up on her sewing machine, or less daringly, tennis togs. Our host, Bart, is the only one not in white. He is the Devil, in a red nightshirt. I see Pierre Trudeau is here: Judy has him in her sights but I suspect he will evade her. Leonard Cohen will not be here as he is in Greece.

But his name calls up in my mind another party and a summer moment: the party, then, is on Judy's North Hatley verandah, and then too there is only the light of candles. Right below is the black lake. It is a warm evening and I am wearing a silk shift that belongs to Cynthia: it is an experienced dress that circulates among several of us. I am talking to two young Australians someone has brought and I notice Leonard is a few feet away talking to someone else. I've met him a few times but don't really know him. He breaks off his conversation and moves across to where I am standing. His eyes gleam up at me for a moment — "up" because he is considerably shorter than I am — and then he places his hand gently on my tummy and strokes me, watching his hand while it does this. Then his eyes gleam up again and he steps back and continues his conversation. I turn back to the Australians. There is a feeling of something unfinished.

Leonard and I never had our magic moment but I remember another evening that starred him. I say "starred" because Leonard was full of himself. That sounds as if he was obnoxious. He was not. He was compelling and convincing as someone with a special destiny. On the particular evening I'm recalling he floated the idea that perhaps he was the forever-awaited Jewish Messiah, come at last. It felt almost believable; he certainly was amazingly sure of his own significance. There were just a few of us present that evening; it wasn't a party. Just Judy, Leonard and Don Owen (we were at Don's place) and another young director. Don worked at the National Film Board and had directed Leonard in a documentary, *Ladies and Gentlemen . . . Mr. Leonard Cohen*. It was almost a love-letter to Leonard, it was so admiring.

We sat on the floor of the small living room, very close to one another. Leonard's intensity was magnetic and Don seemed entranced by him. Well, we all were. Leonard held forth about one thing and then another. He told us in some detail about his experiences with Scientology. He described the way its principle of initiating worked, how he had to hold onto wired-up tinned cans, one in each hand, and was asked questions, essentially being examined for truthfulness. It was unclear, to me anyway, how seriously he had taken the process. I got a sense he'd try most things.

He also described how he wrote his second novel, *Beautiful Losers*, while in Greece. He said he wrote with the blazing sun incandescent on the page, heat and sun creating a kind of madness. A drug was involved as well, I think.

INLAND NAVIGATION BY THE STARS 171

After five years at Miss Edgar's, the last year spoiled by Mrs. K., I was ready for a new adventure. I wanted something quite different. I knew Quebec and I knew Ontario. The middle of the country gave me a dull feeling (quite unfairly as I learned much later when I got to know Saskatchewan) and thus didn't appeal: I applied only to places on the East Coast, Nova Scotia, and in the West, British Columbia. Nothing came of the Nova Scotia applications but I had luck with BC.

PART III

How Beauty Makes Things Possible

29

AT the beginning August 1970 the children and I arrived in
Kamloops for me to take up my new teaching job. When I look back
at that young woman venturing into the unknown, to a place she'd
never seen and where she didn't know a single soul, I am struck by
her boldness.

I'd had an interview in Montreal with the principal of Selkirk
College, to which I'd applied. I'd heard of Selkirk from the poet Eli
Mandel at a poetry event. Eli had a friend teaching there who liked it
and thus I applied. The interview went well and the principal, a very
pleasant Englishman, was impressed by my Hugh MacLennan glowing
reference (also amused by Mr. MacLennan's spelling mistakes in it).
As it turned out Selkirk College didn't need me but unbeknownst to
me the Selkirk principal passed my application along to the dean of
a brand-new institution. This was Cariboo College, at the time in the
early throes of being set up, in Kamloops. Thus one evening I got a
phone call offering me a position at a college I'd never heard of, in
a town in the Interior of BC that I knew nothing whatsoever about.

When I'd applied to Selkirk I had an image of the Rockies and
I imagined being there would feel like a return to the long-missed
beauty of Alaska. Out my classroom windows would be snow-capped
mountains, brilliant against a blue sky; nearby would be rushing
mountain creeks with Alaska-like pale green water tumbling over
smooth grey stones. The children and I would spend all our free time
outdoors, exploring our amazing new environment. I had no image

in my mind of the Southern Interior. The few details I learned were not encouraging: rattlesnakes abounding, no real and snow-topped mountains, just cactus and sagebrush on dry hills. Tumbleweeds. Cowboy country. But I decided to go. It wouldn't be as I'd pictured BC when envisaging the Kootenay Mountains but it still would be an adventure.

We crossed Canada by train, arriving at one in the morning at the station north of town. Only a couple of other people got off and we stumped sleepily along the platform lugging our bags.

Paul stopped to throw up: he'd been sick for the last couple of days of the train trip, a combination of homesickness for North Hatley and for his grandparents, and the dubious train food. An inauspicious arrival.

I helped him along. I was my children's whole human world now.

Low dark mountains were sleeping creatures shouldered against the barely lighter sky. The air was almost still and warm as blood and we could smell sage and other vegetation that was unfamiliar.

So, who did I become in my new world of the West? How much of the old Anne came along with me? My essential self of course but what of old patterns of thought? Would I succeed at last in fitting myself into a successful marriage plot, as a woman surely must? Trying to see that young woman I was then boggles me as I approach describing this period of my life. I am confounded by some of my behaviour, especially the man I would choose so quickly, but I can see that as I grew even more in independence from my original family some of the old patterns held their sway. And hormones: it is impossible to pull their role out of the novel of Anne. They are so powerful, or were for me. They dictated such an unsound choice that I am dumbfounded, looking back.

For a long time the landscape wouldn't let me in to love it. My eyes sought the round green hills of the Eastern Townships and a long narrow blue lake with white clapboard cottages along the shore-line. Instead, our Kamloops house stared north over some trees, then rooftops well below, towards a wide expanse of water where two rivers met. They were the North Thompson (pale green) flowing down from the north and the South Thompson (dark blue) pouring along from the east. At Kamloops they merged and became simply The Thompson. Across the joining bodies of water — and because they were different colours, one could see the abrupt line where they met — were two huge dark, purplish-grey, sage- and cactus-covered small mountains, Mt. Peter and Mt. Paul. They were quite unlike the snow-capped peaks of my imagined Rockies and they bore, if possible, even less resemblance to my North Hatley hills.

Mts. Peter and Paul were on the Indian Reserve and that was where the new college was to bide its time until new buildings were finished south of town. The new premises weren't to be ready for over a year, and meantime, a couple of trailers were pulled into place to hold our offices. Our classrooms were the vacated ones of the Indian school, as the Indian children were by then being bused into the regular public schools in town. These children still lived in a large red brick building set at right angles beside the two classroom ones we were taking over. They still had Catholic Brothers overseeing them. We would see the children sometimes out playing on the sports field but not often. It was an odd situation: two entirely separate educational enterprises cheek by jowl but with no communication and only rare sightings of each other. The Brothers must have kept the children very much under control. At the time just how brutal that control was and had been for generations was still a well-kept secret. The Brothers kept themselves and their charges so removed from us that I never encountered face to face either a child or a Brother over that whole year, though they were a mere stone's throw away.

The brand-new college's faculty was almost all young, hired straight from graduate school, and initially all male. I heard only years later that after the entire faculty had been hired, a woman from the

INLAND NAVIGATION BY THE STARS 177

local branch of the University Women's Club asked if they had hired any women. Possibly embarrassed — or more probably not, in 1970 — the new principal, I'm sure bemused by the question, said, "no." Likely thinking, "of course not. Why would we want a woman?" But then it turned out they did need another English teacher. Perhaps that woman's question was still in the air, and some scurrying on someone's part happened. As I've described, my application was passed along from the Selkirk College chap who had interviewed me. And someone picked it up: "oh well, maybe we could have one." And so I got that surprising phone call.

And there we were, Paul and Jane and I. Paul was horribly homesick, for North Hatley, for his grandparents, for his old life. Jane, still most often sleeping in my bed, and therefore not quite so much feeling herself exposed to a very "wrong" new world, managed better. They both felt very different from the other children in our quite mixed neighbourhood. It wasn't at all like Westmount, which had been solidly middle-class. In fact "class," so significant in Montreal, didn't really exist in Kamloops. This was a good thing but took adjusting to. And after a few days they confided in me that they felt very dark: their Slavic eyes and hair were not the blue and blond of all the other children on our street. The Indian children, who of course were also dark, they didn't glimpse until school began, and those small souls, sitting silently at the back of the class and ignored by the teachers, were alien in a different way.

I use the word "Indian" deliberately as that was the label then. The term "First Nations" came much later. In the first years of the college I had no Indian students. In the last decade of my thirty years there I had a few, never many and almost all women. Especially when they were in my women's course they would come to me in my office hours and tell me about their lives. They were incredibly strong women, the ones who made it to college, and through their stories I began to understand, at least from the point of view of these women, why there were almost no men among them. At least as terrible things had happened to these women as to their brothers, husbands and sons, and in the destruction of families, girls and women are often most vulnerable. And yet if they survived physically (a challenge right there) girls' and women's spirits seemed more resilient.

Huge damage was done in those red brick schools, the one on that Kamloops Reserve beside our first classrooms, that place of silence and mystery, and many others. Everyone in Canada knows about it now or should. But it is hard for people outside the experience, including me, to fully understand how lingering are the effects. For years I knew quite well a teacher in an elementary school in Savona, a small town west of Kamloops. She had numerous Indian children in her classes every year. She claimed there was no point in expecting them to participate, that they sat silently and would never meet her eye. "Everyone knew" that was all one could expect. It was best, kindest really, just to leave them alone. Small wonder few went on to college.

When my daughter Jane was teaching in Berkeley — many years after our arrival in Kamloops when she'd been only ten — she was up visiting me and wanted to try out her own unusual teaching methods with Indian children. She was sure the situation couldn't really be as hopeless as that teacher we knew still described it. By that time a school was on the Reserve and the principal was a fellow who had once been my student; I was able to arrange for Jane to go into the school for a week. She was warned by the principal of the various children — quite a few — who would never respond, owing to being so damaged by their home life. Jane was used to teaching college level math to black children in West Oakland. She worked for a project the point of which was to use math to unlock the native intelligence of children hampered by poverty and low self-image. She figured her techniques might well work with the Reserve school children.

They did. By the end of her week she had all the students in the class waving their arms, each boy or girl desperate to be the one with the answer, coming up to the board, totally involved. Learning. On her last day CBC News came and filmed her and our NDP Member of Parliament came to watch her. She proved her point: Indian children were as teachable as any children. A teacher just had to know how to teach them, which meant how to unlock them. But Jane had to return to her job in Berkeley ...

30

BACK to our arrival in Kamloops in 1970. After a short while another difference emerged for my children: their schools in Montreal, whether Miss Edgar's in Jane's case or Westmount's Roslyn in Paul's, had prepared them in a way that had them so far ahead, academically, that they operated — and wanted to carry on — in another dimension. Neither their classmates nor their teachers could cope with them. Paul in polite puzzlement kept correcting his grade seven teacher, who was also the principal, on matters of fact. Whatever the subject, the principal was frequently wrong. This did not go down well. The authorities switched Paul to another school, distant enough that I had to drive him — a worse school, though in quite a different way: there they were experimenting with "the open classroom," a fad in the early 70s, the result being that the children wandered hither and yon, at whim, in and out of the classroom, into the halls or wherever they wanted to go, talking, playing and wrestling and the noise was constant and frantic. We couldn't ask for another change, and for that year Paul suffered, surrounded by chaotic silliness and learning nothing at all.

Paul was also bullied at that school. Not physically, because he was tall and strong, but once students learned he loved animals they would leave animal parts in his desk — pieces of birds, and of other small creatures they'd killed — for him to find.

As for Jane, she stayed in the neighbourhood school and spent most of her days in the school attic, alone, working in the next book in the series of her Miss Edgar's math texts. Her teacher, a sweet and obliging man, had not the slightest understanding of the math she was doing but let her get on with it.

For some time my children were fish very much out of water or in the wrong water. Eventually they both found their way through. Paul played on several sports teams and discovered other bright kids when he left the awful "open area" school and went to junior high. Jane played hooky by day and whenever I'd let her sat in on college maths and physics classes. Paul attended some college classes in anthropology and math. Finally I let Jane skip senior high and come right to the college, at fifteen. Paul didn't want to do that because of sports.

For my part, after adjusting my expectations of my students, I very soon enjoyed my new role as a college teacher. Adjustment was needed because I started off as if addressing students at the level of my Miss Edgar's girls one year on and most weren't at that level yet. I also addressed them as Miss and Mr., as I had always been addressed at university. They quite enjoyed that but I soon realized that first names were the rule in the West. I had many bright young students and some very keen older ones. Even the ones who didn't expect to like English, and merely "had to" take it, who had never read a book and saw no good reason to start reading one now, I enjoyed as challenges. I enjoyed all of them, the resistant ones I had to win over as well as the eager ones. There were also numerous somewhat older people in town who had waited years for the chance to take university courses. There were even some in their seventies and at least one eighty years old.

There also were young men in the RCMP who needed university English to advance in their careers. They were very funny and liked playing tricks on me. Several times I was followed through town, and once on the highway, by a police car with screaming siren and flashing lights. I would think, "Good grief! Are they after me? What can I have done?" I would pull over and two uniformed men would jump out their car almost falling over laughing. "Fooled you again!"

Quite a few of my students became, and still are, my close friends.

✦

182 ANNE COLEMAN

Working with a faculty of almost all men was new. Another woman was actually hired just as term was starting, so there were two of us, but essentially it was an entirely male culture and very different from the Miss Edgar's staff room. At Cariboo everyone jealously guarded his expertise. I had very much created my own role at Miss Edgar's, inventing my teacher self as I went along, but at the same time there was an atmosphere of friendly sympathy and sharing among the staff. We discussed specific ploys that worked with certain students. We shared frustrations. We shared not only books but our thoughts about them. At Cariboo, while I made friends with many of my new colleagues, no one spoke of what actually happened in their classrooms. There was always an underlying competitiveness that precluded any sharing of teaching tactics or materials. I pondered whether maleness was possibly the whole if it but for a long time didn't accept what seemed too simple. And why would men be so much less secure than women?

A typical example of this new — to me — way of operating was when one fellow, who used the same short story collection I was using, boasted of his very wonderful interpretation of a rather difficult, highly symbolic (rather tiresomely so in my view) story. I think his analysis had been part of his master's thesis. But he refused to reveal it. Yet we were good friends! Actually it took about twenty years for anyone in my department to share helpful information. I was astonished when a newly hired woman, one of the influx around 1990 as we were evolving into a full university, offered me her notes on a play for a drama course I was suddenly and unexpectedly having to teach.

The difference between how men and women operated in the workplace was part of much larger picture that I began to pay attention to. In 1971 I read Germaine Greer and Gloria Steinem and a long list of others. With their help I acquired sharp new lenses through which to look back on my past and then at my present. I had long been aware of the fundamental inequality of the sexes but as with the air I breathed I knew it was unchangeable and also amorphous, its details fogged by custom.

I spoke earlier of smoke, the way we took for granted that the entire world was polluted with it, and the parallel with sexism. They were essential elements one moved in and had to ignore as best one could and deny if possible. I never blinked when my brother got a sports car as his present when he graduated from university (and on a second try, at that), when my reward a few years earlier had been a pen and pencil set (for doing quite well, first try). It took years for me to see that injustice, which my poor brother is now sick of my using as an example. At the time I even shared our father's enthusiasm over the car gift. It wasn't my brother's fault, Chuck has pointed out, and that's true. It wasn't really our father's either. The fault went back to the beginning of time.

Seeing this pattern lifted into the light at last was electrifying. I became a feminist overnight, or at least over a summer, as I read book after book and stared around me with new x-ray vision. I planned and very quickly started to teach a women and literature course — the speed of this made possible by our college being so small and new, without the heavy male hierarchy of larger institutions. My male colleagues didn't protest, largely because it seemed such a trivial matter to them. I remember a close friend laughing at me in a perfectly genial manner when I remarked that feminism was going to be a major movement. He knew it was a passing nonsense and thought I was sweet, perhaps even cute, for taking it so seriously.

Over the next couple of years, with a few other women and even a man or two, I started a women's centre. We put on a number of province-wide conferences; I went out to all the high schools in the district and spoke on sexism in the education system, in their textbooks, their courses, money allocations for sports and on and on. Other women in the province were doing things as well and we shared information and attended one another's events.

After some time the men at the college and in the wider community started to notice and to get very cross when the "cute fad" seemed to be building rather than waning. After a particular panel discussion

I organized at the college on the subject of rape I faced a frightening backlash: the local newspaper, the *Kamloops Daily News*, over three or four weeks used their Friday most widely read edition to pillory me on their front page. My male social science colleagues, especially the psychology and sociology men, got into the act and mocked me at every turn. I received one or two scary and disgusting phone calls. These men from having been incredulous were now angry. Feminism threatened to pull the rug out from almost their entire body of knowledge. Naturally they were vexed. What could their professional lives turn on without Freud and all the patriarchal figures they had built their work on, the "truths" they had learned and for years had been stuffing into the minds of their students — who were mostly young women — swanning about their classrooms as superior males?

Not only the social scientists were cross. One colleague who taught in the business department murmured to me, with a very sinister gleam in his eye, that I needed to be raped myself. It was ten o'clock at night, after my night class, we were the only two left in the building, and he came up very close to me in the hallway to make his threat. I was unnerved. But I stood up very straight and stared back at him. I was taller than he was. He backed off. He was especially angry because as a result of my complaints to his dean about him he had to take down a huge poster he had hung on the wall over his desk. It featured a young woman's thrust-out bare buttocks. Her lasciviously grinning face was twisted back over her shoulder, towards the viewer. Girls as well as boys had to consult him in his office and they, as well as I, thought the poster was out of the question. It's amazing now to remember what a kerfuffle I created with such objections. *Playboy* pin-ups in a number of offices had to bite the dust, owing to me, and there was much grumbling. The men were truly mystified about why I objected; they felt badly done by at the hands of a prude.

Throughout what turned over several years into a small-scale war my students were solidly on my side, and since my main college relationships were with them and my time spent largely with them, I

INLAND NAVIGATION BY THE STARS 185

coped. I thickened my skin and in a way found the war energizing. I did move my office across campus to avoid daily harassment from members of my own department: my women's course had become the most popular second-year course, even running to two sections for a while. To confound me they brought in a new way of determining the second-year courses by vote. When we were just a two-year college these courses were deemed the choicest, from the teaching point of view. Inevitably, as I was the only feminist of the few women teaching literature in my department, and there were more men anyway, my women's course lost the vote. To the men's rage so many potential students phoned the principal over the summer that the departmental vote had to be ignored.

The men's behaviour was mostly so appalling that, looking back, I hardly know what to feel about them or their behaviour. It was more complicated and more damaging than either side really saw at the time, even I, because it was normal. But changing it, as I was working on doing, was going to be dicey for everyone involved. Men had always gotten away with such tactics as a matter of course. They were deeply affronted at having their controlling role questioned and then they began to be frightened too. Women's demands and the gains we were starting to achieve shifted everyone's social and personal landscape. The ground was quaking.

For many of the men involved at our college, especially those in the social sciences, suffering, even, for some, mind-cracking suffering, arose out of their inability to face and adapt to the changes. Several ended up in the psychiatric ward of Royal Inland Hospital, at least one under police guard. One fall semester a whole row must have been confined there — well, perhaps three or four.

One sociologist was so threatening to the college secretaries that they had a police guard. One psychologist put up a notice in my corridor announcing that he was heading down to the US to get guns. (He was banned from buying one in Canada owing to a gun incident involving his common-law wife.) As I was his chief hate at the college this was unnerving. He passed out anti-feminist handouts in his classes urging students to violence, even to use bombs, though the targets were left hazy, apart from, very curiously, beauty parlours. (Surely he ought to like beauty parlours, as fitting more with the old stereotype than the new feminist one. Feminism eroded reason in such men.)

Of course the students, far more level-headed than he, did not follow his urgings. Several brought his handouts to me. The swift result was that he was fired. He blamed me for that and he was at least indirectly right as I had sent his handouts to the principal. He never could see that his own behaviour had brought about his downfall. Disquietingly for me he had considerable support among the male faculty. The Faculty Association took on his case and fought hard for him. They lost, but the old boys' club feeling remained powerfully against me.

There was another, quite different, even more distressing incident. One morning I faced in the coffee room a desperately upset man I knew only vaguely by sight. He came up close and in a trembling voice accused me of causing his wife's suicide. I had no idea who his wife was; as far as I knew I had never even met her. Apparently she had attended a conference where I spoke. He claimed that she had been inspired by something I said — it had to have been something general, certainly nothing about her husband or her, neither of whom I knew — to leave him but was then too fragile to cope on her own. Poor, poor woman. It was a terrible thing and I was shaken and sorry — but was I to blame?

There can be terrible ripple effects of working for change. Tsunami effects even. Revolutions have victims. Were these sad outcomes my fault? I can't come up with an easy answer. I was sure I had right on my side in my fight to free women from patriarchal power and I still am sure. But some people are too fragile for the times they live in and that is very, very sad.

31

THE account of my struggle against the college men makes me sound almost Amazonian. But as I revisit that time I see that it wasn't simple for me. My professional public self felt to me quite strong, clear and bold. But I had had a girlhood and young womanhood within the patriarchal society that I now, apparently, was triumphing over and it is surely a human reality that a person cannot take on a new identity, holus-bolus, top to bottom, by act of will. Or even know how to do it. More important, even want to let go of certain things. One cannot, all at once, see, understand and strip out all the layers of consciousness that made up the old self.

Even before I became a feminist I had assumed I had considerable control of my destiny. I thought of myself as fiercely independent. I made choices large and small, rejecting girdles and the whole idea of womanly wiles and "helpless" games. More or less boldly I had stepped onto a career path and supported myself and my children on my own. It seemed as if the new term "feminist" simply endorsed who I already was. I just had to slap on the label. This was at an early stage of that wave of feminism and I had only books to inspire me, no living woman whom I actually knew to model myself on, no one to point out to me my naivety. Unrecognized by me, societal and family patterns, and my hormones also, weren't trounced so easily.

Love, romance, sex. Another, better, marriage. I still was holding onto the notion that somehow I must get back on track in terms of the love and marriage plot. The relationships with men I'd had in Montreal, fun as they had been, had not brought me to the safe haven of "normal" womanhood, marriage. And on the most basic, hormonal, physical level, my life didn't feel exciting enough without a man in it.

But I was still a dangerous chooser. Being zealously sought after, being "necessary" to someone, having that power to give or withhold myself: the old delusional trap caught me again. I had failed to learn that such "power" is entirely deceptive. One hands the power over to the other person.

But there was I, that summer of 1970, in a new landscape and a new and initially slightly intimidating job. I had no close friend yet in the West. And there was D., a colleague in another department. He was tall and, at that time, handsome, with his curly light hair and blue eyes. He was intelligent. I noticed him at the very first faculty meeting, sitting a couple of rows over in the old, battered, Indian School classroom we had to use. The desk was too small for him. His very long legs had to be angled sideways into the aisle, as did mine in my also too-small desk. It was his profile I especially noticed, the line of nose, upper lip, chin. His profile was my undoing. I knew right then something of what was ahead of us. Danger, of course, but first, lust.

His addictive intensity immediately focused on me was irresistible. Again — oh, foolish girl! — I couldn't resist being needed so desperately.

I could not have been more more unfeminist in my second marital choice. But I managed not to notice.

We began an affair within three weeks of that initial sighting. Then we lived together. The day he moved in with his enormous pieces of heavy oak furniture — inherited from his grandparents — I did feel a sinking dismay. I had lived alone with my children for over seven years by then and now we were being invaded by alien dark pieces that loomed in corners. In particular there was a very tall armoire from Belgium with linen-fold paneling. It was actually a beautiful piece but its presence suddenly there in my living room scared me. It looked like a sarcophagus. My reaction to the furniture was significant and I ought to have paid attention but I didn't. We married in late spring 1974.

And what sort of man, this time around, would be so intense, so downright frantic in his need to "have" me? My own charms aside, with Frank I think the intensity came from the pain of his childhood of war and losses, his boyhood times in prison and the departure into the unknown and subsequent loss of his older brothers.

I believe my second husband's intensity in his quest of me of me had different roots — and that we both were wrong in what we thought we recognized in each other. He thought that, because I'd had other lovers, I could be open to what I considered extreme experimentation. I desired love and intimacy and definitely wanted the relationship to be exclusive. After I'd made it clear — and I had to do it many times over our first months — that I was not open to these paths, he backed off.

Our reading interests couldn't have been more different. Literary for me and what could euphemistically be termed Adult books for him. I did not explore these books beyond some early glimpses but now see that I was not vigilant enough in the environment they created for my daughter.

There was another, admittedly minor, element in D's attraction to me: his mother was like me a tall, handsome, strong, literary woman. Unlike me she was entirely undomestic and unmotherly. She was also a snob. She admitted, when asked, that she preferred, and always had, D.'s twin brother. She considered, and was quite unembarrassed to state it, that he and his wife had class and D. and his first wife did not. Some part at least of D. wanted to have a wife his mother could admire.

His language and his taste in any sort of cultural thing were different from mine. He did not share my background in classical music or art, in aesthetics generally. For years this was one of the things that caused tension between us. I felt it was my responsibility to solve the bitterness this caused. Over the years, though, perhaps owing more to his affection for and admiration of my parents than anything to do with me, gradually he adopted as best he could my and my family's taste in matters cultural. When we built the house in "Narnia" (more on this, later) my taste defined almost every detail and he did not object.

Our politics diverged as well. Well along in the twenty years of our relationship, he became obnoxiously right-wing. As far as I could see, outside of his job, he did nothing and was interested in nothing. When at home he only sat at his computer. If I entered the room where he had his machines set up he would appear to be playing Solitaire online. It didn't take long for any friends we had as a couple to fall by the wayside. Most remained friends with me but avoided him.

Sometimes I challenged him for being so sedentary; sometimes I thought up enjoyable things we could do together, things to plan. I gave him a book on Italy for Christmas and suggested a trip. I got literature about taking a sailing course down at the coast, as some friends of mine were doing with their husbands. He was unresponsive. I stopped trying. For at least the last ten years of our living in the same house there really was no relationship between us. With my uncanny ability to compartmentalize, I ignored the situation and got on with my own life. I had many good friends myself. I loved my teaching. I loved where we lived, my ski trails, my myriad birds. I was happy; D. was essentially invisible to me.

In my girlhood and young womanhood my father could go silent on me or on one of my sisters. And certainly, well beyond "a bad mood," Frank could be crazed with booze, ultimately driving me away entirely. But my difficulties with D were not related to alcohol. Angry moods would erupt almost out of the blue. I never, while I was with him, had any sort of handle on them. Being me, I may have had some sort of understanding slipping about underground but if I did, I left it there, underground.

Even so, initially we had happy periods, especially when we travelled. D. loved my parents, he claimed even better than he loved his own, and often we would meet them on holiday in England, sometimes connecting with Carol and her husband as well. I remember a lovely couple of weeks we spent in a manor house we rented in Devon, the six of us. I visited my parents in North Hatley every summer and D. often came too. Those are all times I remember with pleasure.

I should never have allowed D. to stay. And stay for years. How could I have done that? I can't answer that in any way that satisfies me now. I created happiness for myself by attending to all the other rich elements in my life.

I was making a trade-off with myself. One of the fiercest joys of my life was to live fifteen years in Narnia. Narnia was what we called the 160-acre property that we bought fifteen miles south of town. It was land high above the Kamloops Valley. The road to it twisted and turned, up and up. And up. And then levelled to a plateau. It was mostly upland meadow dotted with patches of forest and with ponds and it dropped down in a series of cliffs to Long Lake. We built a house and moved there just before Christmas 1980.

Forever I will love revisiting in memory my walks, my birds and my ski trails. When I am awake in the night, I follow one of my routes: I step out the door and set off, down the drive and through the gate, eastward past Currie Lake and up Currie Hill by a looping cattle path to the top of the world, where I can see for miles in every direction, great sweeps of grass and small distant lakes set in the valleys like blue eyes staring up and far purple hills. And if it is spring the wind will be tossing the wildflowers: pale purple lupins, pink wild geraniums, darkest blue larkspur and bright pink shooting stars. There will be yellow aconites under the trees and pussytoes where the soil is thin. Every rocky outcropping will be softened by a drift of mauve penstemon. Or instead I might head north from my door and walk into the forest. I pass first the small pond on my left, which is a stone's throw away, barely into the trees near the house. I give it a quick glance but I am heading for the larger Witches' Pond, half an hour away and downhill. This pond is surrounded by a thick barrier of fir trees and you wouldn't know it was there until you push between two trees and find yourself on the very lip of an oval of black, deep water. The sun never sends a beam down, at least not when I've been there. I cast a spell or two, for good luck.

My love for all of that landscape is still alive in me, nurturing me as my imagination takes me back. And I know that on my own I would never have bought all that land, hired a designer to follow my notions of what my house should be (an old Quebec house, in the West), then watched it come to life before my eyes. I would never have lived for fifteen years in Narnia if I had not been married to D. So what do I do with all that remembered joy? Part of me can't unwish that part of my life.

During that odd time I had a sudden powerful urge to acquire a wolf-dog. We already had Rosie, a sweet golden retriever, but I needed something male and potentially fiercer who would be just mine, loyal to me. Sometimes wolf-dogs were advertised in the local paper and I started to watch the columns. I went and looked at a litter: the mother was quite scary-looking, dark-furred with long lean legs and wild eyes. She was half wolf. I picked out my Wolfie. He was one quarter wolf, the rest husky, lighter in colour than his mother. I fell instantly in love and carried him out of that house like a baby.

Wolfie was happy from the start, with Rosie as his adopting mum, and he grew to be beautiful. He accompanied me always on my walks, racing off in wide circles then coming back to my side for long stretches. He liked to walk leaning lightly against my leg as we both stepped along. I saw a program on wolves at that time and it showed how, with their sociable natures, they liked to walk like that, leaning against each other some of the time. Wolfie was gentle with my grandchildren — a crucial matter — realizing they were cubs who had no ill intention if they stepped on his paw, pulled his ear or sat heavily on him suddenly. I think now — it is just occurring to me — that my need to find a wolf then arose from my situation with D.

Wolfie created a balance. He was a male, but strong and loyal. He was good. Can a wolf-dog be moral? Of course not! Moral choices are no part of his nature. But he felt sane and straightforward. He was always delighted to see me. He loved me. I had him for several years and then he disappeared, not long before D. left me. The one thing in which I was helpless in training my wolf was keeping him from escaping and running free sometimes. And he loved to chase cattle. I suspect a rancher shot him, as he was lawfully allowed to do. No one would admit to it. The ranchers liked me and would not have wanted to destroy my animal, but there are risks when a person adopts a partly wild creature and I sadly accepted the fact. Of course I'd prefer to believe that Wolfie ran off to join some cousins, to live in the wild, but I don't think he would have deserted me on purpose.

32

BOTH my marriages ended with someone fleeing. The first time it was I who left, motoring away slowly, terrified at my lack of speed but unable to make out the country road ahead of me clearly without my glasses, and aware for a minute or so of Frank running behind, trying to catch up with me. The second time it was my husband who ran.

Carol used to get cross at me for saying, of that ending, that "he ran away." She felt the words trivialized it. But he did run, after a fashion, literally. It was an awkward sort of scuttle but presumably the best he could do to get himself out of the doctor's office where our final moment took place.

While this ending was decidedly less dramatic, I still was extremely shocked at the abruptness of it. Or what seemed to me to be that. Actually it needn't have been such a surprise had I been paying attention. Someone other than I would have got busy and ferreted out the reason but I didn't.

I had finally convinced him to meet with our doctor to discuss what was happening to us. Why were we married, with so little happening between us now? Did our wise and wonderful Dr. Jane have any suggestions? Well, he came to her office but he didn't stay. I think he agreed to come that day only because having another person present, especially a professional, would forestall facing me undiluted. He entered, announced the marriage was over, then turned and left.

Dr. Jane was distressed of course. She wanted to know what

I would do, right that minute. She was concerned for me. It was snowing out and I lived fifteen miles up in the hills. Should I be alone? I said I would first go and visit my young friend Anita and get some comfort, then head home before the snow got too deep. I remember wondering about the plowing — the one task D. did. Our driveway was long and sloped uphill from the gate. Impassable in deep snow.

As I finally was making my way up into the hills the winter light was fading but the snow conditions were still not bad. I approached our gate, picking up speed a little, to have the impetus to make the slope, but not wanting to slide off the roadway. As I drove past it I saw an owl on the left-side gatepost. A great grey. He can't have been more than three feet tall yet with one of those tricks of memory I see him as huger than that. As I drove up the drive I kept glancing over as he flew alongside, slowly, keeping pace with me. I think he was even looking at me. That is hard to claim for sure at this distance of time — as witness my memory's trick with his height — but I think he stared at me. That was the first appearance of my guardian, as I came to feel he was. Why do I assume the owl was a male? When I told my usually unfanciful mother about his presence she said, "I think it is your father." She as well as I was in shock, receptive to some magical thinking.

That owl seemed a signal to me that the wild creatures, the trees, the wide cloud-piled sky, the rolling grasslands were on my side. It stayed around for a full week. I was mostly home that week, marking exams, and I would catch sight of him floating, low down past a window. Or I would see him through one of the skylights. Was he watching me? Why else was he there? By night he was out of my sight yet I felt sure he was nearby.

After D. left, over the three years when I lived as the only human in Narnia, I never saw that particular owl again; he had done his job. But there were other owls, smaller ones, to whom I would call from my bedroom window and they would ring the house and

196 ANNE COLEMAN

call back to me. Often standing on the lawn I would give low hoots and one would fly low over my head, almost touching my hair. Someone warned me that owls' claws could hurt me but I felt no fear and no owl ever did touch me. This sounds as if my account is entering the realm of magic realism or that I was going a bit crazy. Looking back at myself then I don't see my behaviour as mad. My feet were always on the ground. But I allowed myself to dramatize my situation: I was a woman alone in the wilderness. I was talking to the animals and they were talking back. I was turning into a witch! The spirits of the trees were comforting me! I must have found it helpful, in the way to lose oneself in music or dance can be releasing and healing. I used those things too, dancing alone in my living room to Kate and Anna McGarrigle's songs of lament.

It wasn't till a year later that daughter Jane felt able to tell me how disturbed she had been during our time with D. She had been ten when he came into our lives, a vividly beautiful little girl, small for her age but feisty. She had bright brown eyes that sparked with energy and humour and she could run like the wind. My sweet daughter: I did not watch D. keenly enough. I did not notice what I ought to have had the sensitivity to see.

I blame myself fiercely, and I also blame the era. I hated those books of D.'s, hated that they were in our house. I refused to peruse them or involve myself with them. But in that early-70s era of general sexual arousal and freedom was a new licence for the breaking down of all boundaries to men's sexual indulgence. It was open season for sexual exploration and display.

Two forces pushed and pulled. It was a time of extreme sexual muddle; sexual freedom for men was wildly ascendant yet at the same time feminism was making women examine how they fitted into this picture of male sexual power.

Sometimes I fought back. I remember once actually throwing out some books of his that I'd somehow managed not to avoid looking into — they were stacked on the table on his side of the bed. In fury he retrieved them from the garbage and in raging revenge he snatched up several of my best beloved books. I remember doing my own retrieving of *Letters of E. B. White*, *Middlemarch* and *Emma* from where he had hurled them into the dusty hedge across the road.

My guilt over not protecting Jane from the tensions of my marriage pokes up to this day in dreams of our Narnia house. The house has been trashed; it is full of mess and muddle, piles of tattered papers, filth. The floorboards are rotted and broken. The dreams show that my denial skills could not have been totally successful.

33

IT is a conundrum to me. Unlike in my dreams of a ruined Narnia, the real-life house I created was beautiful, orderly, a-tumble with my grandchildren. My real-life animals — my cats, my dogs, my wolf — were exemplary creatures. And I had my wide meadows, my forests, my birds. I loved my life.

Before D. and I bought the land there, the children and I and sometimes D. as well used to explore everywhere in every direction around Kamloops. Then we found the best landscape of all. It was high, that land, almost alpine level, a high plateau that fell away, as I've already described, in a series of banks and cliffs down to Long Lake. There was another smaller lake, Currie Lake, just before we entered the property. The particular quarter section we focused on included open grassland, forest, hidden ponds. Walking in those upland, wide and rolling grassy meadows, I felt as if, were I to pick just the right moment, I could change a ground-bound step into a leap up into the sky. I was so far above any valley; the sky was so huge above me, an endless blue vault; I was hardly a human. I could be a bird or an angel. We called it Narnia after the books the children and I had loved, because it had such a dream-magic feeling to it. When we decided to move out of town, that was where I needed to be.

I had fifteen years there, longer than I had ever lived anywhere else, and the last three years on my own. We had 160 acres but since the surrounding land was grazing land with no houses save one old homestead fallen to ruin, it all felt like ours. I walked or skied everywhere.

It crossed my mind once or twice while the house was being built that I might find it isolated. Driving home alone in the winter, after teaching a night class, might I feel nervous? There would be many miles without another house, only black wilderness with nary a blink of human light. Once I was living there I knew the silliness of that. Feeling unsafe in Narnia, or on the way to it, was out of the question.

The birds! They are perhaps now, as I think of them, what I miss the most. I have joy in the memory of them — but oh how dearly I wish I could see and hear them again! I actually can't bear to remember them very often. There were swans that came every spring and fall and spent a few weeks coming and going from Currie Lake. I woke in the morning to the great clapping of their wings as they rose from the water and flew low over the house, on their way to wherever they spent their days. In the early evenings I walked quietly near the lake and watched the mass of them floating on the still water, moving slowly, their long necks brilliant white even as the light faded. I wished I could hold the moment forever.

And the sandhill cranes in their hundreds came also every spring and fall, competing for space on the lake with the swans. When the cranes first announced themselves every year, their signalling cries were the voices of spring. Every single spring the sound caught me by surprise. I would stare up and the skies would open wide for me as I searched for them. Their cries were like bells. Where? Where? And then I'd see a great swirl of them, like a blowing scarf across the sky, whirling, unfolding, down and down, and finally arriving, and settling on water, in a dark clutter of wings. The atmosphere was different when they visited in the fall for a few weeks. They were not announcing awakenings and births. They were delivering a leave-taking before they flew away to warmer climes. At night they rested on the dark water. In the morning they took off over the golden aspens, to stalk the harvested fields down the valley for pickings.

Their numbers, over the fifteen years I was there, didn't noticeably decrease but the swans' numbers did. Because of us? I do hope not, when I loved them so.

There were also the bluebirds, and the long-billed curlews with their astonishing cry. The curlews built their nests right on the ground in the grass up on Currie Hill; I had to be careful lest I step on a large mottled egg almost too successfully camouflaged. Spring brought many other birds as well. The red-winged blackbirds were early heralds. One would suddenly dart at the edge of a pond and soon there were more of them, and, later, swallows, killdeer, meadowlarks and hawks.

In winter I cross-country skied every day for several months; we had much more snow than lower down and it stayed far longer. Often I left the college at four o'clock and the day already seemed to be dimming, thick cloud heavily settling in like a lid over the valley. Wanting to ski would seem unlikely. But my drive took me up and up and out of the cloud and into bright sunshine; once home I stripped off my teaching clothes, pulled on my ski clothes and jumped on my skis, all within ten minutes.

I had different trails over open country and through the woods, choosing one according to mood and according to wind or the amount of snow falling. Dusk soon came upon even the high meadows but I had no fear. In the years when I was on my own I sometimes thought, when lifting one leg, plus ski, and then the other, plus ski, over a barbed wire fence — a tricky maneuver — that maybe my bones would be found by a rancher come spring. But I didn't really believe it. Narnia wouldn't kill me.

In late winter, every year after my dear Wolfie was gone, a pair of moose came, a mother and her adolescent daughter. The moose would be about for a few weeks and they would come right up to my windows, or I'd look out and see them between my door and my car. I'd wait a bit till they slowly moved to a little distance — and they were never in a hurry — before going out. They gave off no feeling of menace but I saw no point in challenging them. Why should I? They were perhaps territorial about my ski trails, peeing and defecating on them. My students who were hunters told me they could attack me but somehow I never felt they would and they didn't. There were also coyotes about and occasionally bears.

Once in the early fall I woke up to changed light in the bedroom, sun pouring in where usually a mountain ash tree shaded that window. Looking out I saw that a bear had climbed the young tree for the berries and bowed it to the ground. The same bear on another day pushed his way onto the screened-in verandah to sniff around the barbecue. But then he lumbered off and I didn't see him again.

I liked that other creatures shared my space and I never changed my roaming ways. The land was theirs, but mine too. We could share.

34

I stayed in Kamloops for one year after retirement, then moved to Victoria in late summer 2001.

Free of D., no longer teaching, I would become something new. But first I must find my route forward.

It has seemed my fate that I enter fresh worlds without models. In my own department several of the women were almost other daughters, two of them once my own students who had gone off and got their PhDs and returned to work with me. Now only I was entering uncharted terrain. I was uncertain even about my financial position. It was curiously difficult to find out any specifics about the Canada Pension Plan, the Old Age Security pension and even the university's own pension plan. Perhaps because I was one of the first of the old guard to retire, there seemed to be no machinery in place to help me sort things out. The personnel department had no information. Nevertheless I forged on, figuring there had to be a way I'd survive.

But more than the financial element it was the identity question that troubled me. I brooded in unbusy moments until I no longer could bear the uncertainty of who I was going to become. I decided to act, as was my habit in some things anyway. (Clearly not in ending that second marriage! And I don't feel the rush to hasten towards death's threshold, not yet at least.) I would leap rather than wait for the inevitable to overtake me: the college was offering a buyout if one left early. I took it and jumped.

Through the first part of the summer that followed my retirement

I held myself in a listening posture: how much was I minding? Gradually my spine relaxed. Even before August my body first and then my mind knew that I was ready for what I would become next, whatever it would turn out to be. I'd known from the start of the leaving process that I did not want to stay on part-time even if that were allowed. I did not want to be a fringe person where I had once been central. I was ready for a new role to present itself. I was confident there would be something.

It took a year for my new venture to swim up to the surface. At first it was a glimpse out of the corner of my eye. Then it swam into my sightline: it was time to be a writer.

I'd planned to be a writer in childhood when Carol and I wrote poems and stories. I remember an ambitious "novel" I began at about age ten. It was about refugees in Palestine. I had an image in my head, awoken by something I heard adults discussing. I couldn't take it far as I really knew absolutely nothing about the subject but I had a vivid picture of several people, a woman and her three children, a family in dusty and tattered biblical clothing. They were pressing onwards over a dry landscape, the mother carrying the youngest, the other two clutching her skirts. It sounded grand to claim Palestine as my topic when I told my mother and sisters. I have no recall of how many pages I actually wrote. Did I even get to the fate of the family's father, why he was absent from my scene?

Despite that feeble start the writing plan didn't die. Throughout my school life I wrote, and abandoned, then later wrote and published in the school magazine, stories. At McGill in my second year I won the prize for fiction. I have a copy of the *McGill Daily* with my story on its front page and see that Leonard Cohen won the poetry prize at the same time. Leonard had to have been far more sure of himself and his talent — and with good reason. He swept on to fame and fortune with astonishing rapidity. My writing ambition was overtaken by life, the claim of children and the shifting drama of my first marriage. Whose fault but my own? Ambition came alive again at Bishop's where I published things in the university literary magazine, *The Mitre*, and there was a story that Michael published in the Queen's literary magazine a couple of years later. But then again, life — supporting and caring for my children (I had no support from Frank, back in Yugoslavia, either financial or practical) and my bugbear, my hormones, took over.

Other people, women as well as men, write despite such distractions or circumstances. I can make excuses along the lines of, "I did those other things more intensely, more thoroughly — better! — than those people who managed writing as well." That is much too feeble. It can't be the answer: I had whole summers free and instead of sitting writing I travelled in England, I went back to North Hatley where I swam every day with my children, I paddled my canoe far up the lake. I lay reading in my hammock. I spent long hours talking to my mother and sisters and my friends. I can't have wanted to write enough to give up those things. Was that it? I experienced pangs of guilt from time to time at the wasting of a talent but not enough to be goaded into sitting down and getting at it. Yet surely only children need long summer holidays to swim and play outdoors.

I am speculating: perhaps it was simply that I lacked conviction that I could write something worth publishing. I didn't articulate that even inside my head but did I feel it? If so, why did I? I knew I had talent. I didn't use it. Sitting for hours writing requires an exceptional ego. A person has to have unusual confidence to trust that success will follow and make worthwhile all the time and effort taken from other activities and especially from other people's needs and wishes for one's attention. I had supported myself and my children all the years; I was successful at a job I loved. Why should I lack such confidence?

I see one big reason now: during that long time — all the years after Montreal and thus most of my adult life — I worked among men who did not for a minute treat me as an equal, and however much I told myself that they were wrong, I had to have been affected. The little daily put-downs, mostly unconscious and automatic on the part of the perpetrators, most often with no conscious malice at all, just habit, had to have taken a toll. I faced the same thing at home with a husband who for years punctured my balloons, and even worse, surrounded me with discombobulating lies.

Pretending not to mind put-downs is taxing. Lies fill the air with smoke even when one refuses to acknowledge them. All that denial on both fronts took energy. I needed my lazy summers.

There was something else as well: my feminism was always compromised, according to the tenets of the early 70s. It required a certain convoluted dance in my head. Despite my role as Feminist Suprema I loved certain of the old "womanly ways" of my mother's generation. I wanted them too and still want them. I wanted to be as good a mother as my own mother had been, not out of a sense of duty but because I loved the role. I had to be a double person, a new woman and an old-style one too. Both to the hilt.

I still love, when I get the chance, presiding over an archetypal matriarchal scene: I am having a big family dinner gathering. I carry in the Sunday roast beef. The mouth-watering smell of my sherry gravy floats in the air. My lovely long table darkly gleams, my flowered Portmeirion plates are heated and piled at the ready beside my son's place. If it is summer the windows are open to the view of garden, trees below and distant sea. Most important, around the table there is a multi-generational group of beautiful people I adore, my children/grandchildren/great-grandchildren, probably Karen and maybe Sonya too, eagerly and affectionately looking up at me as I bring in the platter, the "beast" which my son will carve, as the man of the family should. He likely will have both raised and butchered the animal we are about to eat. I could be my mother and I love feeling that she is alive still in me in such a moment.

Virginia Woolf in an essay wrote of her need to kill the Angel of the House each time she sat down to write. The Angel was her beloved mother's ghost, with all that the perfect Victorian wife stood for of wifehood and motherhood. Julia Stephen had been a martyr. She died young, worn out from such an overextension of self in caring for others. I have never wanted to kill my mother's ghost. In my later generation such ruthlessness didn't feel necessary. I wanted her ghost to inhabit me, if that were possible. I just wanted my father's ambitious and independent one in me too.

I revel in my family role and I revelled in my teaching role. They are connected as parts of the same impulse. And now I am enmeshed in five generations. I have never shaken free of, nor wanted to — even when, according to the Movement, it was wrong — relishing the visceral joy of caring for, in the sense of doing things for, the people I love. Part of that has often been enjoying holding forth to a group, bringing them along with me in discussion and making them laugh, whether they be family or friends or students.

Writing had to wait its turn. I couldn't be everything.

I faced my fear of retirement by arranging to go abroad for that first fall. I wanted to be sure I didn't experience horrible pangs when classes began in September and I had no students.

I arranged a stay in Italy.

Carol's daughter Ruthie, after finishing university, had worked for an English lord, Lord Antony Lambton (Tony), for several years running his Tuscan estate. Lord L. himself, and his mistress, the Honourable Mrs. Claire Ward, lived in the palatial house, Cetinale, and the secondary house on the vast property, Cerbaia, was let by the week or month. It was considerably less grand than Cetinale but large and beautiful all the same. One or both houses were sometimes used as movie sets; we even were told that Prince Charles in his bachelor days had stayed in Cerbaia as the Lord's guest while recovering from a polo accident. Of course we knew of Lord Lambton's colourful history: in the 1970s he had been a Minister in Heath's Conservative government and had to resign over a scandal involving several young women. He maintained to the press that the fuss was only because one of the women was black and he fled to Italy, abandoning his wife and four children, taking his mistress.

We saw almost nothing of the Lord during our stay but his invisible presence and that of the Hon. Mrs. W. (mother of the movie star Rachel Ward) added a note of English upper class badness that we colonials always enjoy. We had two maids and a cook in our villa and a magical Holy Wood to walk in (where the Palio horse race took place for a few years in the 1400s when Siena was experiencing excessive violence). Ruthie was by then married to a Sienese doctor, home with her babies but still in the area, which is how I knew of the place. It was not cheap, but among the nine of us we could afford it.

It was a lovely introduction to my retirement and important: it underlined for me the joy I had spending time with my friends. For my Italian venture I collected a group from several different chapters of my life. They didn't all know each other but they were all people I loved. There were Sonya and Rosemary from McGill days, both close to me since our late teens; Rosemary's husband Alex; Jan, Rosemary's cousin from England with whom had I had also become close; Moira and Alistair from Oxford and San Francisco; Jacquie from Kamloops and Trish, a new friend from Vancouver. And of course we saw Ruthie and even Carol was able to visit our villa as she was staying with Ruthie when we first got there.

When I reflect now on my friendships — and there are many others besides the group in Tuscany (Cynthia, Roberta, two Anitas, Joyce, Lynda and Linda and far, far more than I can list here) — I recognize what I'd not brought into proper focus when I was younger: my friends have been more constant in support, more loving, more fun, more enlarging of my understanding of life and people, than the husbands and lovers I've had. During all my "hormonal" years

I had supposed that having a man romantically and sexually was "the" essential to a woman's happiness. In my case this was not so. I'm not attempting a general claim. If I'd been a better chooser and had a long and happy marriage I'd tell a different story. But such marriages are rare miracles. I can think of only a handful that I've observed over my long lifetime.

35

SOON after my move to Victoria in 2001 my friend Cynthia, close to me from our first day at McGill when we were both seventeen, made a discovery. Cynthia was a great saver of things, not really a hoarder as we use the term now, just a saver. Over decades her Ottawa basement was a frequent subject of anxiety and conversation: she had to deal with it, but when? And how to decide what must be gotten rid of? Finally she had to bite the bullet: the house was sold and she was moving west. The grand clearing out began. And she discovered, under a pile of old *National Geographics*, a collapsing cardboard box containing a cache of letters written by me to her over the six years of my first marriage. She packaged them up and sent them to me.

I sat with the package on my sofa in my living room, a high-ceilinged, oak-panelled room with tall casement windows that look down over treetops to the sea. I tore off the old brown paper grocery-bag wrapping — Cynthia, like me, was always frugal — and the room and Victoria present disappeared.

I held in my lap letters, page after page in my handwriting — tidier handwriting than I have now but recognizably mine — mostly written in ink not ballpoint, the paper thin and creased, smelling pleasantly musty like an old library book.

I opened an envelope — and I was at once in an old house in Pointe-Claire.

I was there. Oh my lost house, my lost garden! The house was tall, narrow, brick, covered in vines. In spring those vines seethed with birds. When I walked down the gravel drive towards the back garden a mass of green above my head would move and flutter as birds flew out. Tendrils would catch in my hair.

The long garden was wild. I never really tamed it. In June it was full of pink and white apple blossoms hanging against the grey, ridged bark of gnarled old trees. In July there was a thick tangle of peonies and poppies and honeysuckle. In winter deep snow came up to my knees as with freezing fingers I plucked from the clothesline diapers frozen stiff as boards. I loved that garden. I loved its wildness. Remembering, so long after I last smelled my peonies, I feel again sharp loss. I've never seen a garden since with so many peonies.

For the first time in years and years I was back there, in that garden and that house where I had lived from the summer of 1959 to the summer of 1963, when I ran away. Only four years but they feel much longer than that, a decade at least, surely!

But who exactly was the girl who had written these letters? It was I. Of course it was. Yet it was an "I" I had chosen to — what? Forget? Abandon? Simply lose?

The details described in those flimsy pages were utterly familiar. I knew they were true. Yet I had lost them for fifty years, or most of them, whether on purpose or willy-nilly. I think it simply had hurt too much to acknowledge and hold them in my mind and I'd had to let them go.

Yet they weren't forgotten; I read about that old life of mine, details of my babies and my husband, and my feelings and reactions, the look of my world then, all described for Cynthia, and I remembered them perfectly well. They could have happened within the last year, not fifty years before. But it was as if I had bundled them up and hidden them away, closed a drawer or a door on them, locked it. Never peeked.

And then I remembered as well how, after I ran away from that marriage and was staying with my parents, my mother had insisted that I get rid of things. She saw to it that things incredibly precious to me were just — gone. That sentence isn't even precisely true, not in its use of the past tense! I can feel again the hurt at the loss of them.

My mother disposed of my children's baby clothes.

Jane was only three. How could my mother be so sure I'd never have another baby, never put tiny arms into a certain pale rose sweater, a sweater my friend Monique had given me, a very special sweater from France that she didn't use herself as she had only baby boys? It had a tiny collar and the pink was quite unlike the usual baby wool colour and was so soft. I don't know what that wool could have been. Possum? I can hardly bear to remember it now. I felt then, and now feel again, grief. I remember thinking: does this mean I will never have another baby? How can she know that I will never be happy again? To me then happiness had to be in a marriage, the prospect of another baby.

Yet I went along with it. I had married against my parents' wishes and they had turned out to be right: it had been a terrible mistake. I could not expect happiness again.

This anecdote makes my mother sound cruel. She wasn't. But her distress over all that had happened made her shut down, emotionally. The truth of what I must have suffered was too much for her to face squarely. Her overwhelming impulse was to bury it.

To please her, I must tidy away that mistaken and terrible marriage.

All of it, all of it, must go. Even that dear little sweater with its precious memories of Jane as a baby and the possibility it held of another such little person.

Only when I moved out West with my children when I was thirty-four had I finally stopped thinking about my father's judgment of something or other I was doing. I needed a few thousand miles of distance. Throughout, I never doubted that he loved me but I yearned for a relaxing of that "judging" tension that often tightened the air between us. Often I didn't feel entirely natural with him but rather as if I was acting the part of the good daughter — the good daughter that I really was! — hoping to convince him that I was "coming up to the mark," as if it could only be by a trick, an act, that he'd be convinced. But what was the mark exactly, the mark that I knew I'd never really come up to? I don't think it was simple for either of us.

As I've already described I feel sure that he saw two contradictory, dangerous outcomes for his daughters, grievous missteps we might well take at any age. In the same illogical way that his so-loving indulging of his son made it difficult for my brother to achieve the independence our father would respect, I suspect that on a powerful, never fully brought to the surface level of his mind, he dreaded his girls evolving into either his sister or his mother.

My old letters showed a different truth about my first marriage than the one I had come to accept. There was so much more happiness than I had been allowed to remember. A violent ending had cast a shadow backward and the shadow had remained in the way I consciously thought of that marriage and told its story to others.

The different truth the letters revealed made sense. I bounced back so swiftly and resiliently from those six years of my marriage. Could I have done so if they had really been unrelievedly disastrous? There was considerable happiness in those years. There were terrible times and at the end I knew real fear for my physical safety and, most crucially, for my children's. But Frank had not been bad man; he had been a sick man.

Many years later, when I was still in Kamloops, Frank visited Jane three times, twice when she was at university and once when she was married and living in Berkeley, each time surprising her, arriving unannounced. They had at least one long conversation about early events and he maintained — and she believed him — that he had no memory whatsoever of any violent behaviour on his part. Had it been an alcoholic blackout? Could such a thing cover an extended period? Or perhaps the shock treatment he received so much of? We shall never know.

I'm not even sure when exactly Frank returned to Slovenia.

At the time of my divorce, which took place in the Senate Chamber in Ottawa in 1965 and required an Act of Parliament, I dreaded his sudden appearance. He could negate the whole thing if he burst in, spoke up and said that his infidelity had been a charade. Two detectives gave testimony of catching Frank in adultery, still the only justification in Canada for divorce. The "adultery" had been a faked but the necessary lies were accepted, doubtless everyone there knowing them for what they were. It felt very wrong but at the same time — blackly — very funny, the two fake detectives taking their faking seriously, as if they were starring in a movie. And all in that exceedingly formal red and gold Senate Chamber, by far the grandest place I'd ever been in. I found out much later that my father knew at least one of the Senators; they were unlikely to make trouble for me, and Frank may have already gone back to Slovenia by then. And there he stayed with no contact until those very much later visits to Jane. He lived a surprisingly long time, given the abuse he inflicted upon his body with alcohol and nicotine.

His sudden and pathetic, yet somehow fitting, end came in 2000 when he was seventy-two. The Grand Hotel Toplice had been a sort of mythical lifeline for him all his life. Lost twice over, the first time when it was taken over for German Headquarters during the occupation of Yugoslavia, and the second time after the Communist nationalization, it remained a fixture in his imagination, defining who he really was, and also allowing him, at some vague point in the future, to give something to his children. He believed, or fantasized anyway, that the day would come when it would be his.

After the fall of Communism in Slovenia, in 1990, property did begin to be returned to original owners. I believe a business could be returned with less confusion and trouble than a private property, where several generations might have lived in a home they'd be loath to give up. Workers in a business wouldn't have the same emotional investment so long as they kept their jobs. But Sasha and Jula Molnar had had four children, who themselves had gone on to have families.

Molnars were scattered in Australia, Switzerland and Canada. With all four of the first generation of heirs dead, who owned the Grand Hotel? Jula's will left it to Frank. Frank himself made a total of sixteen wills. In one he even left me a villa, to make up for never having paid child support. I was told this and had a fleeting image of taking holidays in beautiful Bled but later wills soon negated that one.

Against the day he would have the money in his hands, Frank moved into a suite in the Grand Hotel, his second wife (an unfortunate woman who herself suffered terrible bouts of mental illness) into another. He lived to a pleasant daily pattern. He began with a swim in the wonderful hotel pool. (Long ago when I was there I was told that the water was somehow filled with bubbles so that Tito could imagine himself swimming in champagne. I've no idea if the water is bubbling to this day or if the story was even true.) Then he would have a massage from the young and attractive masseuse. He and this woman became very close, according to reports. An old man awaiting a large inheritance, a younger woman prepared to wait?

Picture him: he has had a long lifetime of punishing alcoholic binging; he has chained-smoked for sixty years. He looks a hundred years old.

A sum of money is advanced from the inheritance and the couple — old man, young masseuse — take off on a holiday, a cruise in the Greek Islands. They are having dinner one evening on a terrace overlooking the wine-dark Aegean Sea. He leans over to feed a passing pussycat. He has always preferred animals to humans. He reaches out his arm, a piece of meat between his fingers — and he falls over. Dead.

An autopsy is done in Athens and there seems no particular reason why, despite the life of alcohol and cigarettes, he should have died just then. A toxicology examination is done as well. The results are sent to my son, Paul ,who had them translated. The report has a headline: Poisoned. There are many drugs in his system, including Viagra.

Paul soon learns that his father had just made a new will leaving a considerable sum to the mistress. It is clear to everyone that the much younger and attractive woman has not been seriously smitten with the old alcoholic man. Perhaps facing one more Viagra-enhanced session is more than she can put up with. "Enough!" she mutters to herself (in Slovenian, of course) as she prepares for that last supper, slipping a few pills into her purse. However, his body is rather quickly cremated and nothing is ever proved.

Paul and his wife Dorothy go over for the funeral. They hear tales of how Frank's second wife has been standing nightly under the mistress's window in the Grand Hotel, screaming, "MURDERER!" The mistress attempts to enter the church for the funeral; the second wife weeps, "No! No!" My daughter-in-law, a woman capable of considerable firmness, strong-arms the mistress out. A young man appears, claiming to be a half-brother of my children. He runs a gay nightclub in Vienna. Paul feels no blood tie, but who knows? The whole scene is so like a film script that Paul scarcely knows how he feels: perhaps more a grief for what he never had, yet something hurts his heart. He gives a eulogy, in English, for the father he scarcely knew, then he and Dorothy leave Bled and visit Venice: they might as well have some holidays while over there. Meantime, I am back at Paul's ranch near Kamloops looking after my grandchildren for the two weeks their parents are away. I have plenty of time to reflect on Frank's death as I walk over the meadows, brilliantly green with new spring growth, and up through the forest and the zigzagging mountain trails. This upland world, so wide, so huge, with a sky an immense blue vault above me that yet — as I used to feel in my lost Narnia — is so close I can almost leap into it: this is a different world from my long ago Quebec. There, the hills were small and near, roundly enclosing our lake and valley.

But the comparison triggers memory. Not just North Hatley but Montreal and Pointe-Claire slide into the present along with the shocking truth that I've not properly allowed room: Frank is dead. Just for a moment I know it in my chest, my heart. I am shocked at how real it feels, a dart to my heart. He is so long gone from me. But once I loved him. He was my children's father.

Yes, I loved Frank. I loved him physically and I loved what I sensed was his deepest, essential self, the person who was still there beneath the scar tissue he had developed. There was a sweetness in him, a loving-kindness, tenderness. For stretches of time, sometimes over several months, that self of his was ascendant. Those premonitions of disaster that I'd had before my marriage, the cliff or curtain images I allowed myself to fashion, what can I make of them now? From this vantage of almost sixty years on, I cannot plumb them "really and truly"! There can never be a real and true knowledge of one's motives. But I suspect, now, that I was not a masochist heading, knowingly, towards certain victimhood. I am shifting my understanding of the past as I write. For so long I held onto the memory of how I dramatized, before my wedding, the dangers. I'm almost sure, now finally, that I couldn't really have believed in them. I wanted drama but not suffering. I must have trusted, at bottom, that the goodness in Frank would triumph, that my love would help bring that about. My love couldn't work that miracle and I developed a defence against acknowledging that sad fact. I developed a darker picture of the marriage in order to bear that failure.

If someone you love descends into madness and you have to escape him, the love does not automatically yield to reason and disappear. I escaped with a deep wound myself, one I had no idea how to deal with.

36

DURING the time in Italy my long-delayed idea of being a writer began to stir again though at first I had no focus other than wanting to write something about growing up in North Hatley. It was during our summers there that my senses and my imagination came alive. It was there that I began to sharpen my identity, discovering where I could push out my boundaries while keeping my edges firm and my independence clear. But at first the North Hatley writing had no shape. It was an exploration, a moving in memory and imagination within the landscape and within the maturing consciousness of the young girl I had been, with no particular direction. Memories flooded back. I loved reliving scene after scene of childhood and young girlhood but lacked a central point. There was a chapter in this formless opus that I kept going back to. It was important for me to get it right though I wasn't sure why.

That chapter dealt with a relationship I'd had from when I was about fourteen to the summer I married, at twenty-one. A relationship that I'd not understood and that made me uncomfortable to think about. I'd left it alone, an unexplored room. I had a tender/wincing feeling about it as if I were guilty of something. I had loved someone or thought I had (had I really?) and the friendship or whatever it had been had ended abruptly at my marriage. I had not revisited it since, not for almost five decades. Now a few specific memories of that relationship tantalized me. I wrote them down until I had ten pages or so. I wondered if there was enough there, despite the unresolved nature of what I had so far uncovered, to stand alone as an article. I sent it off to Michael Ondaatje for advice. He responded at once saying, unsurprisingly, that it didn't work as it was, but then, surprisingly, that it could be "a gold mine" if expanded into a whole book.

This was a double conundrum for me: how could I remember enough to make a book and what had it all been about, anyway? I didn't at the time even know the term "creative non-fiction" and it felt as if I'd have to lie to make it into enough of a story. I'd have to invent conversations and incidents. Was that allowed? However, I began. And to my surprise whole scenes unfolded to me. I heard again real words that Mr. MacLennan had said and in my body I felt again how I had responded then. At first in the writing I called him "Hugh MacLennan," but soon that felt wrong and presumptuous. He had always been "Mr." to me so "Mr." he became in my book. An interesting small point here: Hugh MacLennan had a PhD but he considered the word "Doctor" reserved for medical practitioners. It was bad form to use it otherwise. I don't know exactly when this changed. Now every PhD immediately becomes "Doctor."

I wrote my memoir about my relationship with Mr. MacLennan over a summer. For two months I wrote all morning, sitting at my new desk.

The purchasing of the desk was a telling step in terms of the confidence I was reclaiming: I had always adored the kind of desk I associated with a gentleman's library in a large country house in England. I've seen these desks behind velvet ropes when I've toured National Trust houses near Oxford or in Hampshire. Of grand size, crafted long ago of dark and richly polished oak, such a desk has a working surface of leather, worn but polished to a soft gleam. There is sometimes gold tooling, also worn, edging the leather. There are wide pedestals with many drawers. I'd never yearned even secretly for such a desk. To own one was out of the question for such as me, an ordinary middle-class Canadian woman, a colonial. Above all such a desk was for a man. Yet suddenly in my newly freed power I was ready to vault the country, class and gender barrier. And once the idea hit me my need was urgent. I knew of a store in Vancouver that specialized in reproductions of classic furniture. I went, I saw and I bought my desk within five minutes of crossing the store's threshold. It was simple: one desk was simply the most beautiful piece of furniture in the room. It was mine.

So there I sat at my desk — the desk of a powerful person — and began to take my writing seriously, and myself doing it seriously. I would earn the desk.

It was my first summer in my new home in Victoria and I lived my days to a pattern: I wrote all morning, from dawn. In the afternoon my friend Karen and I would drive up the peninsula and swim in the sea. Then she would read my new pages and we would discuss them. She was an invaluable friend. With her musician's ear she noted where the rhythm of a sentence or paragraph didn't work; she pounced on places where I needed more detail or less. Then Michael Ondaatje critiqued my first twenty-five pages and urged me to continue. He like Karen was sure my project could work. I finished the manuscript and sent it off.

Ellen Seligman became my editor at McClelland and Stewart. This was good fortune far beyond what I, such a novice (at sixty-five!), knew at the time. She phoned me one January afternoon when I had more or less given up hoping for an answer. It had been a whole year since the day I'd sent in my manuscript. I hadn't known if one was allowed to nudge a publisher but had sent a tentative and humble email off before Christmas, wondering if my ms. might have fallen behind a radiator. The email brought a swift and brief answer from Douglas Gibson, the President of M & S then, to whom I'd mistakenly sent my book (one does not send directly to the president; anyone else would have known that). He said he had passed it along to Ellen Seligman, the fiction editor. She was Michael's editor. I knew that, but my book was not fiction. Would she take it anyway? And had Mr. Gibson passed it along to her a whole year ago or recently?

It was on a day in early January that I heard. I was lying on my bed after lunch reading one of E. F. Benson's Lucia books as I liked to do every year or so and gazing out the window from time to time at some tiny snowflakes falling out of a grey sky. I was just home from spending Christmas with Jane in Berkeley. I barely dared any more to think of my book, which was somewhere out there — behind that dusty radiator or buried under a toppling pile of slush manuscripts or removed from such a pile and shredded.

And then the phone rang … and my life changed. It was Ellen. She had taken my manuscript to New York with her over the holiday and couldn't put it down. She loved it. She wanted to publish it.

I was a writer.

Working with Ellen became one of my peak life-joys, though our work together, when we got properly down to it, began with a shock. She had been so enthusiastic in that first phone call that when I received the first chunk of edited manuscript I was horrified: my erstwhile clean pages of script were covered with a storm of red pencil marks. They looked like a failing student essay dealt with by an exceedingly exasperated professor. I sat down in despair, shuffling through the papers, noting barely a page without Ellen's red comments. However, the situation was not as it seemed. On closer examination, many of her remarks were questions and positive things, sometimes even simply saying that a person I mentioned was someone she also knew. She had read with a kind of super attention.

And then our long editing phone calls began. I would be at my glorious desk, on my computer, my work in front of me on the screen. Ellen, who was suffering from a sore back, would be lying on her bed in Toronto, her copy held above her head. I hadn't met her then and I never saw her house, let alone her bedroom, but I had a clear picture of her in my mind, lying on a pale, cotton bedspread in a high-ceilinged white room. I even saw tall bed-posts, narrow and dark.

We would talk for three, possibly even four hours at a stretch. It felt intense and timeless. We prowled over the text, every descriptive phrase and line of dialogue. Our exploration was about language of course; it was also simply about me: what exactly happened the summer I was fourteen, or eighteen or twenty-one? Why was I fascinated by the furiously stomping bulls chained in my neighbour's barn? I remember that question and the deep thinking I had to do to come up with an answer. Over and over I would revisit a moment: what had it felt like and what had it looked like, the scene before me, the man I was looking at? She would say, "I think there is more," and "Go deeper." Or she would say, "That's far too much dialogue. Cut most of it."

Yet she never interfered and told me what she would say if she were the writer. There was a word I mentioned early on that she fastened on: what had I meant? She kept returning to it. The process had an element of therapy as she prodded me to dig away among long-buried emotions, to uncover and bring into the light of day, and into language, crucial threads of meaning. At the same time she was always respectful of its being my story not hers and that her role was to help me find it and tell it in my words. Ellen was a marvellous editor and I was supremely lucky to have her.

When the book, *I'll Tell You a Secret: A Memory of Seven Summers*, came out in 2004, it got considerable attention. Several pages in the *Globe and Mail* were devoted to it and there were other good reviews. I became a finalist for that year's Governor General's Award for Nonfiction. I won the Edna Staebler prize for creative nonfiction, given by Wilfrid Laurier University. I went on a book tour to Montreal and Toronto. I was invited to speak at a few universities and the book was even selected for several university courses. It was all immensely enjoyable. I loved that year.

I remember going with Carol to a writers' event at the King Edward

Hotel in Toronto. It was a breakfast event; I was to be on a panel with three other writers. We arrived in the very grand lobby to hear a baying roar of hundreds of voices floating down the wide staircase that led to the mezzanine. I couldn't imagine what sort of sports event could be happening in that place at that hour but we were told to go up. We ascended the stairs — and lo! — the noisy crowd was there for Louis de Bernières, and for me, Anne Coleman, and two local Toronto women whose names I unfairly forget. All these hundreds of dressed up people had each paid a hefty sum to hear us talk, as well as to eat eggs benedict and buttery croissants.

37

IT is a morning in late July 2008. I come in from my morning swim and as I step out of the sunshine and into the dimness of the hall I experience an unusual visual disturbance. I see a cascade of flickering white dazzle shimmering on the right side of my vision. It lasts only a second or two. I've had occasional migraines going back to earliest memory but this isn't at all the same sort of weirdness. It is on the opposite side of my head and the dazzle is only momentary. In fact even as a memory, a second later it's already floating away. I try to remember exactly what it was and I can't. This is odd. Why is my mind so fuzzy?

In case it's some sort of peculiar migraine I walk slightly unsteadily (why?) through to my bedroom and lie down. I cover my eyes with my arm. I almost doze off — but the phone is ringing. I reach out and grab it and it's Jane. I recognize her voice. Of course I do. My daughter. But I can't seem to understand what she's saying. I try to tell her to say it again but I can tell the words aren't coming out right. I realize that, at least. I know I can't talk properly now. That's something firm, knowing I know that. Jane is saying something about "Peter." I hear myself say, "Who's Peter?" Am I supposed to know who Peter is?

Jane's voice comes again: " Mum," she says, very firmly. "You must hang up and call 911. Right now. Will you do that. Mum?"

I say, "Yes," and I hang up and I dial the numbers 911.

I wait for the ambulance. I know that is the next thing: an

ambulance will come and I must open the front door of the building. I think I'll tell my neighbour, a close friend, what is happening. That seems sensible and I can also feel my mind starting to clear a little. Her apartment is just across the hall from mine. She and I both have large apartments on the ground floor of one of the old Victoria mansions. I step across and knock on her door, and then — I have no idea what her name is. She comes out and I tell her I'm going in an ambulance. I don't say I forget her name as it seems rude but I can tell her what is happening and I do. Really I'm definitely better. She looks at me in her serious way and says, "I'll follow in my car. I'll meet you at the hospital." She is frowning and studying me as if she is trying to read my eyes. She must be able to see that something is wrong with me. And then I remember her name. She is Lynn. Of course she is.

By the time the ambulance is whisking me through the city, the obscuring muzzy-mindedness is gone.

When I bring back that day in the hospital, I can see that I was curiously unworried by what had just happened, and then as the morning went on, even by what its consequence entailed, the hours of waiting and all the tests many different people performed on me with needles and machines. Was it shock or was it still the aftermath of the initial event? I walked as if floating, down long corridors, going where I was told. After each drawing of blood, each tightening of the blood-pressure cuff, each intrusion into my body of one device or another, I returned to where Lynn waited for me, Lynn, my friend, whose name I now steadily knew.

I feel no concern for my over-casual appearance and this strikes me as rather funny, though I still don't care. I am wearing the outfit like a pair of pyjamas that I pull on every summer morning to take me to the pool and back, a loose white, open-necked, million times washed

T-shirt and some baggy white cotton cheese-cloth pants I bought years ago from a street vendor in Berkeley. It's as if I'm invisible, or — in the opposite direction — too important to be criticized. I ponder which it is and decide it is the latter. I simply wander about the hospital corridors, obeying directions. Sometimes I am sitting down beside Lynn, just waiting. I balance the heel of one Birkenstock on the toe of the other. I study the way one of my pant legs is rolled up and the other is not, leaving one bare tanned leg on view almost to the knee, the other not. I look around at the few other people also waiting. I am the tallest and healthiest person in the room. Does that mean anything?

The last test involves lying on my back with my head inside a white machine that is a sort of hoop. I vaguely wonder if it's a CAT scanner, though I'm not sure exactly what it does, how it differs from an MRI. I think an MRI is the one that's more of a tunnel. Of course I've seen both scanners on doctor shows. Will this device show up some anomaly in my head's landscape if I've had a stroke? That must be the point surely. I still don't feel alarmed. I wander back along the hallway in my white pajamas. I feel nothing in particular.

I see ahead of me, yet again, the central waiting area and Dr. P. I know his name by now. After each test I've checked back with him. He seems a pleasant, very calm man. Now I walk up behind him where he is standing staring at a green screen. I come up beside him and I stare too. I see and recognize the picture even as I approach.

It is just like on the TV show *ER*, just like the moment when Dr. Mark Green first sees his fatal brain tumour. The image on Dr. P's large screen is clear. We both can see the white outline of a skull. The two halves of the brain are obvious, and there is a large fuzzed area that fills about a third, maybe rather more, of one side of it. I think, "That's not a brain a person would want to have as hers." I think it quite bemusedly, detachedly, but I know it is mine, really, even as I ask him, "Is that me?"

He turns and faces me though he doesn't quite meet my eyes.

"Yes," he says. "That's you." He touches a key and we see another image, the side-view. I've never seen the inside of my skull before. I've never wanted to think of what it might look like, without its normal covering of hair, skin, muscle, fat, any more than I would like to imagine my skeleton, flayed of all tissue. But the pictures, somehow, now that I see them, don't upset me.

He prints black and white copies of each image for me. "It"s a meningioma," he says. I've never heard the word. "It's almost certainly benign. But it's large."

It's obvious to me it's large. I don't know how large is seriously worrying, how large is fatal. But I don't ask. I don't want to know about that word "almost" either. He gives me two doctors' names and addresses and says both their offices will be phoning me to make appointments. They are a neurosurgeon and neurologist.

"The neurologist may have a view about what happened to you this morning," he says. "It could have been a migraine. It may not have been the tumour at all."

He just mutters this as if it's a tentative suggestion only. It seems obvious to me, and I think to him, that the tumour and the "event" are linked. The episode was too different from any migraine I'd ever had.

"I'll want to tell my nephew about this," I tell him. "He's a neuro-surgeon in Denver."

Dr. P. resents this remark, judging by his suddenly pained expression. "If you were in the States," he says, "you'd be in surgery by tonight having it out. We're more relaxed here."

I have no idea if this is a good point or a bad. Should we be relaxed about this?

Dr. P. gives me two sheets he prints up of the Wikipedia definition of meningioma. I hold them lightly between my fingers. I am not ready to read them.

Lynn drives me home. I phone Jane right away to reassure her. And of course I have remembered who "Peter" is, the name I was confounded by in our earlier non-conversation. He has been the cause

INLAND NAVIGATION BY THE STARS 227

of enormous stress for weeks: no wonder Jane was thrown by my blank response to his name.

+

Two weeks pass before I meet with the neurosurgeon. The neurologist has just gone on holiday so it will be even longer before I can see him. Two weeks can feel long as a person waits to get a date to have her head opened.

I talk to my nephew Teddy, via SKYPE, and I show him my scan pictures. Talking to him I remember another hospital detail. "The ER doctor said it was the size of a golf ball."

Teddy looks quizzical, "Maybe more a tennis ball?"

He assumes I'll be having it removed, given the size. I ask him if it can come out a small hole. I have an image I can cope with of its being sucked out. I have no idea of the density of a tumour, if it is a soft, even squishy thing, or hard. And what about lasers? Aren't operations often done that way these days? Again, a nice, tiny and tidy aperture, and a ray darting swiftly in: presto! End of tumour.

Not, please not, a major dismantling of my head.

"No," Teddy says, "I'm afraid the opening would have to be at least as large as the tumour."

"So can they make a flap and just lean it to the side?" I picture a hinge. "Or does the whole piece of skull get lifted right off and laid away on a side table?" It somehow bothers me a lot to envisage part of my head placed at a distance from the rest of it. The rest of me.

"It has to come right off." Teddy makes the gesture I just had made, two hands removing the skull-top and putting it over somewhere to his left. I see a soft-boiled egg. My teaspoon makes a neat tap and cracks the shell. I lift away the top with its half-spoonful of firm white, which I scoop out and eat first. And now the runny yoke is exposed, ready for "soldiers" of toast to be dipped. But this will be my head. There won't be a neat teaspoon-tap but rather — what, exactly? There will have to be a drill, or a small sharp-toothed electrical saw. Maybe both will be required. Or a chisel and a hammer. The laid-aside lid — will it be right side up, showing a rounded, pink, shaved surface no one has glimpsed since I was a newborn with thin wisps of pale curls, or upside down, a shallow saucer of bone? Will there be blood on it, bits of brain?

It is unfortunate to have an imagination in these circumstances. I tame it as best I can. I play with the images that slip past my defences. Doing that keeps them at arm's length. I make blackly funny jokes to my friends about the difference in ball images: a golf ball is smaller but it's so dense and hard, meaner than a tennis ball which is furry, hollow, pleasant in the hand. Far less damaging to be hit with a tennis ball than a golf ball. I think of sad old dead tennis balls, grey, no longer fuzzy, dinged in on one side. I've found them in the back of cottage cupboards. On the other hand, I remember as a child peeling the cover off an old golf ball and discovering what seemed to be densely packed rubber bands. Rotting ones. Not nice at all. So which do I choose to have in my head?

As if I have a choice! It's the way we sometimes talk, my friends and I, now we are elderly, about how we choose to die. We all agree we'll go quietly in our sleep, after a happy day. We will be very old, and tired in a gentle way, and ready. For a moment, as we see ourselves, years hence, sweetly sleeping ourselves away, we hold the illusion we will have that power of decision.

It has to be that the bigger the tumour is, the more deadly, but as best I can I repress the actuality of this unwelcome squatter in my head. A kind of silly dramatizing of it in conversation keeps its reality at bay. That mode of operating — denial, something supposedly bad — has always helped me cope and I do it now.

Though remembering that Teddy mentioned calcification, that there seemed maybe quite a bit of it, I feel a tactile image pushing momentarily a little closer. The thing itself is turning partially to bone? I think now he meant it to be a good sign. Something calcifying doesn't sound very lively. I can allow my imagination to see that image.

INLAND NAVIGATION BY THE STARS 229

Dealing with the upcoming operation is a taxing job for my denial defence system.

My friend Anita has told me that she remembers the aftermath of her heart surgery as of herself drifting in a pleasant dream but knowing she was surrounded by loving care. It was blissful, she says. I remember it differently. I sat by her hospital bed and she whimpered and bleated like a baby, clearly experiencing a horrible combination of discomfort, lostness and fear. She has forgotten that. Maybe I'll forget it too but first I'll have it. In the lead-up to seeing the surgeon I firmly thrust away my memory of how Anita had really been.

When my old friend Clem got his brain tumour he developed a new personality, an unhappy and angry one. This alteration overtook his earlier sunny self for at least a couple of years before he had the seizure that led to a diagnosis so there's no real way of knowing the role the tumour played or how long it had been there invading his brain tissue. So, have I been altering? I still love my family and friends. I didn't turn on anyone, as Clem so upsettingly did. But am I, in subtle ways, no longer the person I've always felt myself to be? I first recognized my very specific individuality, the clear edges of myself, the ways I was distinct in the world and different from anyone else, when I was very young. I want to be her still, that girl. I'd thought I was. But am I? Was the tumour there already when I wrote my memoir of my girlhood and called up that old self so clearly — that old self that I want to be still? My family and friends assure me I am unchanged ...

My tumour, this meningioma, is of another order than Clem's. His was a glioblastoma and viciously malignant. Mine is not truly a brain tumour at all in that it's situated in the meninges, the skull lining. Thus it isn't, like his, invading brain tissue. What it's doing is shoving into it. Pictures flicker like little films: a golf or tennis ball mindlessly shouldering into my head the way a glacier moves into and over and scours a landscape, creating moraines all around its edges. Crumpled ridges of heaved up brain tissue can't serve a person's thinking well, even if the thrusting invader doesn't actually breach the walls. I can keep the films at bay in the daylight, not always at night. We hear so much now about the brain's plasticity, how it can rewire itself. Did my tumour grow slowly enough for my brain to compensate for it?

✦

An MRI has been booked for me. It is my first and is a surprise as no one warned me either of the time it took or the noise, but as with everything else I simply do what I'm told, accepting anything however odd or puzzling. Later I am told I should have been given earplugs and warned of both noise and duration. But I have been swallowed up by the medical process and move along within it obediently. For someone who likes to be in control as much as I do, my unquestioning calm is surprising.

After the MRI I am back to waiting. I do not conform to my normal behaviour as an academic. I don't research meningiomas during this waiting period. The Wikipedia definition Dr. P. handed me is worrying enough in certain paragraphs and my swift glances at a couple of websites I find on Google are too distressing to pore over. There is one site called Meningioma-UK on which survivors compare post-surgery sufferings and share means of coping with their various levels of incapacity. I allow my eyes only the briefest glimpse and repress, repress. Ignorance is helpful. I use my famously strong will to hold onto it.

I wash and iron my silk scarves. I will want to wear them to cover baldness and scars.

My sister Carol says she will come and look after me, post-surgery. I tell her to wait so I can enjoy her visit properly and do things with her. She has been an OR nurse; she assures me she will be coming at or right after the operation. I don't ask her why she thinks this necessary.

But even if I don't want medical details, I do ponder death.

It may happen much sooner than I'd anticipated and I am not ready for it. How should I think of it? One middle-of-the-night revelation is oddly comforting, also surprising: I realize that however unready to die I am right now, I might want to die sometime. If one's life had to go on forever, if one knew one could never, ever, get out, or step off — that could be a worse nightmare. I say "step off" because I picture it as being like one of those boardwalks I've been on that pass over swamps in the rain forest. Mossy, slippery, they go on for miles. They snake off into the mist and there is nothing one can do but plod on. And on. And on. I see my figure, for some reason from the back — I suppose that way I am more anonymous, also more pathetic — hunched and tired, shuffling ever onward, in endless, relentless forward movement. Please, no, God. Let there be an end. Sometime.

But I hope not quite yet. Please God, give me time to be more ready than I am right now. I'm not old yet and I want time to figure out what it's all been about, what it's been for, my life.

The day of my appointment with the neurosurgeon finally arrives. My oldest friend in the city, Sonya, is coming with me. We met when we were eighteen, in our second year at McGill, and we have supported each other through many a drama over fifty-plus years. We have particularly promised to be each other's advocate in such situations as I now face. We know how impossible it is to take in terrifying things doctors say, or even non-terrifying, simply practical things, when one is so ready to self-protect and keep ears blocked. Sonya has supplied herself with pen and notebook and sits at the ready beside me, both of us across from the doctor.

He is leaning back in his chair, his eyes moving as he glances at us and then up at a screen on which my MRI is playing out, page after page turning on a hinge. The black and grey images are hard to see from where I sit, as the machine is high up over my left shoulder, but

I'd not have been able to interpret them in any case. The doctor seems puzzled by our presence.

"So what is your concern?" he asks.

I've prepared a list of questions. I wrote them down so I'd not forget them. They are all to do with the surgery I am sure will be happening. But as soon as I mention the word "operation," he is clearly surprised, as if he can't imagine why I'd be expecting one.

"Oh, there will be no surgery," he says. "That would be a very bad idea. I'd definitely not advise it."

This is such startling news that I am dumbfounded. I can't think now what to ask him. Does he mean it is too late to do anything?

"But — there is a tumour?" I manage that much.

"Yes, indeed there is. It's somewhat over four centimetres across at the widest point. It's not symmetrical; some of it is just four, or even a little less." He goes on, "Some people do insist on surgery. Psychologically, they can't come to terms with having such a thing in their heads. But the risk — in your case a very high risk, with the tumour right up against the venous cavernous — is that you'd have a massive stroke during the operation."

I sit there trying to take this in. My head will not be cracked open like an egg. I am stunned.

It seems he has nothing further to say. We are meant to leave, so we do.

I walk out the door, Sonya at my shoulder. We share our reactions in the elevator. For my part I feel guilt as well as confusion, as if I should be ashamed at my foolishness in taking myself and my tumour seriously. I've made a mountain out of a small molehill. Yet a tumour over four centimetres across — isn't it serious? Is it really just a molehill? And what about all those people on that Meningioma-UK website whose post-surgery stories I'd skimmed? What about Teddy saying it is so large, it will almost certainly have to come out? What about my friend Donnie's sister who is having an operation for a meningioma this very week in Ontario? The only further information the doctor has given me is that I must have another MRI in six months. Above all why did we leave Dr. H.'s office so swiftly and ask nothing? It was as if we'd been obeying a voiced command of his and yet he'd actually simply turned his attention away from us.

As Sonya drives me home I think of the things I'd been too startled and bemused to ask: what had that episode of complete confusion been about then — if it was the tumour (and how could it not have been?) how likely is it, or something even worse, to happen in the future? What about driving — am I safe to do it? How swollen is my brain around the tumour — those moraines I'd pictured — and what are the implications as time passes? How do people with a meningioma this large, and left to itself, tend to function, as years pass? I hadn't managed to summon, let alone voice, any of these crucial perplexities in time and neither had Sonya. What a pair we had been!

Teddy expresses satisfaction with what Dr. H. has said. Even though he'd wondered before if surgery should be the best option, after he examines the MRI — which I mail him and which he watches on a machine at his Denver hospital — he agrees that to wait and see is the best course. The threat of a major stroke during surgery is a real one. And he repeats and enlarges on a detail he'd told me before but that Dr. H. hadn't mentioned: that the extent of calcification visible on the CAT scan (though not on the MRI) really is a good sign of the thing not being likely to grow with any speed, if at all.

My appointment with Dr. S., the neurologist, is for August 10. His office is a half-hour's drive up the island in the little central shopping area of a small rural community. I consider I can handle this visit on my own, assuming nothing too horrendous can be said with surgery out of the picture. Indeed I'm not sure why this visit is necessary, but at least I can ply him with some of the questions I'd not thought of in time with Dr. H. I plan to stop for corn and tomatoes at a farm gate on the way back, so that will be a certain benefit of the expedition.

It rained in the morning and is still cloudy, the air heavy. It will probably rain again. I splash across the little parking lot searching for the right door which turns out to be around the side of the building. I find Dr. S. to be patient, easy to question, careful to be clear in his answers. He looks at me questioningly after each statement he makes, to be sure I've understood him. And what he tells me is enormously reassuring. He has absolutely no doubt that the "episode" had nothing to do with the tumour. How I wished Dr. H. had mentioned this! I would have been spared my anxiety about that sooner. I suppose it was out of his purview.

Dr. S. tells me very firmly that migraines can suddenly manifest in an entirely different manner from how they ever have before, especially if one is under stress. And the particular symptoms are not that unusual even if never experienced by me before. Because of the placement of the tumour, on the right lobe of my brain and towards the front, it can't possibly have caused my hearing and speech problems. My dread of further periods of scary mental confusion, periods that could intensify and lengthen, become something much more manageable. Migraines will likely still happen to me, even ones like that last, but I will know that is what they are. No one loses her mind permanently during a migraine, not that I've ever heard.

I leave Dr. S.'s office. I can't get over how different his manner was from Dr. H.'s. Had there been something about Sonya and me that had put the neurosurgeon seriously off — our unusual height and straight posture making us seem "entitled," in an unpleasant way, as well as our holding notebooks and pens at the ready? Or had he just been in bad mood about something else entirely? I'll never know.

As I recross the wet parking lot I have a lovely sensation throughout my body: a tight wire of tension is releasing. I literally feel lightened, as if I am full of light. And I see that I am surrounded by a world also suffused with light. The summer fields, the wide, cloud-piled sky, are all awake. I drive home slowly, taking the long route by the sea and stopping for corn and tomatoes and new potatoes as I'd planned to do. The sun is now fully out and the clouds are drifting off westwards to pile behind the mountains across the bay.

I choose my vegetables, taking my time, taking all the time in the world. I gaze at the now blue water and the fields of ripening grass that slope down to the shore. I do these things not as I have in recent weeks, consciously striving for small ways to comfort myself. I do them with full joy. I pat a tomato and sniff my fingers for the warm and spicy smell. I peer into an ear of corn to see its glistening yellow kernels.

Death was very close for a bit. I felt his cold fingers. But he has retreated. He was just teasing me. For now.

38

BESIDES writing, there was another road-not-taken long ago that I at last stepped out along in retirement. After I graduated from McGill back in 1957 my father offered me the chance to study in England, perhaps to take a B.Phil., maybe even a master's degree, at Oxford or Cambridge. It was a bribe. He hoped that if I went the lure of Frank would fade. But it was too late. I was Frank-ensnared and had to play out that drama to its fated end. How different my life might have been had I gone to England then! Probably I would have had a different husband, different children. But it is impossible to want different children! My mind cannot go there. I also wonder now if there could have been something else keeping me from accepting the chance to study in England, as well as the Frank-plot's demands. I had been encultured to think of English universities as superior to our Canadian imitations. Many of my professors were indeed English but likely, we supposed, of the second rank, not wanted at Oxford or Cambridge where surely they would have preferred to be. I may well have feared a colonial inadequacy to test myself in the realer (in the Platonic sense) universities of Oxford or Cambridge. I suspect there was something of that.

In any case, however differently things could have played out long ago, when I discovered the Oxford Experience, a summer program offered by Christ Church, I was able to live a version of that barely entertained dream. For seven summers — the first one in 1998 and the rest from 2010 to 2015 — I went and took a range of courses.

I dearly loved those two-week stays. Yet for the first time since I began doing this, I have not arranged to go in this summer of 2016. I am not sure why, if it is the prospect of turning eighty in July, or if it is simply that I've had enough of long-distance flights, or if the unsettledness of Europe right now plays a role. Or is it that writing this memoir has pulled all my attention? A bit of each, I think.

My late-life Oxford summers were perfect: I had two spacious, airy, high-ceilinged and deep-window-seated rooms in Peckwater Quad, a lovely Palladian building in Christ Church.

Every early morning I crossed my own quad and then Tom Quad and slipped out the just-opened main massive gate under Tom Tower. St. Aldate's Street was quiet, unlike its later noisy trafficky self, and I made my way down it to the also just-opened gate to Christ Church Meadows. I loved the fact of those heavy, solid, ancient college gates, the way life turned inward in the evenings, locked itself up against outsiders. Almost every window faced the quad rather than the surrounding street and the lanes. From dusk to dawn the ancient buildings, the quads and gardens, the Cathedral, all were only for the initiated. The tourists (mostly European and Asian youths) who swarmed in by day were locked out.

When I walked through the Quads at night, the past drew near in my imagination: the seething long history of striving and scholarship, the ghosts of ousted Wolsey and fat, terrible Henry, and also of gentle Charles the First with his mournful face and long curls and his Henrietta Maria under siege in Christ Church before they chopped off his head. Much later came Alice and her strange friend. And all through the centuries the students in their black gowns and severity (some) and in their wildness and drunkenness (others), like Evelyn Waugh and his circle and many later still. In regular term time now there is plenty of bad behaviour but much hard work too and there are also girls now. But for generation after generation, hundreds of years of generations, it was all men. The portraits of the famous who line the Great Hall are all men. But then — there was I, at long last, and I felt at home as if it were as much my place as theirs. I was a student too.

At dawn the ghosts slink back into the shadows of the cloisters. There is not another soul about, either living or dead, as I walk the Meadows footpath, north along the wall of Masters Garden then east behind Merton. I look up at the open casement windows and wonder who is within, waking up — an ancient crotchety scholar or a pair of young lovers? No one ever looks out.

Then, after passing Rose Cottage and the lane up to the Botanic Garden, I turn southward under the shade of thickly hanging foliage and walk along the Cherwell riverbank. The water is dark and moves swiftly, sleek as an animal. Then I reach the point where the vista opens up and I see the Thames itself, much wider and sparking with sun everywhere the water is stirred by a duck's passage. There are houseboats moored across the water, each houseboat its own little world, with potted plants and even lettuces and herbs on the roof, and a sweet-faced young man in pyjama pants comes out on deck to sniff the morning air. I watch for a moment his sleepy face and I imagine his life; in a second see it all: his girl is still asleep below, her cheeks rosy and warm, her fair hair tousled on the pillow. She wakes and yawns and smiles to herself. He will go inside again and make her a cup of tea. (How? I don't know the cooking arrangements on a houseboat, what sort of stove they'd have. I lose the image.)

I head west along the Thames. There are several people in sight here: two girls jogging, an old man and his dog. On the smooth sun-glinting water a couple of single-scull shells slice along. I hear the sound of their oars, even one young rower's breathing as he passes closely by. The morning is awake now, for some at least. I leave the river and walk north again up the much wider footpath under trees that make a tunnel up to the Meadows building. I see three pale long-horned cows on the meadow. They make me think of Paul and his Charolais bulls so my son is in the moment too.

Those were perfect English, Oxford summer mornings, just as I had long dreamed them and now had them. And still have them.

39

IT is 2016, just over a year since Carol died.

My sister was there from my very earliest awareness of the world. Two and a half years older than I, she was my best friend, the sharer of doll-play, tree climbing, naughtiness, the one who stepped ahead of me into life, giving me someone to follow or to test myself against. Of course we fought as children but mostly we were in league with each other.

When we were very small, Carol perhaps five, I three, she used to plan to run away. She and our mother used to have battles royal. As I mentioned at the beginning of my tale, perhaps because they were alike, their relationship could be stormy. Carol, pink-faced with outrage, would set out to leave forever and I would come along, just to the top of our block. I don't recall her having any supplies with her but even so I always took the final goodbye seriously. There we would stand on green spring grass under a weeping birch tree and she would sing a song of farewell. The only lines either of us could remember as adults went "have no food at night, sleep in haystacks bright." Then I would trudge homeward crying and Carol would perhaps go farther around the block (we were not allowed to cross Ava Road) but after a little while she would return too.

Each time I believed in her runaway and in a way I think she did herself, in a "magical thinking" fashion. We had a similar suspension of disbelief about flying: we were sure that we should be able to fly as we jumped from the corner of the verandah over the rockery — a big jump — if we could just get our flying power operating before our feet met the ground. We never managed, yet might the next time. When Carol was dying the word "haystacks" became a code for her final leave-taking. I used it in my last email to her. Once she was on her way to Switzerland we could no longer Skype as we had done daily all year, so our last messages were by email. I have kept hers:

"Don't be sad, I know I am doing the right thing. Kids terrific, Ruthie an angel. Much love, Carol."

Reading it again, and then typing it out here, I think of her typing it, over in a Swiss hotel, her last words to her little sister. Short because she could type only with extreme difficulty by then, her hands had become so feeble. It makes me cry. She was so very brave.

We each had an idea of what the worst possible ending would be. For me it was (still is, if it comes back, for I have had an episode of it) colon cancer, for Carol, ALS. She had nursed a patient with it long ago when she was a student nurse. She was glad to remember, all the years later when she suffered from it herself, that she had felt only compassion for the woman and none of the fear and even disgust a different young girl might feel in cleaning someone up in such distress and incapacity. I remember back then asking her how it was possible for her to do these things without getting disgusted (we both as children had been appalled at anyone throwing up) and she said that it always felt at the time like a privilege to be helping another person in such an intimate way and it was impossible for disgust to enter in. The suffering was all theirs, not hers. Carol became a nurse any patient would have been lucky to have.

She was already very sick herself when I went in for my colon cancer surgery but she was the first person on the phone to me when I came round. We both wished we could be roomies, side by side in our beds, but I was in Victoria and she in Toronto.

The first signs of Carol's illness snuck up on her, as ALS does. The illness cannot be diagnosed except by elimination of every other possible thing it might be. She began to have falls. For some time one can argue with oneself that there was a reason for the fall, like the wrong shoes. We both had the same kind for a while and both of us took a tumble in them. I remember joking with her, saying, "Well, my Mephistos hurled me to the ground too!" We vowed to throw the shoes out, which worked for me, falling-wise, but not for Carol. Her falling went on. Explained as an unexpected curb or a patch of ice.

The most horrible fall, which still makes me quiver to think of her experiencing it, was when she got up in the night to go down for something to eat and fell right down the stairs into the tiled hall, breaking off her two front teeth. I can't bear it, that image of her lying on the tiles, bleeding from her mouth. Yet this memory with its precise detail is a puzzling example of the peculiar tricks memory can play: Carol's daughter Ruthie remembers the broken teeth happening in quite a different way. It seems more likely Ruthie would be right — she was in the same city at the time, although not in the house — yet my images are so vivid. Could I have misheard my sister or did my mind all on its own create a more elaborate scenario? Or could Carol have told me something she could not bear for her daughter to know? Carol! Why can't I ask you?

But it began to be apparent that living in her charming four-story Cabbagetown house was becoming dangerous for her. From then on everything happened nightmarishly fast. From being able, in the summer, to go about the city with a cane, even get on and off the subway and more or less have her normal life, by mid-autumn she had to face terrifying and still mysterious facts.

Carol had been so healthy. She had been athletic, a tennis player when younger, and until the illness began its insidious assault, had walked long distances with her dog or dogs (she usually had more than one) every day. She was slim and fit, hadn't smoked for decades, didn't drink and ate exceptionally healthily. She was almost but not entirely a vegetarian. I think we both more or less assumed we'd live as long as our mother, who died at almost ninety-three.

INLAND NAVIGATION BY THE STARS 243

Her move to more practical premises had to happen quickly given the rate of her deterioration. Over the late fall her children took over the sorting out and selling of her house. By the time the snow flew she was bed-bound at her daughter's house.

Through the months of her illness Carol was astonishingly uncomplaining. The disease moved up her limbs. It took her body inch by inch. Before this we had often dramatized to each other little incidents in our daily lives. It was the family habit to create stories, to surprise and intrigue each other, to make each other laugh at our own or others' absurdity. But Carol did not dramatize her illness. It was real and there was no point or purpose in drama; that would make matters worse, also be exhausting. When coping with true horror she had done this before: in her grief after her husband Vince's horrific and untimely death she explained to me how easy it would be to let go, to scream and wail and flail about, but if she were to give in to that urge all control might go out the window. She could go on screaming forever.

In our daily conversations throughout the ALS nightmare we talked frankly. I learned of each fresh indignity as it came along but we also, and indeed mostly, talked of what she was reading or watching on TV, and often about our lives, our childhoods together, our girlhoods, our lives as wives. We both remembered so much, though often our memories of the same event or person were quite different. Even in the recent past Carol had usually needed to have the upper hand about such things. She would be adamant her version was the true one. Simply she was the Big Sister and knew best. I would eventually back off even if I knew I was right.

I'm not describing fighting or even quarrelling. It just was the pattern laid down when we were small. Carol needed the last word. During her illness that no longer happened. Our talks were reflective not competitive and we laughed a lot. Our brother talked to her every day too and sometimes all three of us talked together.

Carol stayed beautiful. She had high cheekbones, huge eyes — "speaking" eyes — and an amazing smile. Her hair, cut shorter than usual by her daughter, for easier care, was still thick and curly.

Once she had her diagnosis Carol was determined not to put herself and her family through the end phase of the disease. She began working on a plan to be taken to Switzerland. The process was appallingly fraught with hoops to jump through constantly multiplying. Fearing she would be too disabled to go at all made her last months a nightmare but the trip was arranged at last. She wanted only her four children with her. She needed it to be simple.

On the way to the airport she looked out the taxi window. It was October. "Oh my goodness," she said in a quiet voice. "I missed summer." That always makes me cry to think of it, she loved summer so much.

After the enormous vexation of the red tape, and above all her terror that she would not complete it in time, the actual end was easy for her. The doctor gave her a first medication to calm her — though she was very calm — and then shortly thereafter, the second. She gave a small yawn, closed her eyes, and was gone.

How I miss my sister! A whole year has passed and I still have things I "need" to tell her, things I "have to" ask her. There is so much of my life that was also her life and no one else's. I miss her company and the fun of her conversation. I miss her love for me. When things happen to me that are good I want to share them with her. She was always so generous in being happy for me. And when I face scary things, especially medical things, I want her reassurance and her comfort. But her facing death so fearlessly, knowing it was coming nearer and nearer, and that she would soon go into that darkness or (I wish!) that light, makes it possible for me to face it too.

Carol had not wanted a service. Or so she had maintained to Chuck and me. But at the very end she decided she did. I don't know exactly why she changed her mind. She had been anti-church for years. I am very glad she wanted it after all as it was important for all of us to gather and talk of her, and the church itself was important: Grace Church on-the-Hill, in our familiar Forest Hill. It was the church where we had gone as children, and where she had been married, and where her husband's funeral had been. The service was beautiful and fitting. It was not "closure," a word I hate. Carol will never be "closed" while those who loved her remember her.

For my visits to her in the years since she moved to Toronto's Cabbagetown in the late 80s, we rarely ever even drove through Forest Hill. But Ruthie's house, where Carol had spent her last months and where we all gathered after her death, is there and the friend I stayed with lives in Lawrence Park, close to Havergal, my old school, I found it comforting to be in the Toronto that took me back to our childhood. No, it was more than merely comforting; it was a return to something fundamental and healing. I was amazed by how strongly being in Forest Hill again affected me. I thought I'd more or less repudiated Toronto as mattering to me, long preferring first Quebec and then the West. But as I walked through the streets everything was dearly familiar. There were the brilliant, Ontario-fall colours, quite unlike a western October's limited pallet of yellows and ochres. And the houses were different in every detail from the West Coast houses my eye is used to now. Instead of wood, they are all brick and stone, with timbering, and they are set in an unusual close-togetherness with just narrow alleyways between them.

Alleyways! We don't even have the word out here in the West. I knew those alleyways intimately. I had spent countless childhood hours with Carol, bouncing a ball against the brick walls of a Forest Hill alleyway. There was a chant that began, "Ordinary, moving, laughing, talking ..." I could play the game this minute if I had a ball and a brick wall.

I don't want to live in Forest Hill again but being there at that time of heightened emotion had a dream quality, a good dream. It was the place where I'd woken up to life, the place of my so lucky beginning.

With Carol gone Death has stepped closer to me. My two elder sisters have slipped away into mystery, both much earlier in their lives than our mother in hers or even our father, who died before her, at eighty-two. Ruth went quietly and unexpectedly, alone in her hospital bed. Carol took a glass into her own by then frail hand and sipped from it, with her children at her bedside watching. It will be my turn next.

Going on before me in the spring after Carol's death were two of the people I've written about here, still alive when I began the writing. The first was long expected: Doug Jones. I had not seen him for years so he was a memory already for me though an important one. But I am glad to be able to comfort his daughter, my sweet Tory, and through her I have a link with him as we look at his pictures together and speak of him. The second death was a shock: wonderful Ellen Seligman. I had longed to have the chance to work with her again, to experience her sharp intelligence and her warmth and understanding.

40

I am nearly a decade on from that frightening few weeks when I starkly faced the fact of my mortality. In the middle of the long summer nights of that period, Death felt so close he was breathing on me, and cold and nasty breaths they were. I have had other brushes with him since. Yet between such visitations, in my pleasure in my daily life I feel as alive as I ever have, all the more so for having recognized there is a limit.

But do I have to admit I'm old now?

So many sensations are the same as they have always been:

Sex, with all its delights and secrets, is a completed chapter except sometimes in dreams or when the Pearl Fishers' duet or a Chopin nocturne touches a sweet nerve. But the other senses compensate. I am content to be free of sex's power now.

Above all I still love the people I love as keenly as I ever did. People who bore me or sap my spirit I still shake loose or drift away from as I always have. Gently, I hope.

I can only trust I can keep my keen response to the world right to the end. My sisters did. Carol kept her funny bone right to the point she slipped over death's threshold. We were laughing in our last conversation. Crying too but the laughter was also real.

Whatever my essential core of energy is now, wherever it goes later, I have dearly loved being alive in this body. My life has been a gift. When

I try to arrive at its "point" it has to relate to that: the preciousness of life and how I have always, whether consciously or not, but mostly quite consciously, paid attention to what I find lovely and lovable.

My brother is now seventy-five and still wants to go everywhere he's not yet been. I respect that desire of his and hope he gets to see as much of the world as he can possibly fit in. But for my part I don't need now to see everything. I have travelled widely and am glad I have but I don't need to fly to China or go on a cruise around the Hawaiian Islands. What I do want is to pay full attention to what I am seeing, even if it is right here in Victoria as I set off for my morning swim and the chestnut candles are suddenly alight in their creamy radiance, just since yesterday. Each season pulls my attention to something new. This May it was a pink dogwood. I passed a lane and there it was, as if just invented. And this morning I noticed an amazing handkerchief tree across from the library that quite unaccountably I've missed in other years.

But when I think of how we are encouraged constantly these days to live in the moment, to focus on the here and now, I know that that is not what I mean, or not precisely, because in the middle of any experience, however engaging, I am not only in the present. I can't be and I don't want to be. My present is shot through with the light and the glinting images and the shifting shadows of memory. This spring, as I've done other springs, I am experiencing echoes of Forest Hill rock gardens and lilac, Pointe-Claire peonies, Narnian wild penstemon and lupins. The tiny white daisies by the seaside path this morning called up the first time I saw lawn daisies and I had a flash of Carol and Vince and me: it is a May morning in 1978. We are standing on a lawn in Salisbury, looking up at the ancient and massive cathedral which soars against a Constable sky of piled clouds. All around us are tiny daisies in the grass that none of us ever noticed anywhere before. We are all in the charmed state of being in love with England. We love everything we see. We are about to walk across this sunny daisy lawn and enter the coolness of the cathedral.

INLAND NAVIGATION BY THE STARS 249

Am I sentimental in experiencing many moments as palimpsests? People often use the term "sentimental" to disparage emotion they don't happen to feel, rather than the falsely worked up emotion the term is meant to describe. It is a tricky term for surely we can't judge the validity of another person's feelings. Perhaps we can know for sure only if we ourselves are being sentimental.

The writer and feminist critic Carolyn Heilbrun despised nostalgia. She thought it absurd to spend time reflecting on her past, as if any such reflection would be sentimental or at least a waste of time. Well in advance she vowed to die at sixty, to kill herself before her world narrowed with age. In the actual playing out of her life she allowed herself an extra decade. She even wrote a book called *The Last Gift of Time*, about the unexpected pleasures of her sixties. Then she killed herself at seventy. As far as I've been able to discover she wasn't ill or sensing oncoming dementia; she had a husband and other family members who loved her. Could it be, I wonder, that in trouncing her past so successfully as she went along, successfully forbidding nostalgia any houseroom in her brain, she depleted her old age just too much?

Writing this memoir has compelled me to face what my life has all been about, to winkle out the central theme of what I likened at the outset to a novel. As a literature teacher I would analyse my life. In the writing I have been tugged in one direction and then another, sorting through what has been important, what I have learned, what people and things have enriched my life or tested me sharply, what I have survived by the skin of my teeth, and where I have flown, where I am tough and what are my weaknesses. Family life and motherhood have been the central thread, a thread of industrial strength, and teaching was part of the same impulse. I loved my job and my students as if it and they were extensions of my family. And I played it all out against the beauty of the natural and human-created world I had the good fortune to inhabit and that I loved. Love is my central theme and my happy good fortune is that I found it in many places.

And my sins. Do I have sins in my past? I am not sure of as grand a word as "sins," but I have judged people too harshly sometimes, entirely unfairly sometimes. Revisiting past scenes has shown me this fault of mine. I have revised judgments and will tell people so — those who are still alive. I allowed my daughter to be hurt by my second marriage choice. There is no way around that one. Though she has forgiven me I don't forgive myself.

I expect that most people do a sort of magical thinking about death. I certainly did myself and do even now much of the time, and I do it about age as well. Mostly I don't really think of myself as old, not in the way I used to think being "old" was, anyway. I am just myself: Anne. Mum. Gran. Great-gran.

So — am I old? I can't be, surely, not I. I keep shoving off the doomy threshold into a more distant future. Sixty was going to be old, then seventy, then eighty. Now I'm wondering about ninety.

For a while I preferred to use the word "elderly" to describe myself; it didn't feel as old as "old," to me. But people have told me that "elderly," for them, is even older than "old." I don't care who knows my actual age. I just don't see that word "old" as describing me, nor "elderly" now either. I'm refusing both labels.

So what word does describe me, at this stage? Even aside from actual medical events I am a little less than I was, in my body. Certain changes have crept up, each tiny erasure or loss slipping away subtly, unnoticed until perhaps months have passed: an inch of height gone, only signalled because a pair of old pants was mysteriously crumpling at my ankles. Or the realization that I don't swim as many lengths of my pool: I did a couple fewer lengths after a holiday lapse, assuming I'd work up to my old total in a bit. I didn't. I'm still two down.

Is this just a reduced attention span for a repetitive exercise or do I get tired sooner? I don't analyse these things. There is a walk I used to do that involved a tricky stretch where I had to leap from rock to rock, below a cliff and above the sea. One day I realized I'd not done it for ages — had it just been the rainy winter weather? Yet I didn't want to do it again. At the same time I am still to some degree vigorous. I do swim every day and walk for at least an hour. I garden. I accept my new weaknesses but ignore them and don't allow them to define me.

The core of me, my independence, my sense of my enormous luck, my love of a multitude of people and things — those certainties of self are all still in place. I am still Anne. I am still that child/girl/woman who probably has always talked too much in too loud a voice but still loves doing so, who was told long ago that her strides were too long but still steps out, and fast, in exactly the same way. I am still, in crucial essentials, the same person as that small curly-haired girl, aged two, who woke in her crib, climbed up and over the side and trotted down the hall to her mother, who was pleased to see her.

As well as the discovery of the tumour in my head, the event I described in some detail and which precipitated these reflections, I've had other ominously death-portending events. Each episode or discovery was scary until it was, at least temporarily, resolved. But it was not as scary as I might have imagined it would be. When I am in the eye of the storm there is a kind of pause that happens — is it fatalism? I don't know. But it is like an indrawn breath. It is as if I tell myself, "I will not take this in fully." And what is more, I obey! This is quite unlike the kind of intensity of fear I feel when something threatens one of my children. There is not the slightest comparison between my anxiety over my tumour and my terror over my son's malignant melanoma surgery, which happened not that long after.

A heart flutter took me by surprise a year or so ago. It should not have been a surprise as heart issues took my father and both his siblings and also my eldest sister, Ruth, and among those of us still alive, my brother, my nephew, my son and now even a grandson have atrial fibrillation, but somehow I assumed my own heart would follow my mother's. We all take our pills and for my part I seldom think of it in terms of me, though I hate being the conduit of such a weakness that I've passed to younger people I love so much.

Another mortal jolt arose from a routine check, a colonoscopy. I watched the screen with fascination as the gastroenterologist created a science fiction film of my innards. Owing to the sedative I remained intrigued and entertained as he explained what he was finding: a large — though that was partly the magnification — unattractive sea-monster lump that was certainly cancerous. The not-fascinating upshot was surgery of course. It went well and required no chemotherapy.

These events, all three — head tumour, heart flutter discovery, colon cancer — were all easier in the facing of and follow-up than I ever would have expected when I was younger. The word "cancer," especially, has such an evil ring, and colon cancer is the kind I always assumed I'd hate most, for the humiliating aspects as well as its possibly dire ones. I'd long thought even the colonoscopy would be horribly embarrassing and painful. In the event it wasn't either of those things and was even interesting. The only unpleasant moments of the surgery were, first, when the anaesthetist had to try over and over to insert her needle between my too-tightly packed vertebrae and then, later, a six-hour stretch in recovery while nurses tried to bring up my alarmingly low blood pressure. That was not painful but merely a feeling of extreme lassitude. I hadn't the energy to think of the word "death" but I hated it.

Thus I have had signals of my future, or, I guess, non-future. But I don't dwell on them. More will happen. A final one will happen. I don't let that prospect dominate the space in my mind room. Once in a while I think of that image of the wooden walkway leading off into the misty distance and reaffirm to myself my conviction that I don't want it to go on forever. In those moments I tell myself that my parents and both my sisters have stepped ahead of me across death's threshold. They could do it. When my time comes I can too. But one can't really imagine the state of "not being" so mostly I don't even try to.

I love my life now. In my elderly-hood, old age or whatever others call this stage, I rejoice in the beauty of Victoria and in the sweetness of my daily routines. At or before dawn (depending on the season) I drive through the still, grey and sleeping city to swim at my club. On my way home I take the sea route to discover the sort of day that is shaping in the sky and the smoothness or wild turbulence of the water. Home again I sit and eat my breakfast of fruit and homemade granola and gaze out my tall casement windows. In the foreground is a wide lawn and an enormous, mossy-barked oak tree, a squirrels' playground. Quite often, rather surprisingly even in full daylight, an owl sits on a branch turning its head and blinking. Beyond the lawn is a hedge and below it a pond of many lily pads and sometimes two ducks. Then the hillside slopes steeply allowing me a vista that reaches far into the distance, over the roof of the nearest neighbour's pink house, over other neighbours' plum and cherry trees and all the way to the sea and to the snow-topped mountains across the Strait.

Every morning I walk, often using my Nordic poles. I take various circling routes usually at least partly by the sea and in the afternoons I take a second, shorter walk around Government House Gardens. I am a volunteer gardener there once a week but I need my daily wanders as well to notice every new bud, blossom or shoot. This is a different kind of Canadian landscape from my beloved North Hatley's valley, with its round green hills, its pretty lake. It is even more unlike my Narnian wide-skied wilderness thronged with moose and bears and a million birds. Each feeds my need for beauty whether in memory or in the present.

But I don't gaze only at the natural world. My life is sociable too: I FaceTime and phone-chat with my daughter and my son most days (and visit them often also). They are my very best friends but I have many others and of all ages, some still from McGill and Bishop's days, and others gathered along the way, many now here in this city. I savour my daily chats and laughs with them, our frequent lunches together and gatherings to discuss books. I have close bonds with all seven of my grandchildren, and now with my five great-grandchildren. Well, to be fair, Oliver is still too young to be sure of who I am.

And there is reading. I spend several hours every day reading.

Victoria is a city of classical music and on a spring or summer evening I love walking to a concert under flowering cherry trees and by hedges and lawns down the few blocks to the Cathedral, often meeting with a friend at Cook Street corner.

The house I live in is one of the old Rockland mansions of Victoria and I have the largest apartment in it. It is on the ground floor and the huge oak-panelled room which was the original dining room serves as my living room. Sun pours in through two tall banks of casement windows that face southwest to the sea and through French doors that face east onto a long verandah of terra cotta tiles. The verandah is partly shaded in summer by wisteria, grape and kiwi vines. My library, facing northeast, was the original library of the mansion and has built-in bookshelves and a wide window seat from which I look across the front lawn over hydrangea bushes to thick green hedges, azaleas and rhododendrons. This room is where I write at my beautiful desk.

My apartment is furnished very much in my mother's English country house style with Persian and Turkish rugs, old Quebec pine pieces that I finished myself long ago and many old family things from my parents and even from my great-grandmother. I have "real" fireplaces in both my living room and my library. My two book groups enjoy coming here for meetings as it is so cosy and pretty and I often have three or four friends in for tea. I also like filling my long table with larger groups for lunches or suppers.

I am at my desk in my library right now as I write and as I look up from my computer I see links all about me that pull me back to people I love or places I've been.

On the desk's leather top are these treasures: a blue and white china lamp with a cream shade that my son got me at a 10,000 Villages shop; a small oval hand-hooked mat from Quebec that my sister-in-law gave me years ago on which sit a tiny soapstone frog I got in Zimbabwe and a carved sandstone scarab paperweight from Cairo. There is also a wooden pear from my stay in Tuscany that opens and contains paperclips. When I am thinking, I like to hold it. I also like to place my palm over the cool stone of the frog. There is a painted papier-mâché jar that Carol gave me for Christmas ages ago and it is filled with pens and sharp pencils.

Across the room is a sofa that I can open into a double bed when people visit. By the fireplace there is a small rocker with delicately turned spindles that Frank and I got on our honeymoon in Maine, the first old pine piece we acquired. On it sit two very old dolls each with long histories. In front of the fireplace is my old dolls' trunk; it is a miniature steamer trunk of metal painted navy blue with brass fittings, wooden trim and leather grips. On the floor are two Persian rugs patterned largely in red and blue. Tucked beside the fireplace is a high chair I got at the Hudson Bay when my first grandchild, Sarah, was born. So far all seven of my grandchildren and two great-grands have used it, as well as grandchildren of various friends. At the moment it is occupied by Rupert, a stuffed dog Aunt Hazel gave Jane when she was four. It came from the North Hatley summer bazaar and was made by my childhood friend Mary LeBaron.

On the mantelpiece is my great-grandmother's steeple clock and two small wooden dolls, intricately made and dressed in Slovenian national costume by my first mother-in-law, Jula Molnar. The woman doll, who wears an embroidered shawl over a blouse with full, pleated sleeves. holds a lace handkerchief. The man, who is very dapper with his suede coat over one shoulder and high leather boots, holds a furled red umbrella. These are two of the dolls Jula made to earn money after the Grand Hotel Toplice was nationalized. They stand one on each side of a photograph of an owl my brother took in Botswana.

On the walls is a set of seven old French botanical prints. There are also African things a black and white photograph of my father as a young man sitting on a zebra he has just shot for meat to feed his "boys." Two of the "boys" stand on either side of him and a third crouches holding up the animal's head. The three are barefoot and wear only ragged pants, while my father is also barelegged, but wears also a shirt and two hats, one on top of the other. Other African items are an extraordinarily intricately carved walking stick I bought while hiking in the Matopo Hills near Bulawayo and a carved voodoo doll. I got two of the dolls in order to give one to my son who is a veterinarian as they are meant to effect a cure when waved over a sick animal.

Of course as this is my library it has some of my books — though every room in my place, even the hall between the library and my second bathroom, has bookshelves. On the left side of the bank of windows I have mostly history books but also dictionaries and other books of reference and atlases. My father's three volumes of hockey history, *The Trail of the Stanley Cup*, are here too. On the other side of the windows are novels, also some children's books.

My present life, then, is quite remarkably pleasant in situation, activities and sociability. However long this chapter of my life lasts I can say I am happy as I turn its pages.

I read recently in a memoir — it was Julian Barnes's *The Sense of an Ending* but I think he was quoting someone else — a remark about how shapeless a life actually is, that really it's "just one damn thing after another." Yet probably none of us wants to believe in the mereness of that. I don't, anyway. I have travelled my path as if my doing so matters.

I sought drama, even danger. The heroine of my story could and would survive anything. And she did though at a some cost.

INLAND NAVIGATION BY THE STARS   257

Epilogue

I walk along a beach, feeling the damp sand under my toes, under my instep. I smell the water, salty, fishy. There are a few dark skeins of unknown weed and a long hose and bulb of kelp, torn from its ocean bed by the recent storm. An otter, not far out, keeps pace with me. His sleek back arcs up. Then he slips under and disappears, resurfacing farther ahead. I have always walked on beaches, noticing. Perhaps my first memory of a shore is an image of tiny dark stars of weed on white sand. I can date it: it is my third birthday and my sisters are carrying me into Lake Simcoe.

I strike out into the cold sea at Yellow Point, feel on every inch of my skin the sharp shock of it and then the bliss of the second lap, when I'm used to it or it to me and I turn on my back and see there's an eagle on the tip of the tallest pine tree. My body is in this moment and also in thousands of other moments. They echo back and back to other summer waters, lakes, a river, another ocean. I could be entering Lake Massawippi. I could be six, or ten, or sixty — any age. The blue summer sky, silky with streaks of thin cloud at the horizon, is the same element there and here. My body slides through water as it always has. I am the same.

I step across a lawn in the morning and the springy grass is bright green and warm in the sun, dark, cold and wet under the trees. I place my palm against a tree trunk and sense the life inside. I have always loved the variousness of the world, always loved the beating pulse in every living thing.

I sniff a newborn's hair as the tiny, damp and snuffly person falls asleep on my chest. I have known this down the years: my sisters' babies, my own babies, my grand-babies, now my great-grand-babies. It gives me the same sweet and tender animal delight.

I follow my routines with pleasure, my daily swims, my gardening, my meetings with friends, my frequent concerts. I sit at my wonderful desk and I tap away at my machine, writing. I look up frequently at the brilliant red rhododendrons outside. They are massed at the lawn's far border. Nearer than the rhodos, pyrocantha are in thick flower at my open casements. They draw the bees. Every little while one buzzes in, bumps against the window frame and against the glass of the one closed window. It finally finds its way out, or I help it, scooping it in a folded paper.

There is a further, wider dimension to my life than just my personal joy in it. There is that high and many-branched tree that is my family. Every year just now it is putting out new shoots. I want to be a person my grandchildren and great-grandchildren (a group already numbering twelve) will remember or, those still unborn, be interested to hear about. I hope they will see that I did my best, used the gift that was my life and fulfilled my talents. I hope they may be pleased if they inherit some of my qualities and forgive me if they have any of my weaknesses. (My early-life shyness, my varicose veins!)

Of course I wish above all that my love could somehow hold them safe. Maybe, at least, be a comfort in a tough situation sometime. Alive or dead, I am on their side.

Acknowledgements

I have had excellent advice from my editor, Donald G. Bastian, who helped me immeasurably with reorganizing and cutting, and, crucially, with his enthusiasm for my project, and I want to thank my student of long ago, Eloise Lewis, happily re-found after almost fifty years, for connecting me to Don. Also I had many early readers who gave me feedback and encouragement: my children, Jane and Paul, and my brother Charles, all of whom read many versions of the manuscript. Friends were terrific, especially Linda Breault, Susan Vorner-Kirby, Roberta Hamilton, Caroline Miller, Pat Coppard and Suellen Cox. Jenny Bradshaw was consistently supportive, even while she could not take the book on herself.

CPSIA information can be obtained
at www.ICGtesting.com
Printed in the USA
LVHW051701231220
675006LV00012B/1065